T0333444

MY SINS
GO WITH ME

*Also by Martin Sixsmith
from Simon & Schuster:*

Ayesha's Gift

An Unquiet Heart

MY SINS
GO WITH ME

A Story of Heroism and Betrayal
in the Dutch Resistance

MARTIN SIXSMITH

**SIMON &
SCHUSTER**

London · New York · Sydney · Toronto · New Delhi

First published in Great Britain by Simon & Schuster UK Ltd, 2024

Copyright © Martin Sixsmith, 2024

The right of Martin Sixsmith to be identified as the author of
this work has been asserted in accordance with the
Copyright, Designs and Patents Act, 1988.

1 3 5 7 9 10 8 6 4 2

Simon & Schuster UK Ltd
1st Floor
222 Gray's Inn Road
London WC1X 8HB

Simon & Schuster: Celebrating 100 Years of Publishing in 2024

www.simonandschuster.co.uk
www.simonandschuster.com.au
www.simonandschuster.co.in

Simon & Schuster Australia, Sydney
Simon & Schuster India, New Delhi

The author and publishers have made all reasonable efforts
to contact copyright-holders for permission, and apologise for
any omissions or errors in the form of credits given.
Corrections may be made to future printings.

A CIP catalogue record for this book
is available from the British Library

Hardback ISBN: 978-1-4711-4983-2
TPB ISBN: 978-1-4711-4984-9
eBook ISBN: 978-1-4711-4986-3

Typeset in Palatino by M Rules
Printed and Bound in the UK using 100% Renewable
Electricity at CPI Group (UK) Ltd

MIX
Paper | Supporting
responsible forestry
FSC
www.fsc.org   FSC® C171272

CONTENTS

PREFACE

My sins go with me is a line from a poem by the writer Hendrik Marsman, who drowned while trying to escape from Nazi-occupied Holland to join the Dutch forces in England. It is poetry from an era of courage marred by baseness and betrayal, when the Netherlands produced men and women of the greatest heroism, and others willing to sell their neighbours for a few guilders. I heard it first in 2019, when the ship I was sailing on docked in Cape Town and I watched an elderly woman passenger descend to the quayside to be greeted with a kiss from an equally elderly man. When we resumed our journey, I asked her who he was. 'A fighter-pilot,' she said. 'The last time we kissed was in Holland, seventy-five years ago ...'

Anna-Maria van der Vaart was ninety-nine, remarkably independent despite her failing eyesight, elegant, calm and self-possessed. As we sailed north from Cape Town, she told me about the downed Allied pilots she sheltered in the darkest days of the war; she described the persecuted Jews who found refuge in her home and how she stood up to the Nazis by participating in auda-cious acts of resistance. Like many English speakers, I had heard a lot about the French Resistance and about Soviet partisans, but my knowledge of what happened in the Netherlands extended little beyond the heartrending story of Anne Frank. When I asked Anna-Maria why that might be, she said, 'You've just given the answer. The Dutch turned more Jews over to the Nazis than any other nation. There were traitors in every Resistance cell.'

The juxtaposition of valour and treachery struck me as poign-ant and tragic. When we docked in Southampton, I set out to uncover more. In interviews with those who survived, in Dutch and German archives, personal diaries, photo libraries and occasionally contentious memoirs by men with things to hide, I came across a drama on a scale I could never have imagined.

I have told Anna-Maria's story in this book together with those of the Resistance members with whom she had contact or whose deeds she recollected, the people she helped to survive and others who were determined to destroy them, to give as wide as possible a picture – both of those who resisted and those who threw in their lot with their fellow Aryans from Hitler's Germany. I have tried to understand the decisions taken by both sides and have learned that it was not a simple choice, not just a question of courage and honour versus cowardice and greed. In writing their stories, I have adhered to the facts where the facts are known; where they are not, I have filled in the gaps with a probable narrative of what happened in the shadows.

Martin Sixsmith, 2024

1

INVASION 1940

Rotterdam, 14 May 1940

The house shook and the bedroom filled with light. Anna-Maria ran to the window as incendiary bombs from successive waves of aeroplanes set ablaze the wooden roofs of the medieval city. Individual fires, manageable at first, spread and joined together until the firefighters could no longer cope. Columns of heat, roaring into the night, sucked up air from the surrounding streets, tossing roofbeams, bricks and bodies into the sky. Rotterdam burned for a week.

In the afternoon, giant snowflakes appeared, swirling and growing until Anna-Maria could make out the silk of the parachutes and the grey-green uniforms of the men beneath them. She tried counting but couldn't keep up. At 4 p.m., the Netherlands capitulated.

* * *

Generaloberst Rudolf Schmidt, commander of the 9th Panzer Division who accepted the Dutch surrender, apologised for the carpet bombing. The intention had been to destroy only military targets, he said; an order to recall the bombers had arrived too late.

Hitler told his troops to treat the Dutch with courtesy, as potential allies in the war of races that lay ahead. The two countries had history and culture in common, similar languages and similar outlooks. In the First World War, Berlin had channelled its westward offensive through Belgium, allowing the Netherlands to stay neutral, preserving her colonies abroad and prosperity at home. When the Germans went to war again, the Dutch had hoped they would 'go around us' as they had in the past. The Nazi invasion was a surprise attack, with no formal declaration of war. Initial resistance by the Dutch army had provided Goering with a reason to deploy the Luftwaffe, a timely opportunity to showcase the prowess of his men and their machines.

* * *

Like most Dutch people, Anna-Maria didn't hate the Germans. She had friends over the border; she spoke their language. She was twenty years old, a student at Leiden University, passionate about music, passionate about the theatre. Politics were for grown-ups.

Anna-Maria aged twenty

The grown-ups were worried. In the days after 14 May the organist of St Boniface's Church on Wijnstraat in Dordrecht, south of Rotterdam, climbed to the top of the wooden neoclassical bell tower to watch the smoke rising from the city. Adrianus Roest loved God and he loved music, but he was a good burgher who knew the value of money. He had spent his life building a prosperous grocery and coal delivery business. When the Germans seized the Sudetenland, then Austria and Poland, Adrianus had decided it was time to sell up. He told his wife Catharina that if the Nazis came to Holland, money in the bank would be easier to hide than grocery stores. But now the invaders were here and there were rumours that they were confiscating bank accounts.

It took their son to suggest a way out. Pim Roest was a year older than Anna-Maria and, like her, a student at Leiden. Pim was the captain of the university hockey team, outgoing, bright and popular. At night he played saxophone and trombone in the New Cormorants Jazz Band. It made him seem grown-up and suave. When Pim invited her out, Anna-Maria felt chosen.

'What if we got married?' Pim said to his parents. 'You could use the money from the bank to buy us a house and some furniture. Surely the Germans won't go around stealing people's houses.'

The Roests agreed. They spoke to Anna-Maria's parents who liked Pim and were keen on the idea.

Pim Roest

* * *

By the time she turned twenty-one Anna-Maria was a married woman. In 1940, with the country under German occupation, the wedding could have been a subdued affair, but Pim was full of energy, full of fun, determined to make the best of things. The New Cormorants came to the reception in the townhall and Pim led them through a string of dance classics, delighting parents and children alike.

Wedding day, 1940

The New Cormorants, including Pim Roest (back row, centre)

For Pim and Anna-Maria, whose relationship had been limited to a few dances and hurried discussions in the cinema, married life was a chance to discover each other. Anna-Maria told him about her childhood, her family and the experiences that had made her who she was.

'I'd like a nice three-storey, brick house,' she said, 'to remind me of growing up in my parents' home in Oude Delft. One with a pavement just six paces wide between the front door and the canal. One where our children can put on their skates and step out onto the ice.'

She spoke about the winter thrill of skating to school, speeding down the frozen canal, arriving in class with glowing cheeks.

'And at weekends, we played ice hockey. My father was the referee and when we came back, my mother would make us hot chocolate. Then we moved to Dordrecht. I was good at maths and science and that's how I ended up studying medicine at Leiden.'

Oude Delft

* * *

They found a pretty redbrick in Terbregge, a village outside Rotterdam, with a garden and land. Because the family who owned it were hoping to emigrate, it was going cheap.

When Pim asked the land agent why the price was so low, the man raised his finger to his nose. 'Jews,' he said. 'They were keen to come here in the past, but not so eager to stay now that our friends from Berlin are sorting out the Rothschilds and all the other bloodsuckers.'

When it came to negotiating, Pim asked what a fair price for the house would have been before the invasion and told the owners that he would pay as close to it as he possibly could.

* * *

At first, little changed. Her country was occupied, she was married, but life carried on. Anna-Maria was young; she didn't want tragedy or drama. She pursued her medical studies, acted in university productions, sang and danced. When the troupe she belonged to enjoyed some success in Leiden, they took the show on the road, touring in Amsterdam, Rotterdam and The Hague.

The Germans, for their part, seemed happy to allow the Dutch as much normality as it took to persuade them to throw in their lot with the new regime. Their first official proclamation, carried in newspapers and on noticeboards in public places, stressed the two nations' common history and common blood.

Dutch soldiers have fought well in battle and the Dutch population has adopted a satisfactory attitude towards our troops. There is nothing to prevent us meeting each other on a plane of mutual respect. The German people are fighting a battle for survival, a struggle which the hatred and envy of our enemies have forced upon us. Our intention is that the Dutch nation, akin in blood to the German nation, shall not be subject to living conditions less favourable than those necessitated by the commonality of our fate ... Dutch society will, as far as possible, be left unimpaired; Dutch law will continue in force; the existing civil service will continue in post and the independence of the judiciary will be preserved. All officials and public employees will, however, be expected conscientiously to comply with the orders they are given and the Dutch population to obey these orders with discipline and goodwill ... If the Netherlands nation fulfils the duties resulting from this common task, it will be able to secure its liberty for the future.

Headquarters of the Führer, 25 May 1940

German troops welcomed in Amsterdam

* * *

Even before the invasion, some sectors of Dutch society liked the idea of Nazism. Economic decline and fears of fictional threats – Bolsheviks, Jews, Masonic conspirators – had emboldened Holland's own Nazi party, the National Socialist Movement, Nationaal-Socialistische Beweging (NSB). Under the leadership of Anton Mussert, a chubby opportunist who advocated the annexation of the Dutch-speaking part of Belgium, the NSB aped its big brother in Berlin, promising to rescue the Netherlands from the bondage of foreign capital and restore the dignity of its people.

The Party held rallies and torchlit parades, and demanded the expulsion of immigrants and the Aryanisation of the fatherland. When NSB candidates were elected to the Dutch parliament in the mid-1930s, they flouted parliamentary rules, made anti-Semitic speeches and brought physical violence to the debating chamber.

Left-wing intellectuals mocked Mussert and derided his little-man megalomania. But in May 1940, he reaped his reward. The Germans banned all other political parties, anointing the NSB as the only tolerated voice of native opinion. Mussert went to Berlin to meet Hitler and discuss the future. He asked if he could be named Prime Minister, but Hitler demurred. The ruler of Holland had to be a German or an Austrian, the Führer said; he would shortly be installing a new Reichskommissar. But if the NSB pledged its unwavering support for Nazi rule, Mussert could be in charge of imposing Berlin's diktat, with the honorific title 'Leader of the Dutch People'.

* * *

Anna-Maria heard the whispered debates about how people should respond to the occupiers, about the contested legitimacy of the NSB and the fears that resistance to Mussert's petty demagogues might provoke the Nazis to harsher measures. She spoke good German and she admired German culture. Goethe had been the literary companion of her teenage years; she loved the old Berlin cabaret numbers that she danced to in her stage performances. She resented the thought that her country was no longer her own, but like most people in those early months she just got on with things.

When her troupe went on tour, they drew big audiences, including German civilians and Germans in uniform. Anna-Maria was twenty-one, slim and attractive; she could see the admiring looks from the men in the front row. When an envelope was delivered to her dressing room, she half-knew what to expect. 'You are so lovely,' the note began in copperplate German. 'You are so ravishing when you sing. You remind me of the girls of my homeland. Please would you do me the honour of taking dinner?'

The other girls laughed. Anna-Maria threw the note in the bin.

* * *

At the end of Sunday mass, as the priest and choir processed down the nave, Pim's father Adrianus Roest modulated unexpectedly from the comforting B-flat of Bach's 'Sheep May Safely Graze' to the brassy G major of 'Het Wilhelmus', the national anthem of the Netherlands. With the instinctive response that anthems command, some of the congregation began to sing, 'I swear undying faith to this land of mine,' then, joined by others,

> Undaunted, ever-free, let no despair betray you;
> The Lord shall surely guard you, though now you
>   are oppressed.
> He who keeps the faith, who gives his life, his all,
> Shall see this land restored!

The priest asked Adrianus to join him in the vestry.

'Yes,' he said. 'Inspiring. A moment of release. But the organ you play is a hundred years old, my son. It is the voice not just of the man who plays it; it is the voice of the Church and the voice of God. We need to think of the consequences before we take such responsibility upon ourselves.'

Adrianus Roest

* * *

Nineteen-forty was Anton Mussert's year of miracles. Invested by the Führer with authority in a nation where many had mocked him, he demanded submission and obedience. The NSB was empowered to vet civil servants for loyalty to the country's new rulers. Those deemed suspect were fired, with no right of appeal and no pension. Mussert's men evicted councillors and mayors in all the major cities, making new appointments from their own ranks.

Anton Mussert receives instructions from Hitler in Berlin

In June, Berlin gave instructions to begin the reorganisation of the Dutch police and military. Hitler wanted to retain Dutch goodwill, so Mussert was told to interview and re-engage all those who were willing to serve the new order. Thousands of soldiers captured by the Germans were asked to sign an undertaking not to engage in activities hostile to the Reich and, having done so, were released. The *Opbouwdienst*, the Reconstruction Service, distributed new uniforms, new conditions of employment and a new oath of loyalty. Ninety per cent of serving police officers accepted.

* * *

Adrianus and Catharina Roest were frequent visitors to Pim and Anna-Maria's new home. When Catharina, a good Dutch mother-in-law, asked indiscreet questions about their intentions and when she and Adrianus might become grandparents, Anna-Maria smiled.

'I've got two years of medical school left,' she said. 'And I'm acting in my spare time. I'd hardly look right in a cabaret skirt with a swollen belly.'

* * *

Dutch society continued to function. Businesses and schools, cinemas and theatres, post offices and public transport remained open. The bulk of the German army had moved on to France, leaving the Netherlands in the hands of a sitting garrison and the forces of the NSB. Newly introduced blackout regulations were one of the few reminders of the war.

Queen Wilhelmina

The Dutch royal family, exiled in London and broadcasting calls for resistance over the BBC, was a rallying point. Orange, the royal colour, became a mark of civil disobedience. On Prince Bernhard's twenty-ninth birthday in June, people wore carnations in their lapels and flew the Dutch flag. The Germans responded by removing royal portraits from public buildings and changing street names.

Carnation Day in The Hague, 1940

A family that christened its new baby after the royals and put a birth announcement in the newspapers listing her names – Irene Beatrix Juliana Wilhelmina – received messages of congratulation from all over the country. The Germans sent the mother to the Ravensbrück concentration camp.

* * *

Adrianus had a visit from an old schoolfriend. He and Ruud Wilders had been close as teenagers, but Wilders had made a career in law enforcement, Adrianus in groceries and the Church.

'Adrianus,' Wilders said, 'I'm a good detective and that's why I've reached the top – commanding officer for north Amsterdam. Signing up for the Opbouwdienst will mean working with the Gestapo. But I don't see that there's a better alternative.'

'The problem is that the NSB have adopted the Nazi creed of hatred,' Adrianus said. 'They claim they want Holland to be pure and proud. But what they mean is, "Let's destroy the Jews and the foreigners and anyone who doesn't think the way we do." That's not compatible with the beliefs of a Christian – or any honest man.'

'The country you and I loved as children has changed,' Wilders said. 'Don't you remember how everyone used to pull together? That's all gone. We may not like it that the Nazis are here, but we're going to have to deal with it.'

'But we have to deal with it in a way that leaves our conscience free,' Adrianus said, 'that lets us sleep at night.'

'We can stand against the Germans and try to drive them out,' Wilders said. 'But look how they crushed us when we fought. Or we can work with them to get the best deal for Holland. We don't have to sign up to all their excesses: we can co-operate just enough to have some influence over them, to have some say in what happens to our country. You only have to look at what the Germans have done to the Poles who stood against them, to the communists, the Jews, the partisans. We mustn't let that happen here. And we have one big advantage – the Germans came to Poland with hatred in their hearts, but they've come here with open minds. We have a choice, Adrianus – we can turn Holland into a new Poland or we can work to protect the majority of our people and the fabric of our society.'

'I'm sorry, Ruud,' Adrianus said. 'If we believe in the teachings of Christ, we can never support a regime like this. It's a Christian's duty to avoid bringing suffering on his fellow man ...'

'Yes, yes,' Wilders said. 'I agree. But the vast majority say the same as I do: that we carry on doing the job we've always done, keeping law and order, preventing crime, making the country safe so the government can do the best for the people. I'm going to the Opbouwdienst with my men and we're going to sign up.'

* * *

Pim brought home a brochure that had been distributed to students at the university. It was full of photographs of young men and women engaging in outdoor sports.

'Swift is the tread of our feet; grand is our dream of the future,' Anna-Maria read aloud, leafing through the pages. '"Drums beat loud throughout the land; come, march with us!" It all sounds very uplifting. Are you thinking of going along?'

'Don't be naïve,' Pim said. 'The NSB want to turn us into Nazis and tell us how to think. They want to make Holland a province of Greater Germany. And there are so many people falling for it.'

'Oh, I don't know,' Anna-Maria said. 'There are some nice photos of girls in uniform here. Don't you think I'd look good in one of those short skirts and tight blouses?'

Pim saw she was laughing.

* * *

The first months of occupation had been quiet, with a widespread acceptance of, even enthusiasm for, the German presence. If resentment showed itself, it did so in symbolic acts such as flying the Dutch flag and humming the national anthem. When cinemas replaced American films with German newsreels, some audience members booed or walked out.

By and large, the authorities turned a blind eye. When a group of students were caught with a pamphlet claiming that the Germans were planning to force Dutch people to work for the Third Reich, they were arrested and charged, but the regime decided against punishing them.

By the end of the summer, tea and coffee, then bread and flour could no longer be purchased without ration cards; meat rationing was introduced and petrol stations closed. A National Employment Bureau – the *Rijksarbeidsbureau* – was opened to ensure the provision of labour for industries prioritised by the Reich, and compulsory identity cards were introduced. Censorship was tightened. All but a handful of official news-papers were closed and a ban imposed on listening to the broadcasts of the BBC. When people continued to listen, the Germans confiscated their radios.

Underground publications began to appear in greater num-bers. When their distributors were caught, they were no longer released but sent to a newly constructed holding camp at Amersfoort in the central Netherlands.

Suspects awaiting trial in Durchgangslager Amersfoort

In October, Jewish-owned businesses were ordered to register with the authorities. Two hundred thousand public employees were told to complete a questionnaire about their family history and sign a so-called Aryan declaration, swearing that they did not have Jewish ancestry. Only a handful refused to comply. Restaurants and cafés were encouraged to display '*Joden niet gewenscht*' placards, barring Jews from entering.

2

RESISTANCE BEGINS

For Anna-Maria, the turning point came with the boy next door. She didn't know his name, but in the months since she and Pim had moved to their new house she had seen him playing outside. He looked fifteen or sixteen, well dressed and nimble on his feet. In the evening, she watched him ride off on his bike and return after dark with parcels tied to the crossbar.

She spotted the danger before he did. Bent down fixing his bicycle clips, the boy had failed to see the soldier in the doorway, failed to hear the click of the rifle bolt.

'You! Off that bike!'

The soldier was pointing his weapon, signalling the boy to come to him. The child hesitated and made as if to obey, but Anna-Maria sensed what was about to happen. She ran out as the boy jumped onto his bike and the soldier's trigger finger tightened.

'Stop! Sir! Please stop!'

She was in the soldier's eyeline, close enough to see his moment of hesitation as she threw herself in front of him. Two shots exploded past her ear. As she raised her hands, she glimpsed the boy disappearing into a side street and the soldier's drunken eyes as he swung his rifle into her face.

* * *

On 23 November, the chancellors of Holland's universities received instructions that Jewish employees – from professors to clerks to cleaners – were to be fired with immediate effect.

It was not unexpected. But students at Delft College and Leiden University were angered by the injustice of it and announced they were going on strike.

Student strike committee meeting, Leiden University, 23 November 1940

Pim and Anna-Maria supported the demands that were presented to the Education Ministry, including the reinstatement of all lecturers and employees, a pledge from the authorities to renounce religious prejudice in public policy and guarantees of political independence for institutions of higher education.

Two days later, detachments of armed police arrived. The striking students were evicted and the universities closed.

* * *

Anna-Maria's nightmares began the moment she fell asleep at night. She would be back outside the house, running towards the man with the rifle, trying to intercept the flying bullets with her outstretched hands, feeling the stab of pain as they passed through her palms, the shots detonating in her ears and the terror that woke her screaming and covered in sweat.

* * *

'We can't not do it,' Pim said. 'We wouldn't be able to look each other in the eye if we refused.'

Anna-Maria agreed. 'It's time to stand up for something. To *do* something, after all these months.'

The men with the bundles had come to Leiden as soon as the strike was crushed, looking for volunteers among the students. The newspapers – flimsy cyclostyled sheets, half-typed, half-handwritten – were taken up at once. The founding edition of

De Waarheid – The Truth – bore the same date as the university strikes; its bold sub-heading proclaimed it would lead the Netherlands on 'The Road to Freedom'.

Distributing *De Waarheid* was not without danger. There were no signatures on the articles, but the newspaper's title proclaimed its loyalty to the Soviet Union's *Pravda* (meaning 'truth' in Russian). Communism had been as contested in pre-war Holland as National Socialism, but the Nazis were here now and the communists were calling for resistance. Political dislikes were put on hold in the common cause.

Pim took care of the collections, going alone to pick up the fortnightly consignments and dividing them into parcels to be taken to the locations on their list. The regime had announced that possessing subversive literature would be considered a capital offence, so the fewer people who knew you, the safer for everyone.

'There's no point in you knowing where I go,' he told Anna-Maria. 'The Germans will have their spies inside the network.'

* * *

Berlin had given Mussert and the NSB the chance to deliver a subservient Holland and they had failed to do so. From now on, the Reich would take care of its own interests.

Hitler had named an Austrian Nazi as his plenipotentiary in the Netherlands, Reichskommissar Arthur Seyss-Inquart. As the acting Chancellor of Austria in March 1938, Seyss-Inquart had been the man who invited Hitler to invade his homeland, overseeing the plebiscite that served as justification for the Anschluss and the incorporation of Austria as a province of Germany, and implementing the Führer's policies on the Jewish question. Assigned next to the Nazi administration of Poland, Seyss-Inquart had presided over the confiscation of Jewish property and the deportation of its owners to the camps. His mission now was to do the same in Holland.

Arthur Seyss-Inquart

Seyss-Inquart's first move was to locate and identify the country's Jews. His Decree on Jewish Registration was thorough to the point of obsession.

DECREE BY THE REICHSKOMMISSAR FOR THE OCCUPIED TERRITORIES OF THE NETHERLANDS.

By virtue of article 5 of the Führer's proclamation of 18 May 1940 relative to the exercise of governmental powers in the Netherlands, I hereby decree as follows.

Persons who are entirely or partly of Jewish race and who are residing in the occupied territories of the Netherlands are to be registered in accordance with the following regulations:

A person is considered to be entirely or partly of Jewish race if he is descended from even one grandparent of full Jewish blood. A grandparent is automatically considered as being of full Jewish blood if he belongs or has belonged to the Jewish religious community.

If there should be any doubt as to whether a person should be considered to be of Jewish blood as stated above, the decision will be made by the Reichskommissar for the occupied territories of the Netherlands or the office indicated by him. This decision is final.

Registration must indicate:

1. First and last name of the person to be registered
2. Place, date, month and year of birth
3. Home or residence, indicating exact name of street and number of house.

The State Inspectorate of Population Registers [*Het Hoofd der Rijksinspectie van de Bevolkingsregisters*] is responsible for making all registrations and shall keep the residence records of the concerned persons in the register in its offices.

Any person who is due to register and does not fulfil his obligation to register will be sentenced to a term of imprisonment of up to 5 years.

Issued: The Hague, 10 January 1941
Reichskommissar for the occupied territories
in the Netherlands, Seyss-Inquart.

Arthur Seyss-Inquart, January 1941

* * *

Pim and Anna-Maria shared the deliveries of *De Waarheid* between them. For the most part, they kept to their own handover points. It meant fewer names at risk if either were caught. There were more uniforms on the streets and policing was becoming aggressive. Duties that had been carried out by Mussert's NSB now fell to the Wehrmacht and the SS. Stop-and-search squads patrolled the cities.

In early February 1941, Pim had a message from their contact at *De Waarheid*. A wave of late-season bronchitis had left the network short of couriers; would he or Anna-Maria be willing to make an extra delivery in Amsterdam?

Pim said he would do it. He was told to be at the south-eastern corner of Waterlooplein, a square in central Amsterdam, at 7 p.m. on Thursday the 13th. He would recognise the girl to whom he was to make the handover by the folded copy of *Volk en Vaderland*, the Dutch fascist newspaper, that she would be carrying under her left arm.

Pim got there early and found the square crowded with people. Waterlooplein was not one of his usual haunts, but it seemed to him that there was an uncommon bustle; people appeared on edge, as if waiting for something to happen.

He spotted her just before seven, a young woman with dark hair in a blue overcoat carrying the folded newspaper. She had evidently been given his description because she nodded and signalled to him to walk towards the canal. As they were passing the Rembrandt House, approaching the water's edge, the woman dropped her newspaper and began to run.

Pim saw the black-uniformed WA men running towards him. He fled along the Zwanenburgwal, with the canal on his left. Emerging onto Jodenbreestraat, he found himself outside the Tip Top Cinema and pushed his way through a crowd of bodies into the foyer.

'A ticket. A ticket, please,' he heard himself say in a voice that was too loud. He looked around and saw that the foyer was full of German soldiers. The clerk said something. Pim didn't understand.

'I said, "Do you have a Wehrmacht pass?"'

The man was speaking slowly, as if to a foreigner.

'It's Thursday' the clerk said. 'Wehrmacht only today.'

With counterfeit composure, Pim adjusted his tie and walked out. The street was filled with noise; people were running, some of them with bloodied faces. Pim slipped into the crowd and made his way to the station.

* * *

The WA, The Weer Afdeling, were Holland's blackshirts, uniformed thugs dedicated to targeting Jews and foreigners; they made their own rules, only partially controlled by Mussert's NSB. In early February, WA men had marched through Amsterdam's Jewish quarter, assaulting the inhabitants, forcing restaurants and cafés to put up *Joden niet gewenscht* signs, daubing slogans on synagogues.

WA men march through Amsterdam

On Tuesday 11 February, two days before Pim's mission to Amsterdam, WA members had smashed doors and windows at the Alcazar Cabaret, where Jewish singers were performing. They had entered the auditorium and driven spectators into the street to run the gauntlet of sticks and clubs. Passing German soldiers had joined in the fun, helping the WA men to break into Jewish homes in the neighbouring Jodenhoek district, terrorising the occupants and stealing their possessions.

WA men and German soldiers terrorise Jewish neighbourhoods

In response, young Jewish men had formed self-defence squads with the assistance of communist-organised workers from the industrial suburbs of Kattenburg and Jordaan. It was they who were waiting in the Waterlooplein when Pim arrived there on the evening of the 13th and they who were the target of the WA units Pim had run into on the Zwanenburgwal. The fighting that began while Pim was in the Tip Top Cinema had intensified during the evening, with injuries on both sides.

Clashes in central Amsterdam

When German troops cleared the area, they discovered the body of a WA man, Hendrik Koot. Koot had been felled by a brick thrown from the crowd, but the official media reported his death in more lurid terms. 'Jewish Atrocity' headlined *Volk en Vaderland*. 'A brutal murder by cowardly terrorist Jews ... the victim of countless wounds and beatings.' A Jew had been spotted, claimed the WA, kneeling over the body with blood dripping from his lips, having bitten through Koot's ears and nose and throat.

* * *

For two days after he returned from Waterlooplein, Pim barely spoke. On the third day, he went out, returning in the evening with a parcel wrapped in brown paper.

'I was scared,' he said to Anna-Maria. 'Not scared to die, but scared that I would die without you. And scared that you would have nothing to remember me by. I thought of the danger we are running and, even worse, that it might be you who died and I who would be left with no token of our love. I got these – one for you and one for me.'

He handed her a necklace with a silver guilder bearing the head of Queen Wilhelmina, the symbol of resistance declared illegal by the Germans.

'The next time something like Waterlooplein happens,' Pim said, 'we will have these round our necks. They will give us something to believe in, something to remind us of each other in that most terrible of moments. And, I hope, the courage to be brave when that moment comes.'

3

The ghetto

The death of Hendrik Koot gave Reichskommissar Seyss-Inquart the pretext he had been waiting for. On 12 February, he sent police and troops to cordon off the Jewish quarter of Amsterdam. Signs were erected announcing that this would henceforth be the *Judenviertel*, the *Joodse Wijk*, the Amsterdam ghetto. From Herengracht to Rapenburg and Kloveniersburgwal barbed wire and makeshift fences appeared, delineating the closed zone in which the dangerous Jewish terrorists would now be confined.

One week later, a clash between WA men and members of a Jewish defence unit at an ice-cream parlour in south Amsterdam ended with injuries and arrests. One of those arrested, Ernst Cahn, was tortured and shot by the WA. He was only the first.

Jewish ghetto, Amsterdam

* * *

Opposition to the occupation was centred on the underground newspapers, each with its own politics. The shared dangers of producing and distributing them forged bonds between the men and women who did so, an intimacy of risk that led to the formation of distinct Resistance groupings.

De Waarheid carried the message of Soviet socialism, but not all who worked for it were communists. Pim and Anna-Maria did it for the sake of their homeland, not the cause of Moscow. A collective horror at the treatment of Holland's Jews helped promote co-operation.

When a suggestion came from their handler at *De Waarheid* that Anna-Maria's theatrical touring could be a cover for taking the newspaper to towns not yet served by the network, she agreed. Her medical studies had been suspended following the Leiden student strikes and she was acting full-time. Now when she travelled to venues where her troupe was to perform, she took *De Waarheid* with her.

Anna-Maria in The Perfect Murder

There had been no lessening in the number of amorous German officers in her audiences, she told Pim, and no let-up in her determination to repulse them. Pim laughed.

'If only they knew what you were really up to!'

'They seem not to have the slightest suspicion,' Anna-Maria said. 'It's as if the Reich has drummed into them what the enemy looks like – male and dark, with a big Jewish nose or a hammer and sickle tattooed on his buttocks. The thought that a blonde, blue-eyed, nice young lady could be a terrorist never enters their heads!'

* * *

Seyss-Inquart got word from Berlin. The Führer was concerned about the rise of Jewish provocations in the Netherlands; a firm hand was needed to deal with them. Heinrich Himmler, the head of the SS, wanted his representative, Höherer SS-Polizeiführer Hanns Albin Rauter, to be accorded full authority to crush the revolt.

Hanns Rauter

Hanns Rauter had risen through the SS's intelligence arm, the Sicherheitsdienst (SD), to become, at the age of forty-five, one of the youngest officers at his elevated rank. Wounds received in the First World War had left him with a damaged shoulder and a burning hatred for the enemies of the fatherland. His nickname, Vulture of the Alps, reflected both his lanky frame – six feet four inches – and his service between the wars in the right-wing anti-Semitic Freikorps, where his motto had been *Gladius Ulter Noster*, 'The Sword is our Vengeance'. Himmler regarded him as capable and ruthless.

After duty in Poland, Rauter had come to the Netherlands as 'Himmler's man'. He was the SS chief's eyes and ears, instructed to keep tabs on the enemy, but also on Seyss-Inquart. The potential for friction between them was present from the outset. On Himmler's order, Rauter had been given authority over all branches of the German and Dutch police, with the power to issue his own decrees.

At their meeting to formalise his new responsibility for the Jewish question, Rauter let Seyss-Inquart take the lead. 'The Jews for us are not Dutchmen,' Seyss-Inquart said. 'They are enemies with whom we can come neither to armistice nor to peace. The same goes for anyone who supports them or who supports the so-called Resistance.'

That evening Rauter wrote to Himmler, assuring him that the unrest in Amsterdam would henceforth be met with a 'commensurate' response.

Arthur Seyss-Inquart (left, back to camera)
and Hanns Rauter (furthest right)

* * *

The 10 January decree on compulsory registration had sowed fear in the country's Jewish community. People had heard what the Nazis were doing in Poland and the demand for Jews in the Netherlands to identify themselves seemed a harbinger of similar horrors.

Polizeiführer Rauter ordered the Jewish 'terrorists' who had brought death and destruction to the streets to surrender their weapons. But he let it be known that he wanted a negotiated solution. He was appointing a prominent Jewish businessman, the diamond dealer Abraham Asscher, and a university professor, David Cohen, to form a Jewish Council – the *Joodse Raad* – to serve as the community's voice in relations with the occupying powers.

Abraham Asscher (left) and David Cohen (right)

Asscher and his fellow members of the Jewish Council had spent the 1930s caring for Jewish refugees fleeing Nazi Germany for what then had seemed the safety of the Netherlands. They had few delusions about Rauter's intentions, and misgivings about negotiating with him, but doing so seemed the only chance of mitigating the suffering ahead.

* * *

Marlies Friedheim, aged twenty

Marlies Friedheim felt sorry for the WA man Hendrik Koot and the terrible way in which had he lost his life; what must the poor man's wife and daughters be going through? And now all the worry about what might happen next ... Already there was fighting on the streets and the Germans were threatening to crack down.

Marlies was twenty, a student at Amsterdam's New School of Art, the *Nieuwe Kunstschool* on Reguliersdwarsstraat. Ceramic design and pottery were her refuge from the world. The art school's founder, Paul Citroen, was a reassuring presence. Citroen was twice her age, but he treated her as an equal and a friend, recognised her talent and her intelligence.

'The Germans need the Dutch to be on their side,' Citroen said. 'The last thing they want is to turn the country against them. They aren't going to go round murdering people.'

* * *

German troops round up Jewish men, Amsterdam, 1941

Hanns Rauter signed the order. 'Four hundred Jews is the minimum,' he said to his aide-de-camp. 'Any resistance and we shoot them.'

On 22 February 1941, German troops entered the Jewish quarter of Amsterdam. Armed detachments of the Ordnungspolizei converged on the Jonas Daniël Meijerplein, driving before them the men they met on the street, cornering them in the square against the canal, kicking and beating them until order was restored.

Hanns Rauter read their report with satisfaction: 389 Jews had been taken alive and were now in custody, awaiting transport to the internment camp at Schoorl, thirty miles north of Amsterdam. From there, it would take a week to transport them to Konzentrationslager Buchenwald. Conditions on the transport and treatment at the camp, the report confirmed, would be rigorous.

* * *

Marlies Friedheim was one of 25,000 German Jews who had moved to the Netherlands. She had grown up in Essen where her parents had put her and her brother, Hans, into a Lutheran school, hoping to shield them from Nazi persecution. But by 1935, when Marlies was fifteen, it was clear that flight was the only option. Now, the nightmares were starting again.

'I know I've been naïve,' she told Paul Citroen. 'I always want to believe the best about the world. But, Paul, does it mean they are coming for us?'

Citroen was also Jewish. He had moved from Berlin to Amsterdam a decade before Marlies, gaining an international reputation as a painter and photographer.

'We have to take the world as we find it,' he said. 'But we must be positive. It is a gift from God.'

Citroen had a way of lifting her spirits. There was an aura of assurance about him that promised protection.

'All my optimism – or stupidity, call it what you will – comes from my parents,' she said. 'When we lived in Germany, they used to say, "Hitler won't last. We'll just be patient and keep our heads down." I told you how they sent me to a Christian school; and for a while it worked. But the Nazis stirred things up. The last Christmas before we emigrated, when I was fourteen and my brother Hans was sixteen, we went out to see all the St Nicholases and Devil Krampuses going round the houses where there were children. We did it every year and we loved it. We celebrated Christmas because my mother didn't want us to feel different. But that year when we were out, a gang of boys appeared and we heard them saying, "Come on, let's beat up the Jews!" Five of them attacked my brother. I tried to separate them, but I couldn't do it, so they punched him and kicked him. When we got home, his mouth and his nose were bleeding. My mother wanted to ring the police, but my father said it's no use – we have no rights any more. That's when my mother decided we couldn't stay in Germany.'

Marlies paused.

'After the incident with my brother, we had a phone call from the mother of one of the boys. She said how sorry they were and that they hadn't brought up their children to be like that; that they always respected us living there and they had punished their boys. She even came to the door to apologise. The older generation weren't as anti-Semitic as the young ones, who were told right from the beginning in school how bad the Jews are.'

'And that's when your parents decided to come to Holland?'

'Yes. My father had transferred some money here and he had a business in Amsterdam making eiderdowns and bedspreads. When we came, in 1935, we had a house in the country. My mother planted vegetables to feed us. At the beginning, we could still write to our friends in Germany, but we can't any more because the authorities open all the letters ...'

* * *

Three days later, Hanns Rauter discovered the law of unintended consequences. He had ordered his men to carry out the Amsterdam pogrom in daylight and in public, because he wanted to make an example of the Jewish terrorists who had dared to challenge the Reich. The operation had succeeded in terrifying Holland's Jews, but it also roused the rest of the country.

On the morning of 25 February, Pim and Anna-Maria were woken by a knock on their door and the familiar whistled signal that material for distribution was being left in the porch.

When they opened the bundles, they found pamphlets written by the outlawed Dutch Communist Party and printed by *De Waarheid*, calling for a national strike.

```
ORGANISEERT IN ALLE BEDRIJVEN DE PROTEST-STAKING !!!
VECHT EENSGEZIND TEGEN DEZE TERREUR !!!
EIST DE ONMIDDELLIJKE VRIJLATING VAN DE GEARRESTEERDE JODEN !!!
EIST DE ONTBINDING VAN DE W.A-TERREURGROEPEN !!!
ORGANISEERT IN DE BEDRIJVEN EN IN DE WIJKEN DE ZELFVERDEDIGING !!!
WEEST SOLIDAIR MET HET ZWAAR GETROFFEN JOODSE DEEL VAN HET
                                        WERKENDE VOLK !!!
ONTTREKT DE JOODSE KINDEREN AAN HET NAZI-GEWELD, NEEMT ZE IN
                                        UW GEZINNEN OP !!!!
B E S E F T    D E    E N O R M E    K R A C H T    V A N
         U W    E E N S G E Z I N D E    D A A D    !!!!!
    Deze is vele malen groter dan de Duitse militaire bezetting!
Gij hebt in Uw verzet ongetwijfeld een groot deel van de Duitse
                            arbeiders-soldaten met U !!!!
STAAKT!!!  STAAKT!!! STAAKT!!!
    Legt het geheele Amsterdamse bedrijfsleven één dag plat, de werven
de fabrieken, de ateliers, de kantoren en banken, gemeente-bedrijven
en werkverschaffingen!!
```

Protest against the persecution of the Jews!!! Strikes in all enterprises!!! Unanimous struggle against this terror!!! Show your solidarity with the abused Jewish workers!!! Protect Jewish children from Nazi violence!!! Shelter them in your homes!!!
STRIKE!!! STRIKE!!! STRIKE!!!

By late afternoon, strikes had broken out in Amsterdam, in Utrecht, Haarlem, Hilversum and Zaandam. The Rotterdam docks were at a standstill; trams and trains stopped running. Workers on bicycles halted traffic and called at people's houses, urging them to join the protest. Thousands gathered in Amsterdam's Northern Market then marched in procession to Dam Square.

Taken by surprise, Rauter phoned Seyss-Inquart to report on the uprising but received scant sympathy. The Polizeiführer had caused the problem, Seyss-Inquart said; the Polizeiführer should fix it.

It was not until the following day, 26 February, that Rauter had forces in place, and early evening before the order was given to engage. Repeated charges with truncheons and bayonets dispersed the protestors. The Ordnungspolizei arrested 200 people and took them to the Lloyd Hotel where they were beaten. Strikes continued, but the Germans were ready now. As soon as a demonstration broke out, troops were on the spot, firing at protestors, throwing hand grenades, dragging people out of the crowd.

Rauter wanted retribution. Eighteen strikers were charged with sedition and sentenced to death. A firing squad was convened for dawn on 13 March in the dunes of Waalsdorpervlakte on the coast near The Hague. On the eve of their execution, the poet Jan Campert wrote the stanzas of his poem '*De Achttien Doden*' – 'The Eighteen Dead' – on the wall of his prison cell.

A cell is just two metres long,
A scant two metres wide;
But smaller still is the plot of earth
Where we shall now reside.
The place unknown, the nameless way
Eighteen of us must tread;
None of us shall see the day,
None share the morning bread.

Oh radiant coast of Holland,
Light of my native land,
Now blighted by the curse of war,
Besmirched by devils' hands.
What can the man of honour do
In that dark silent night,
But kiss his wife and kiss his child
And fight the lonely fight.

I knew the hardships, knew the worst,
When the fight we first began.
My heart, don't fail me at the last;
Let me live and die a man!
And you who read these lines,
Think on my comrades here,
As we have thought on life and love
And on this land so dear.

But now the dawning comes on bright
Through the window barred on high;
Oh God, I beg you: Make it light,
That moment when we die . . .

Coffins of the executed hostages on the dunes of Waalsdorpervlakte

* * *

The families of the 389 Jewish men transported to Buchenwald sought news of their fate. Some of the prisoners were reported to have died in transit, others on arrival at the camp. Those who survived had been transferred to work in the quarries at Konzentrationslager Mauthausen, where further deaths had occurred, reportedly from work-related accidents and suicide.

Jewish men transported from Amsterdam on arrival in Buchenwald, 28 February 1941

Abraham Asscher, chairman of the Amsterdam Jewish Council, was ordered to deal with the men's relatives whose grief was turning to anger. Asscher was a diamond trader, not a politician; his deputy at the Council, Dr David Cohen, was a professor of ancient Greek. Their pre-war record of aiding Jewish refugees gave them credibility in the Jewish community, but questions were being asked about their new role as mediators for the Germans. The Jewish Council had advised people not to support the February strike, arguing that doing so would provoke reprisals. Asscher and Cohen hoped the work of the Council might offer a means to influence the occupying power; for Hanns Rauter, it was a tool to facilitate the coming holocaust.

4

THE DILEMMA OF RESISTANCE

The organ loft at St Boniface's had a mirror that allowed the organist to follow the choirmaster without turning his head. In his afternoons of solitary practice, Adrianus Roest used it to keep an eye on the west door; the church was never locked and not everyone respected its sanctity.

The man in the dark raincoat praying in the rear pews had his face in shadow, but Adrianus recognised him. He clicked the switch to turn off the bellows, closed the console door and descended the stairs to the nave.

'Hello, Ruud,' Adrianus said.

Wilders pulled himself to his feet. 'Adrianus.'

The two men shook hands.

'We can talk in the vestry,' Adrianus said. 'The priest is away, so consider me *in loco sacerdotis*.'

'I want to say a couple of things for your benefit, not mine,' Wilders said. 'When we last spoke, you were toying with the idea that the Germans could be beaten. But you should stop fooling yourself.'

'You seem pretty certain ...'

'I am certain. I've seen it from the inside and they're not going to be stopped.'

'From the inside ... ?'

'I told you. The Germans called us in, all of us at commander rank and above. They asked who spoke German and we all did, pretty much. So they went on seniority and experience. I got called to Seyss-Inquart's office ...'

'You're working for Seyss-Inquart?' Adrianus was shocked.

'I'm in intelligence. Eyes and ears,' Wilders said. 'They're worried about the pushback they're getting from society – it's come as a surprise to them.'

'How do you know all this?'

'Because I've seen it happening. And there's no shortage of Dutchmen willing to spy for the Germans. Hanns Rauter runs an army of double agents, with people in all the Resistance groups; there's very little that Rauter doesn't know.'

'And *you*?' Adrianus muttered.

'No,' Wilders said. 'I don't know about it because I'm with Seyss-Inquart. And *he* doesn't know about it because he and Rauter hate each other. Rauter runs the anti-Resistance stuff and keeps most of it to himself. But if anyone dear to you is involved in the Resistance, you should tell them to get out now!'

* * *

Hanns Rauter enjoyed the favours of Himmler and Himmler had the ear of the Führer. Rauter's reports on the setback of the February strike had been carefully worded to convince them that responsibility lay at the door of Seyss-Inquart, while Rauter's own reputation remained intact. The Sicherheitsdienst intelligence agency, the Ordnungspolizei and the Gestapo in the Netherlands all reported to him. He controlled the operations of the Waffen-SS and the Dutch police; it was his version of events that Berlin believed.

Hanns Rauter

By the middle of 1941, Rauter was ready to challenge Seyss-Inquart and the issue he chose was the NSB. Anton Mussert's Dutch fascists had been useful in the early days of the occupation, but Hitler had lost patience with them. Rauter set himself up as the NSB's nemesis. He decried Mussert's opposition to Holland's incorporation into Greater Germany; he closed down the NSB's intelligence service and denounced its director as an agent of the British. In reports to Himmler, he implied that Seyss-Inquart was showing a dangerous level of loyalty to Mussert and warned that it was damaging the interests of the Reich.

With his star in the ascendant, Rauter unleashed the Gestapo. All necessary measures, he decreed, should now be deployed to eliminate the Dutch Resistance.

* * *

Spring 1941 was the high point of Anna-Maria's acting career. What began as a hobby had become a serious undertaking. The troupe now included established actors who had lost their jobs when the Germans closed the professional theatres. Costumiers and set designers who had graced the stage of the Stadsschouwburg were willing to work with students, simply in order to carry on working.

Anna-Maria (left) on stage

In May, the company began rehearsals for a production of the classic drama *Gijsbrecht van Aemstel*. The plot, involving a fourteenth-century siege of Amsterdam and a Dutch nobleman driven from his homeland by foreign invaders, had contemporary connotations, but the censors showed little interest.

When a preview in Leiden was well received, venues in six other cities booked them for multiple dates. At each of them, Anna-Maria acknowledged the applause and passed on the bundles of *De Waarheid*. She and Pim were getting on well; life had settled into a rhythm.

At first she didn't notice them. The same two men, in the same front-row seats. But having spotted them, she knew at once that they had been there before, in the tell-tale mufti of the plain-clothes Gestapo – short hair, dark suit, white shirt, sober tie. And they were looking at her.

The same two men . . .

* * *

They came for her after the performance; waiting at the stage door, smirking, jostling her as she tried to pass.

'Don't be like that, Miss.' They were speaking German. 'Don't snub your admirers!'

'Admirers?' Anna-Maria replied in Dutch. 'I don't want admirers like you!'

'But we only want to take you to dinner,' the men were saying. 'Come and have a good time with two nice German boys!'

'Why don't you stop the charade?' Anna-Maria said. 'Why don't you tell me why you are really here?'

The men laughed.

'Well, if that's what you want, then of course. It is our duty to inform you that distributing subversive literature is a serious offence – in fact, a capital offence.'

Anna-Maria's hand rose to the silver pendant on her breast.

'We know about your sideline in communist propaganda. We know who your accomplices are. There's no point denying it.'

The man paused.

'I can see you're scared,' he said. 'You're probably thinking of the firing squad and the bullets ripping into that pretty chest of yours. But don't worry, Miss; we're here to tell you there's a way out. You don't have to die; that would just be stupid. All you have to do is come and work for us. No one needs to know. And we'll look after you. You'll be protected, you'll be paid. But just to be clear: if you refuse, we're taking you to the interrogators at Euterpestraat.'

* * *

Adrianus rang.

'Pim, thank God. And Anna-Maria, is she there, too?'

Pim heard the strain in his father's voice.

'No, Dad, she's in Amsterdam tonight. It's the last performance of *Gijsbrecht*.'

'Ah . . .'

'Dad? What is it?'

'Nothing; nothing, son. Only, please – ring me when she gets back . . .'

* * *

In the rear of the black Mercedes, Anna-Maria felt the shoulders of the Gestapo men against hers, the silk of their jackets soft on her arms, their steady breathing and her heart racing out of control.

The driver joined in the banter.

'So, what do you make of our offer, Miss? Quite a bargain, don't you think?'

In the rear-view mirror Anna-Maria returned his stare and shook her head.

'I'm not sure that's wise,' the man said. 'My colleagues have told you what happens if you refuse. If you refuse, we can simply shoot you and get commended for it; or we can take you to the forest and enjoy ourselves before we pull the trigger . . .'

A safety catch clicked.

'I'll never work for the Nazis,' Anna-Maria said. 'Never! If you are going to shoot me, then shoot me!'

She struggled to sit up.

'Look!' she said. 'Look at the pendant! This is my queen in this life. And as for the next, the Queen of Heaven is my protector!'

* * *

Alarmed by Adrianus's call, Pim rang the theatre.

The stage manager confirmed that Anna-Maria had completed the performance. They had been expecting her at the end-of-tour party, but for some reason she hadn't shown up.

* * *

The car slowed to a halt. Anna-Maria closed her eyes, waiting for the bullets.

A woman's voice spoke in Dutch.

'Forgive us,' the voice said. 'That was unpardonably cruel.'

Anna-Maria looked up. A tall, middle-aged woman with dark hair was leaning into the car.

'It was cruel,' the woman said. 'But we needed to test you . . .'

* * *

Ruud Wilders took his copy of the *Aanwijzingen* from his desk drawer.

'In the interest of the people,' Wilders read, 'public servants shall remain at their post. Officials shall discharge their duties to the utmost of their ability, mitigating the burdens of the occupation, acting as intermediaries between the occupying forces and the population.'

Like many of his colleagues, Wilders took comfort from the *Aanwijzingen in Geval van een Vijandelijke Inval* – 'Regulations in Case of Enemy Invasion' – that had been drawn up in 1937 when the Dutch authorities were already fearful of incursions by their eastern neighbours. He turned the page.

A public servant shall be permitted to leave his post only in case of dismissal.

On that point, the Regulations were categorical.

> A public servant shall, however, protest against any measure
> introduced by the occupying power that would run counter
> to international law.

How could a public servant – even a lawyer or a policeman –
be expected to judge which of his actions are acceptable under
international law? You might have thought that aiding the
Germans in mapping where Amsterdam's Jews lived would be
considered unacceptable. But Mayor Edward Voûte had agreed
to it when he ordered the National Records Office to comply
with Seyss-Inquart's demand for a register of Jewish addresses.

It seemed public servants must judge for themselves where
the line lay between national duty and collaboration.

Wilders was finding it hard to sleep.

Arthur Seyss-Inquart (left) and Mayor Edward Voûte (right)

* * *

The woman helped Anna-Maria out of the car. They had drawn
up beside a row of recently built Amsterdam townhouses with
iron balustrades and windows blacked out against the attentions
of the RAF. One by one, the men from the Mercedes embraced

the woman, who ushered them through the door of number 6. A painted sign decorated with ceramic roses proclaimed that they were entering 'Beauty Salon Health and Lust for Life'.

The woman took Anna-Maria's arm. 'It's my hobby,' she said, pointing to the sign. 'Well, my business actually. No point in letting the war get in the way of beauty or life … or lust.'

Anna-Maria did not smile. The woman pulled her close.

'I am so sorry, my dear,' she said. 'I am Mies Boissevain. The men you thought were the enemy are my sons. Welcome to Corellistraat.'

Mies Boissevain

* * *

When the phone rang the following morning, Pim had already reconciled himself to hearing the worst. The sound of Anna-Maria's voice overwhelmed him.

'Pim, dearest …' she began. 'I'm all right … Don't worry. Come to the Amsterdam tram station. They're sending someone to meet you …'

* * *

For Holland's Jews, 1941 was the year of reckoning. They were told they must now carry identity cards classifying them by their religion. The new cards were designed to make them harder to forge; their ration books were stamped with the letter J; plans were put in place for the mandatory wearing of the Star of David. Unemployed Jews – their numbers swollen by the closure of Jewish businesses and dismissals from public employment – were liable to be taken to work camps.

Some 160,000 Jews lived in the Netherlands, of whom 140,000 had Dutch nationality. The others were refugees, including 16,000 from Germany and 2,000 from Poland. Over half of all Jews lived in Amsterdam, 20,000 in The Hague and the rest scattered in towns and villages across the country. By October 1941, 140,001 'full-Jews' had been registered and 20,885 'half-' or 'quarter-Jews'.

Hanns Rauter presided over the new measures and he had willing accomplices. The Dutch civil service was zealous in registering Jews and denouncing Jewish employees, the judiciary in implementing German justice, the District Labour Offices in assigning Jews to work camps, the railways and police in transporting them.

The Jewish Council was bribed, bullied and threatened into doing Rauter's bidding. Abraham Asscher and David Cohen were told that co-operating with 'regulatory procedures' would avoid the necessity for harsher measures in the future, and they chose to believe it.

Rauter wrote to Himmler.

The rounding up of the Jews will make us rack our brains to the utmost, but I will not fail to make use of all my powers ... It is not a nice job; it is dirty work, but it is a measure that history will remember as hugely important ... There is no room for tenderness or weakness. He who does not understand this, he who is full of pity or foolish talk about humanitarianism and idealism, is not fit to lead.

In a speech to the staff of his department, Rauter added, 'I shall gladly do penance in heaven for my sins against the Jews on earth.'

* * *

The New School of Art had continued to take in Jewish students when other schools were turning them away. The German authorities sent Citroen a letter threatening closure. 'It's not hard to see why,' he told Marlies Friedheim. 'I'm Jewish, the lecturers are Jewish and most of the students are Jewish, including you. What will you do if they close us down?'

'My dad says there's no point worrying about things you can't control,' Marlies said. 'The worst might never happen; and if it does we can face it then ...'

* * *

The house was full of people, a domestic bustle in which Anna-Maria seemed already at home. She introduced Pim to Madame Boissevain.

6 Corellistraat, Amsterdam

'Welcome,' Mies said, 'and apologies for the manner of our meeting. I have explained to Anna-Maria why we needed to put her through such an ordeal. In this business you cannot be too careful.'

'Business?' Pim said angrily. 'You knew who we were, you know how reliable we've been in distributing the paper . . .'

'Yes,' Mies said. 'But the work we do is much more than delivering newspapers. It demands the ultimate dedication. And Anna-Maria has shown she has it.'

'What sort of work?' he asked. 'And what made you pick us?'

'We will tell you about the work when we know each other,' Mies replied. 'As for what made us select you, people make recommendations. A contact in the theatre told us of certain skills that Anna-Maria can offer us. But please – let's start on the right foot. Come and eat.'

*Mies Boissevain (front, second from left) with her
husband Jan (back, centre), sister and children*

In the Corelli Street kitchen, over a stew of vegetables from
the garden, there were explanations and introductions. The
Boissevain sons who had abducted Anna-Maria were Janka,
twenty-two, Gideon, twenty-one, and Frans, twenty. Mies's
daughters, Annemie and Sylvia, and her sister, Hester, made
up the party. Tensions eased. Mies spoke about the origins of
her beauty salon business. She had started it in 1933 while they
were still living in their old house on Keizersgracht in the canal
district. It wasn't anything to do with making money, Mies
said – the Boissevains had always been wealthy; it was more to
prove to her husband, Jan, that a woman could make a living
and earn enough to support herself.

'I have always believed in women's rights,' Mies said. 'And
the thing is – you may have noticed this – I don't like being told
what to do!'

Gideon, Janka, Frans, Annemie and Sylvia burst into laughter.
Pim and Anna-Maria smiled.

'Good!' Mies said. 'Now I'll show you where we make
the bombs.'

Basement, 6 Corellistraat, 1941

* * *

The Opbouwdienst's task of transforming the institutions of Dutch society to serve the Reich had been completed with remarkable ease. Tens of thousands in the army, police and civil service had signed up to work for their new masters. Encouraged, Reichskommissar Seyss-Inquart announced that a new body, the National Labour Service, the Arbeidsdienst, was being set up to provide employment for all Dutch men and women.

When an initial appeal for voluntary registration produced disappointing results, Seyss-Inquart made the scheme compulsory. All citizens between seventeen and twenty-three were required to present themselves for six months of training and physical labour. Women were given work near their homes, sewing uniforms or peeling potatoes for the army; men were assigned to work camps, where they were used in the construction of roads and canals or in agricultural labour.

Arbeidsdienst display of marching with spades

Seyss-Inquart had promised that Dutch citizens would not be conscripted into the military, but the men found they were being made to drill with a shovel on their shoulder and undergo training in digging trenches and tank traps. Forced marches, lasting up to four days, caused resentment. When the Hitler salute was made obligatory for the Arbeidsdienst, resentment turned to anger.

* * *

Pim and Anna-Maria stayed the night at 6 Corelli Street. Mies had shown them the cellar and explained that Group CS-6, named after the Boissevains' home address, was dedicated to active resistance, sabotaging German munitions plants and storage depots, blowing up railway lines and collecting information to send to London. When Mies asked if they were willing to participate, Pim and Anna-Maria said they were.

'Then it means you must stay for a while longer,' Mies said. 'We need to introduce you to some important people.'

In the days that followed, Mies told them about her own

family and about her husband, Jan Boissevain, whom she had married at the age of twenty-five in 1921. His French surname was the legacy of seventeenth-century intolerance, when Louis XIV had driven out France's Protestants and Jan's ancestors had come to Holland. The Boissevains had gone on to make their fortune in investment banking, with Jan's grandfather Adolphe moving to North America in search of further riches. Jan himself had been born in Montreal – he was known to the rest of the family as 'Jan Canada' – and had returned to the Netherlands to marry Mies.

Jan 'Canada' Boissevain (rear)

Jan Boissevain now owned of one of Amsterdam's leading banking and insurance companies, where, Mies said, things were becoming difficult. The Germans had told Jan to fire his Jewish employees, but he had refused. He had received threats from Hanns Rauter's office and was spending as much time as possible at work in case of a German raid. Three of Jan's Jewish workers had been attacked by SS thugs and had gone into hiding.

'In fact,' Mies said, 'I can introduce you to them – they're in our attic.'

* * *

Anti-Semitism had many faces. It was the generational antipathy of East European peasants, the political opportunism of the Beer Hall demagogues, the pseudo-scientific absurdities of manipulative racists, the fervent soul-loathing that had Adolf Eichmann claiming he would 'leap into his grave laughing' with the 'extraordinary satisfaction' of having five million deaths on his conscience.

For Arthur Seyss-Inquart it was lists and numbers; the deportation of the Jews was a task to be carried out with sound logistics and no questions. A good bureaucrat, he set up a committee. The Central Office for Jewish Emigration, the *Zentralstelle für Judische Auswanderung*, was formed in March 1941, its offices expediently located beside the Gestapo headquarters on Euterpestraat. Its director, Sturmbannführer Willy Lages, and his deputy, Hauptsturmführer Ferdinand aus der Fünten, recruited some staff from the German military, but the majority of its one hundred or so employees were Dutch.

The Zentralstelle's initial mission statement was to 'monitor all Jews, analyse Jewish life and co-ordinate emigration'. The work was mundane. Clerks and stenographers spent their days collecting and collating information, amassing the data that would be needed for the future operation that no one spoke about.

* * *

Pim rang his father to tell him not to worry: he and Anna-Maria were away for a few days and things were all right. Adrianus knew things weren't.

He took the train to The Hague and walked the half-mile from the station to the Binnenhof. He told the sentry he wanted to see Ruud Wilders in the cabinet of the Reichskommissar and the sentry, recognising Wilders' name, directed him to the pass office. Adrianus was escorted to a room in Binnenhof 4, overlooking the waters of the Hofvijver. He refused Wilders' invitation to sit.

'You were warning me!' Adrianus said. 'You were warning me because you knew Pim and Anna-Maria were in danger. You knew ...'

Wilders motioned him to keep his voice down. 'Did Pim tell you he was working with the Resistance?'

'No,' Adrianus said. 'But I know my son – and I know his wife. And you knew it, too. I detest what you are doing, Ruud!'

* * *

Janka and Gideon Boissevain told Pim they were going for a day at the beach. When they asked if he would like to come, he knew it was not for a picnic.

The village of Bergen aan Zee on the coast of the North Holland Peninsula had been a resort since the turn of the century. Miles of uninhabited North Sea dunes and expanses of forest attracted ramblers from the Netherlands and Germany. Germans from the Ruhr cities, Essen, Dortmund, Dusseldorf, had built a children's colony there before the First World War, the *Kinderheim von der Deutsche Hilfsverein*. Bergen was served by a light railway from nearby Alkmaar, but Janka said it would be too dangerous: much of the coast was now a military zone and the Ordnungspolizei policed the trains; safer to cycle to Alkmaar, then cover the last five miles on foot.

They waited until the curfew emptied the Alkmaar streets and set off westwards. There was no moon, but Gideon and Janka knew the way, through fields, across streams and marshland, keeping clear of the roads and lanes until the clay turned to sand and the salt air told them their destination was close. A path dug out of the dunes appeared and disappeared, shifting with the wind and silt. Between it and the sea a single cottage stood in darkness. At Gideon's whistle, the door opened.

Kees Dutilh, 1941

Kees Dutilh had been keeping watch. Watching the Germans was Kees's occupation – their trucks, their planes, their ships in the North Sea approaches from Rotterdam in the south to Wilhelmshaven and Bremen in the north. Kees's eyes were the eyes of the northern Resistance – walking the coastline, talking to locals, logging anything that might be important to the Allies. And he had found something of the utmost importance.

Over ersatz coffee, brewed on a stove that filled the room with smoke because smoke could not be allowed to rise from the chimney, they discussed how to proceed. Since there were four sites, Janka said, a simultaneous operation, one site each, seemed prudent. At least one of them might evade the patrols; and one dossier sent to England would be better than all of them perishing together.

On stencilled maps, Kees sketched out the forest trails and wrote directions for distances to cover and turnings to take. The cameras were sensitive, he said, but they would need to get close. If any one of them had not returned by 6 a.m., the others should leave at once.

* * *

Janka got back first; then Gideon and Pim. An anxious wait for Kees ended as dawn broke.

In the cottage's makeshift darkroom, they took turns to unload the film from their cameras. With carbon paper from beneath the floorboards they made copies of their observations, one for each of them to carry back.

Gideon, Janka and Pim had photographed the nearer masts and estimated their heights at between 250 and 300 feet. Kees, who knew the area, had trekked north to Schoorl, where he found the Klimweg newly tarmacked and the site it led to, on the crest of a 150-foot dune, surrounded by wooden fences. He took the first photos from the shelter of a copse and then got closer. A hurried inspection through a gap in the fence revealed the scope of the thing – thirty feet high with motors mounted on a circular track that moved the apparatus through 360 degrees in less than a minute.

When the four of them plotted the locations they had reconnoitred, they formed a straight line emanating from the Schoorl radar tower, configured to guide the Junker-88s and the Dornier-335s on their way to England.

German radar installation, North Holland Peninsula, 1941

5

THE FINAL SOLUTION

The Zentralstelle bureaucrats were assiduous. The mass of names and addresses that had been collected in response to Seyss-Inquart's Decree on Jewish Registration was processed and stored in filing cabinets in the Dutch public records office. When Seyss-Inquart issued his next decree, the Zentralstelle's mandate was expanded: from now on, its mission would be to 'restrict Jewish movement and prepare for the *Endlösung der Judenfrage*, the Final Solution'. The Reichskommissar's *Anordnung über das Auftreten von Juden in der Öffentlichkeit* – Regulation Concerning the Presence of Jews in Public Life – bore the hallmarks of punctilious pseudo-legality, with enough exceptions, provisos and qualifications that its fearful targets might somehow convince themselves of its reasonableness.

SECOND REGULATION OF THE COMMISSAR-GENERAL FOR PUBLIC SECURITY: CONCERNING THE PRESENCE OF JEWS IN PUBLIC LIFE.

Paragraph 1.

Jews must be in their homes between the hours of 20:00 and 06:00.

Paragraph 2.

Jews may not be present in homes, parks, and other private institutions that are used for recreation or entertainment of non-Jews, unless this is essential on the basis of an existing lease or labour contract.

Jews married to non-Jews are not included in this regulation.

Paragraph 3.

Jews may enter shops that are not marked as Jewish businesses only between the hours of 15:00 and 17:00. Pharmacies are excluded from this rule.

Jews may not order home deliveries.

Paragraph 4.

Jews may neither enter nor use the services of barber shops or paramedical institutions unless they are marked as Jewish.

Paragraph 5.

Jews may neither enter railway stations nor use any means of public and private transport. The following exceptions are stipulated:

- the riding of bicycles within the town limits of Amsterdam;
- the transport of the seriously ill in an ambulance;
- the use of transport on the basis of a permit issued by the Security Police.

Jews who in these cases are allowed to use public transport must be seated in the last compartment (smokers class). They may enter and seat themselves only when there is sufficient seating space for non-Jewish passengers.

Paragraph 6.

Jews may not use public telephones.

Paragraph 7.

A Jew for the purpose of this regulation is any person who is a Jew or is considered a Jew under Paragraph 4 of Regulation 189/1940 concerning the registration of Jewish enterprises.

Paragraph 8.

Implementation orders and additional exceptions to those noted in Paragraphs 1–6 will be advertised in the *Jewish Weekly*.

Paragraph 9.

Persons who violate or circumvent the regulations in Paragraphs 1–6 shall be punished with a maximum prison sentence of six months and a maximum fine of 1,000 guilders. Any person who encourages, aids or abets circumvention of these regulations will face the same punishment.

* * *

The message came by courier, a boy of sixteen who arrived on a bicycle with a code phrase he had been told to slip into the conversation.

'Jazz is great,' the lad announced. 'Especially when it goes with swing.'

'Yes,' Pim replied. 'And Ellington is the king of swing.'

'Okay,' said the boy. 'You're to come with me. Two of you, right? And they've given you both bikes?'

Pim and Anna-Maria, 1941

* * *

The directors of the Zentralstelle prepared for the work that lay ahead. Willy Lages and Ferdinand aus der Fünten took on extra staff including young Jews, because – they told their colleagues – a Jew is best equipped to see through another Jew's wiles.

Using the index of names that had been compiled in the Amsterdam Registry Office – the *Bevolkingsregister* – Lages instructed his staff to select different categories based on age, education and skills. The first selection of Jews would be deployed for work in the Netherlands; the bulk of the country's food production was being sent to Germany and extra hands were needed on the farms. As for subsequent selections, their fate would be determined later.

Willy Lages

Ferdinand aus der Fünten

* * *

Marlies's father asked the family to join him in the kitchen; there was something in the *Jewish Weekly* they needed to be aware of. As Mr Friedheim read out Seyss-Inquart's decree, Marlies saw her mother's face darken.

'It's the pettiness of it,' Mrs Friedheim said. 'All the little things, the drip-drip-drip of oppression. They do it to us *because they can*. They're showing us they have power over our lives and we have no defence against them.'

Mr Friedheim tried to smile. His wife did not.

'They're toying with us,' she said. 'Of course we can cope with sitting at the back of the bus and all the other trivial stuff. They're letting us know that something much, much worse is coming ...'

'There's no point in fretting,' Mr Friedheim said.

'No point in fretting!' Mrs Friedheim said. 'How are we going to live now that the Germans have closed down your business and blocked our bank account? We're at their mercy!'

* * *

Pim, Anna-Maria and the boy cycled east to Almere then north along the Ijsselmeer, over the bridges of the reclaimed lowlands and into the canal-threaded fields of the Noordoostpolder. After the confinement of Amsterdam, the air smelled of freedom, their wheels crunching through soil that for millennia had lain submerged on the bed of the Zuiderzee, splintering ancient fossils risen from the depths. The fields were neglected and the pumps struggled to keep the sea at bay, but the richness of the silt continued to breed tulips in patchwork reds and creams and yellows. The polder was new and still not fully drained: uncharted, shifting land that offered hiding places for those who needed them. Half a mile before the ice-age promontory of Urk, the boy signalled them to stop.

'Wait here,' he said. 'I will go and tell the boss. If I'm not back in forty minutes, you should turn round and go home.'

* * *

Mr Friedheim opened the letter in his study.

'It's not good news,' he said when they had all gathered. 'But it could have been much worse. Nothing in here about us old folks, but you two' – he gestured to Marlies and Hans – 'are going to the countryside.'

* * *

The boy returned.

Pim and Anna-Maria followed him down a side road until they reached a wooden building with a greenhouse, evidently part of an old tulip farm, now abandoned.

'We're to wait,' the boy said.

Five minutes passed, then another five.

'All right. Come in!' The voice came from inside the building.

After the daylight they found the room dark. A heavy-set man with his face in shadow motioned them to stop.

'Names!' Then, answering his own question, 'Roest and Van der Vaart, right?'

Pim and Anna-Maria nodded.

'Ages?'

'Twenty-three. Twenty-two.'

'Experience with *De Waarheid* and CS-6 ... Okay ... Political?'

Pim and Anna-Maria shook their heads. The man emerged from the shadow.

'Fine, fine. Doesn't matter anyway. Believe what you want. All that's for afterwards.'

When he took them by the arm and led them outside, they were surprised by the size of him; well over six feet tall, a boxer's muscles bulging under his clothes. He walked with a limp. As they set off into the field, Anna-Maria saw that he swayed from side to side, as if one leg were shorter than the other.

'We have people on the lookout everywhere,' the man said to Anna-Maria. 'Your stage manager told us about the admiration you get from the Germans. That could be useful for us. The boy will take you back to CS-6. And they'll introduce you to your minder – Uncle Anton talks to me and I talk to London.'

* * *

On the way back, the boy wanted to chat.

'What a guy! The boss is the toughest man in the whole of the Resistance. He's killed twenty-seven Germans all on his own, back in the fighting last year. Everyone's scared of him. And he's smart – no one ever knows where he is or what he's doing. He's always one step ahead of everyone!'

'Why does he limp?' Pim asked.

'Some people say it was the Germans,' the boy said. 'But *I* know what happened. When he was growing up in Rotterdam, he loved motorbikes and he worked in a garage where they had the most powerful bikes in the world. One day he took out this bike that they'd really souped up and he did nearly 250 kilo- metres per hour, then he hit a patch of oil on the road and he smashed all the bones in his body. But he was tough. He built up his strength again and his muscles. He limps, but it doesn't make him any weaker.'

'You really admire him!' Anna-Maria said.

'Everyone does,' said the boy. 'He's been working for the British ever since the Nazis came. He's infiltrated the Germans for them; he drives petrol tankers for the Wehrmacht from here to Lille and Paris, so he can keep an eye on the German troop movements and all their trucks and tanks and he sends the information to London.'

'What's his name?' Pim asked.

'I don't know. No one does. We just call him King Kong.'

'King Kong'

* * *

Marlies and her brother Hans arrived on time for their appointment at Euterpestraat, each – as instructed – with a single suitcase containing clothes and personal possessions. Inside the Zentralstelle, there was chaos. Corridors were packed with anxious men and women, some with children and babies who cried incessantly. German officials, Dutch police and clerks from the Jewish Council were checking papers, calling out names.

It was the following morning before Marlies and Hans were issued with their travel documents and loaded onto the back of a military truck.

* * *

Mies Boissevain met Pim and Anna-Maria at the front door.

'Bad news,' Mies said as soon as they were in the hallway. 'There've been arrests in Haarlem. Two of our people. I hope to God they don't talk. The Gestapo are ruthless and Johannes and Henk know where we are . . . The most terrible thing is that someone betrayed them. It's best if you two go home. But first you have to meet someone.'

Mies ushered them downstairs and opened the door to the cellar.

'This is Uncle Anton,' she said. 'Anton will be your link with King Kong and the Resistance Council and with us. You need to talk to him about how things will work for you.'

Cellar, 6 Corellistraat

In a room tunnelled out of the clay beneath the house, a man was sifting through a sheaf of documents by the light of a paraffin lamp. He put them aside, gave a slight bow and extended his hand.

'Welcome, welcome,' he said. 'And congratulations. King Kong speaks well of you.' The man was rather handsome, Anna-Maria thought, with an exaggerated civility.

'Now, I believe the boss told you that you will be working with me. It doesn't mean we will be seeing a lot of each other. I am constantly on the move, I don't stay in one place more than a couple of days. But we have other ways of keeping in touch. From now on, your instructions will come from me and I shall need to know everything about your movements and activities.'

The man recited a series of addresses and telephone numbers, which he asked Pim and Anna-Maria to commit to memory.

He listed different codewords to be used in different situations, from routine messaging to emergencies.

'I apologise that I cannot prolong this meeting,' he concluded. 'But you may have heard that we are dealing with a contretemps involving two of our operatives who have had the imprudence to allow themselves to be captured by the Gestapo.'

'Uncle Anton'

* * *

Janka and Gideon drove them back to Rotterdam. They spoke about Uncle Anton and Janka said he was a trusted comrade, an electrical engineer from Rotterdam whose knowledge of radio technology had made him an important figure in the Resistance's communications with England.

Anna-Maria said how much she admired Mies.

'She is remarkable,' Gideon replied. 'We love her very much.'

'But she must be worried about the risks you are taking,' Anna-Maria said.

'What would we be doing if it wasn't for the war?' Janka said sharply. 'I'd be at the phone company, messing around with valves and diodes, and Gi would be wasting his days underwriting policies for Dad's insurance business. Fighting back is dangerous, but it's meaningful.'

They were approaching Gouda when Janka spoke again.

'We all die. Die at twenty, die at seventy; it doesn't matter. What matters is what we leave behind, what we do to justify the life we've been given.'

'But what are Johannes and Henk going through right now?' Gideon said. 'How bitter in those final minutes to know that your death comes from the treachery of a comrade.'

* * *

The official media announced the arrest of Johannes Bierhuijs and Henk Schoenmaker on 11 May. *Volk en Vaderland* described them as crazed saboteurs bent on destroying the institutions of civilised society. When their cowardly attempt to dynamite the Prinsen Bolsen marshalling yard in Haarlem was disturbed by a Wehrmacht railway guard, said the newspaper, the two terrorists had opened fire. The guard, Hans Hebel, was left wounded and fighting for his life, the first German to be targeted by the so-called Resistance, an act that demanded the severest retribution. A reward of 5,000 guilders had elicited an immediate and commendable response from Haarlem's law-abiding population. The perpetrators had been turned over to the police and sentenced to death.

'German justice,' concluded the article, 'is inexorable; there can be no escape for those who challenge the authority of the Reich.'

* * *

Marlies and Hans Friedheim were dropped at the gate of a dairy farm near Hollandsche Rading, thirty miles south of Groningen. At the farmhouse door, an elderly couple took their suitcases and ushered them into the kitchen. Plates of scrambled eggs and fresh vegetables were laid on the table, with mugs of impossibly creamy coffee.

'We are so pleased to see you,' said the farmer, Cornelis Griffioen. 'I had a stroke last year and Aafje' – he gestured to his wife – 'suffers with kidney disease. We thought the farm would go to ruin, but now you are here to help us. You cannot imagine how happy you have made us!'

6

V-Men: traitors and spies

Twenty-two-year-old Johannes Bierhuijs and twenty-seven-year-old Henk Schoenmaker would both be executed in the dunes of Waalsdorpervlakte where the February strikers had been shot before them. But what *Volk en Vaderland* did not say was that a third man had been arrested. In addition to Bierhuijs and Schoenmaker, a monk named Josef Klingen was also in the Gestapo's custody.

The confidential report of the Sicherheitsdienst, compiled by the bureau's director, Untersturmführer Joseph Schreieder, revealed that the 5,000 guilders reward had been paid not to a concerned Dutch civilian but to a professional informer – a *Vertrauensmann* or V-Mann – codenamed De Wilde who had infiltrated the ranks of the Resistance.

'For his role in the arrest of Johannes Bierhuijs,' Schreieder reported, 'V-Mann De Wilde received 5,000 guilders in the form of 50 banknotes of 100 guilders. De Wilde needed money urgently so I paid it to him from my own cash in advance and settled the account later with the finance department.'

According to Schreieder, the arrested men were all members of a Resistance group based in Heemstede, south of Haarlem, known by the name ECH/3, the designation of a type of Philips radio tube, because they were transmitting information about German military activities to London. Schreieder's version of the operation to dismantle ECH/3 made much of his own intelligence skills:

I suspected that ECH/3 was operating out of the Saint Jean-Baptiste de la Salle monastery on Herenweg and that it was led by a monk, Brother Josef Klingen from Alem. I tried an initial raid on the pretext that Klingen and his associates might be listening to illegal broadcasts from London, but failed to find any radio equipment.

I therefore sent V-Mann codename De Wilde to infiltrate the group. He was instructed to pose as a Resistance sympathiser who could help them communicate with the British. De Wilde demonstrated his capacity to ingratiate himself at a meeting with Brother Josef and his associate, Henk Schoenmaker. De Wilde is at his best in such circumstances; he understands the art of fooling people and gaining their trust. Schoenmaker and Brother Josef believed the infiltrator at his word – a fatal mistake.

Schreieder expressed satisfaction at De Wilde's success, but his account of subsequent events hinted at tensions between them.

V-Mann De Wilde reported to me what he had discovered. 'Today I have very important announcements,' he declared, self-assuredly taking a seat at my desk. 'What news do you have?' I asked him. 'Brother Josef has a transmitting device not much bigger than a flashlight battery. He carries it always with him, under his monk's robe.' 'Does it make radio contact with England?' I asked. 'Yes,' said De Wilde, 'Brother Josef says that he transmits with this device and that he there-fore always keeps it on him.' 'But surely he cannot establish radio communication with England at any time he pleases,' I objected. 'With radio traffic, everyone must adhere to fixed transmission times. Surely you should know that!' De Wilde hesitated and after some thought replied, 'That is true. But, in any case, Brother Josef claims he has radio communication with England.' 'Then it is your job to find out more about this radio communication!' I said, ending this part of the conversation. 'Do you have any more news for me?' 'Yes,' De Wilde replied. 'The pistol used to shoot the railway guard in Haarlem belongs to Brother Josef. Brother Josef himself confirmed to me that he lent the gun to the shooter!' I asked him if he had uncovered the identity of the shooter and De Wilde said yes, he had.

De Wilde gave Schreieder the name and address of Johannes Bierhuijs. Using De Wilde's information, the SD was able to arrest Bierhuijs and charge him with the attempted murder of the Wehrmacht guard. But Schreieder was not finished.

I wasn't sure what to think of De Wilde. I wasn't confident about his motives; I still knew too little about him. Admittedly, he had provided me with enough material to proceed with an arrest, but his messages to me were too vague. He had been in contact with the ECH/3 group all this time and I was worried that Brother Josef would become suspicious. I could not stretch out the game any further; I decided to move in.

We needed De Wilde to come with us when we carried out the raid, as none of us knew the suspects by sight. I ordered De Wilde to ask Brother Josef to meet him at the garden gate. Six men were assigned to the actual arrest, the others to head off possible escape attempts.

I waited in the car on a side road. After five or ten minutes, I was told that Brother Josef had come to the gate, along with his associate Henk Schoenmaker, and was speaking to De Wilde as planned, thus giving us time to close in and make the arrests. We also pretended to arrest De Wilde, in order to prevent suspicion falling on him.

I then entered the monastery and confronted Brother Josef. He denied all knowledge of any radio transmitter. We searched for it high and low – in his cell, in the library, wherever a device might be hidden. We were working on it for hours. 'It has to be here!' De Wilde swore. Finally, one of my men found it in the library: the transmitter had been camouflaged inside a large hardback book with a wide spine. Other radio parts were also found.

I had the prisoners taken to the car and transferred to the Scheveningen Strafgefängnis, the prison that the Resistance refer to as the 'Oranje Hotel'.

Scheveningen prison

I Personally attended the interrogations, which began the next day. Brother Josef and his friend Bierhuijs both had a deep hatred of Germany and both refused to talk. Bierhuijs wrote a letter that he thought could be smuggled out of the jail, but which we intercepted.

'I trusted De Wilde,' Bierhuijs wrote, 'because Brother Josef trusted him ... After the shooting in Haarlem, De Wilde took me to a hotel, where I stayed overnight. He asked me if I knew anyone who might help me. I mentioned Charles Boom, and De Wilde made me write a letter to Boom explaining why I needed to escape. Then De Wilde said we should go to see a friend of his, but when we got there I saw there were armed men pointing their weapons. I was grabbed from behind and knocked unconscious. When I woke up, I was handcuffed to two detectives who began hurling accusations at me. They put me in a car and took me to the Binnenhof, where the interrogation recommenced. I was tied to a chair and the men started saying that my friends had all confessed, so I should do so too. But I followed the drill of not confessing anything without indisputable proof that they knew it already. They interrogated me until half past twelve, but I said nothing.'

'As for Brother Josef,' Schreieder concluded, 'I saw that he was determined to deny everything; but when I made it clear to him that De Wilde had told us all about his espionage activity, he confessed. He also admitted that he had lent the gun to Bierhuijs and said he had done it out of love for his queen and country. His courage was unbroken. He remained faithful to his comrades to the very last minute.'

* * *

When Brother Josef's arrest became known, 3,500 people signed an appeal for clemency. The Germans ignored it. His final letter,

written on the eve of his execution, was delivered to his family
after his death.

Josef Klingen, 1941

'This is my last letter,' Josef wrote. 'It is hard to say goodbye in
this fashion; but I am ready to appear before Him, from whom
I received this life and to whom I am happy to give it back. I
embark with confidence on the great journey.

'I take responsibility for everything. I made mistakes, but my
life has not been wasted. In these moments, for I write half an
hour before my death, I have a priest with me and I am ready.

'Give my love to my family and my friends. Tell them I am
determined to die like a man. Dying is not difficult when one
is prepared for what lies ahead.

'Live with God. And please give my regards to my old colleagues in the radio business.'

* * *

Anna-Maria went back to her theatre group, but they were
finding it hard to get permission for the plays they proposed.
The censor discovered reasons to refuse the most innocuous
suggestions. In the end, approval was granted for Herman
Heijermans' nineteenth-century comedy *A Christening Cake*,

with its imbroglio of unknown half-brothers and farcical misunderstandings. The censor's apparent ignorance of Heijermans' Jewish ancestry made the choice all the more satisfying.

There were messages from Uncle Anton, but mostly routine check-ins – pebbles left on a windowsill, telephone calls from an anonymous voice advertising a café or department store, to which Pim gave the pre-agreed responses. The arrests in Haarlem had made the Resistance more cautious; there was a lull.

* * *

For Marlies and Hans Friedheim, the winter of 1941–42 was happy. They got used to working outside and learned how to bring in the cattle for milking. They began to recognise individual cows; Marlies had names for her favourites.

Days spent in the open gave them an appetite and they ate well; the farmer, Cornelis Griffioen, was grateful and generous. The farm seemed a place outside of time, a bulwark against the hatred and prejudice of the world. Everyone took dinner at the same table and when the farmer said grace, he would look to Marlies and Hans with a smile of inclusion.

* * *

The rivalry between Reichskommissar Arthur Seyss-Inquart and SS-Polizeiführer Hanns Rauter had not abated. A lack of clarity in the division of authority between party and state organisations allowed both men to assert their precedence. As Generalkommissar for security, Rauter claimed Jews and Resistance workers as part of his remit, circumventing his nominal superior, Seyss-Inquart, taking orders directly from Himmler.

When Berlin sent instructions for the Netherlands to raise forces for the Waffen-SS, both men took up the challenge. In order to frame military service as a patriotic duty rather than a German imposition, Seyss-Inquart asked the Dutch NSB leader, Anton Mussert, to front the recruitment operation. Rauter responded by denigrating Mussert in his reports to Himmler. Instead of using a discredited underachiever, Rauter argued, how much better to engage a genuine Dutch hero.

Hendrik Seyffardt (centre left) with Hanns Rauter (centre)

At a hastily arranged briefing for the official press, Rauter presented seventy-year-old General Hendrik Seyffardt, in full dress uniform adorned with medals. Seyffardt had had an illustrious career as Chief of Staff of the Dutch army, but had retired eight years earlier, in 1934.

'I consider it my duty,' Seyffardt declared to the assembled media, 'to return to service in order to oversee the recruitment of Dutch fighting men. The *SS-Vrijwilligers Legioen Nederland* – the Volunteer SS Legion of the Netherlands – will bind our country to the cause of Germany and all like-minded European nations already fighting for freedom and civilisation. I consider it not only a duty, but a privilege to participate in the fight to preserve our precious European values.'

Hendrik Seyffardt

* * *

Jan Boissevain had not returned from work. He had been spending so much of his time in the office that Mies assumed he was working late; but the following morning he was still missing. When Gideon and Janka went to the bank, their father's secretary said Mr Boissevain had left as usual and everyone had assumed he had gone home.

Jan 'Canada' Boissevain

In retrospect, it seemed inevitable that they would come for him. The SD had issued repeated warnings to banks and investment houses that continued to employ Jewish workers, but Jan – with patrician scorn – had thrown them in the bin.

The Boissevains were a dynasty; their banking exploits had

brought them wealth and influence in high places. Pre-war government contacts who had remained in post informed Mies that her husband was being held at the Euterpestraat headquarters of the SD and the charges against him were considerably more serious than employing Jews.

* * *

Hanns Rauter (left) with Hendrik Seyffardt (centre)

Hendrik Seyffardt made speeches and radio broadcasts, toured the country, commissioned heroic posters and stirring slogans. 'Dutchmen! For your honour and your conscience!' the posters commanded. 'Join the Waffen-SS in the struggle against Bolshevism!'

A clamorous anthem appealing to the common values of two brother nations was played in cinemas and from loudspeakers on the streets.

> Dutchmen and Germans advance in line abreast;
> For liberty and truth we share the common quest.
> March on! Cut through the storm, cut through the tide;
> Let our manly anthem thunder far and wide.
> Mighty Panzers roar, screaming Stukas dive;
> Together we shall keep the flame of truth alive.
> In Russia's barren fields, Dutchmen now stand guard,
> Allied with German heroes, with fire in our hearts.
> Day and night we watch, and tomorrow farther still
> We take the Krieg beyond those barren Russian hills.
> Germany shall be great, her people strong and free;
> Our Panzers, Stukas, soldiers – our pledge of liberty!
> Dutchmen and Germans advance in line abreast;
> For liberty and truth we share the common quest!

At recruitment offices throughout the Netherlands, 50,000 Dutchmen enlisted in the Vrijwilligers Legioen Nederland, more volunteers than in any other occupied country. Seyffardt personally addressed every regiment before their departure to the Russian Front. Their courage, he declared, was the guarantee of Holland's survival.

'The Führer has promised the Dutch nation a future of respect, of equal status and equal rights. But we must earn that respect. We must earn that status. All true Dutchmen must fight alongside Germany in the struggle for victory!'

Dutch SS troops in training, 1942

* * *

Uncle Anton paid an unexpected visit. The executions of Johannes Bierhuijs, Henk Schoenmaker and Brother Josef – and now the arrest of Jan Boissevain – had rattled many in the Resistance. Anna-Maria thought Anton himself was looking tired and drawn.

'Traitors in our ranks are a poison for all of us,' he said. 'A matter of life or death. I want to let you know that it is being pursued at the highest level – I mean by King Kong himself. And I want you to be reassured that there is no question of any danger to the two of you.'

'I'm not sure how you can say that,' Pim said. 'Have you caught the man who betrayed Johannes and Josef and Henk? Do you even have any idea who he might be?'

'We have an idea,' said Anton. 'We know he is a V-Mann that the SD have infiltrated into the Resistance. We believe he uses the name of De Wilde, although that is undoubtedly an alias. Piecing together all the intelligence, we think he probably reports to Schreieder or even directly to Rauter. We're keeping tabs on someone fitting his description coming and going from the Binnenhof. But in the meantime, the decision has been taken to resume full scale operations.'

* * *

The Ordnungspolizei searched Jan Boissevain's office and took away files and documents that none of them understood. Mies, who understood a little, said nothing. The most successful financial frauds are those in which the perpetrator alone knows the whole truth. In a lifetime at the highest levels of the banking world, Jan Boissevain had encountered many such schemes and now he was practising one of his own. Jan and his first cousin, Walraven van Hall, had scammed the Dutch National Bank out of millions of guilders.

Walraven 'Wally' van Hall and his family

* * *

Schreieder and De Wilde met in the Binnenhof for the formal debrief on the Brother Josef affair. It had been a success; Schreieder had been congratulated. But antipathy simmered between the two of them. As the older man, the man with rank, the man who paid the money, Schreieder expected more respect. De Wilde had a self-confidence about him that rankled. Schreieder's report did not hide his suspicion that De Wilde's personal greed might one day compromise his effectiveness as a V-Mann.

The Brother Josef affair was De Wilde's first major case. In the course of the operation, I observed that he made nearly every mistake a novice V-Mann can make. De Wilde has to learn above all that he must stay aloof from opportunities for personal gain, such as theft and the like. I fear this is very difficult for him.

I have pointed out these failings to him and instructed him to improve his level of vigilance. Having made these representations, I have nonetheless engaged De Wilde to continue in our employment. He will receive a salary of 225 guilders per month, plus reasonable expenses incurred in connection with his work, including food and drink consumed on operational duty, travel costs and hotel expenses. These are to be claimed separately. De Wilde will henceforth work exclusively under my supervision.

Schreieder's success in the ECH/3 case brought him promotion to Hauptsturmführer and then to SS-Sturmbannführer in overall charge of Department IV E of the Gestapo in the Netherlands. His relationship with De Wilde, and with one other V-Mann, would become a potent weapon in the Gestapo's infiltration of the Dutch Resistance.

Joseph Schreieder

* * *

The scam had begun the previous year. The February strikes to protest against the persecution of the Jews had been followed by the widespread sacking of workers who had taken part in them. When Jan Boissevain and Walraven van Hall were approached by members of the strike committee seeking financial assistance for the jobless workers and their families, the two bankers had agreed to help.

They began by asking fellow investment managers to make contributions out of their own funds but it was not enough, so Jan and Wally made contact with the Dutch government in London to discuss more elaborate measures. Would Queen Wilhelmina agree to the issuance of bonds backed by her government and redeemable after the war that could be given to wealthy individuals in exchange for cash? Asked to specify the purpose for which the money would be used, Wally van Hall replied that it would provide succour and assistance to the cause of the Dutch nation – a cause that included the bankrolling of the Dutch Resistance.

The bond programme raised extra funds, but still more was needed; poverty was increasing, the Resistance expanding. Wally and Jan approached their fellow bank owners with a new scheme. At their request, eight private banks agreed to tell the Dutch Central Bank that they needed to increase their cash reserves. Some of them cited growing demand for private borrowing; others, such as the Twentsche Bank in Enschede, argued that the danger of Allied bombing made it prudent to diversify the location of the national cash supply. The eight million guilders that were furnished by the Central Bank were promptly redirected to underground opposition groups; Walraven van Hall had become 'banker to the Resistance'.

Walraven van Hall, 1942

When the overseer of the Central Bank, a senior NSB official, began to question the need for such large cash advances, Jan and Walraven came up with yet another ruse. Wally asked the Bank's sympathetic chief cashier, Cornelis Ritter, if he would extract some high-value Treasury bonds from the Bank's vaults and Ritter agreed to do so, replacing the genuine bonds with forgeries supplied by Jan and Wally. The bonds were then converted to cash, raising over 50 million guilders.

The biggest fraud in Holland's history would finance the National Support Fund, the underground organisation that kept the Dutch Resistance afloat for the duration of the war. But suspicions had been raised. Walraven van Hall remained at liberty, but someone had blown the whistle on Jan Boissevain.

7

The Resistance fights back

Koninginneweg, Amsterdam

Pim and Anna-Maria walked the length of Koninginneweg. They located number 121 but continued past; a car parked opposite with two men in it made them wary. When they returned, the car was gone.

In the entrance hall a man smoking a cigarette greeted them.
'Fine weather for wildlife.'
'Yes,' Pim replied. 'Especially for the birds.'
'Okay. Upstairs. Top floor on the left.'
In a low-ceilinged fourth-storey room, a group of people were chatting, the air heavy with cigarette smoke.

'We're meeting here,' Uncle Anton said, 'because Jan Boissevain has been arrested and we believe Corelli Street is under surveillance. Our thanks to Reina' – he nodded to a young woman sitting on the arm of a sofa – 'for the use of her apartment. It's not just the location that has changed; we are also introducing changes in the way we operate. You all know the reasons for this. And it won't be me taking CS-6 forward; I have several groups to look after and my job is to keep all of you in step with King Kong and the Resistance Council. CS-6 needs better security and better leadership. Here's the man who will be doing it.'

A lean, shortish man in his early thirties, with a battered, outdoor complexion, got to his feet.

Gerrit Kastein, 1942

'Gerrit Kastein,' he said. 'Good evening, comrades. Militair Contact have decided that more discipline is needed. It's not just you, it's the whole of the Resistance. Recent events – recent betrayals – have shown the danger of lax vigilance.'

'Excuse me, *comrade*.' The interjection came from a languidly reclining fellow in cord trousers and a velvet jacket, the emphasis on *comrade* unmistakeably sardonic. 'What exactly is Militair Contact?'

'I think you know what it is,' Kastein replied. 'Militair Contact is the armed wing of the Netherlands Communist Party, my party, the CPN. I believe in it. But at this moment, I believe in

Holland and freedom and victory. I want all of us – communists, socialists, Christians, royalists – to co-operate. Can we
agree on that?'

There was a murmur of assent.

'Thank you,' Kastein said. 'The CPN and Militair are on the
Resistance Council now and we're sharing our expertise, so all
of us here will be working together. I want to reassure you that
everyone has been vetted, either by me or Uncle Anton or by
King Kong himself. I introduced myself by my real name and I
would like you to do the same. We will continue to use aliases
for outside communication and written documents, but within
the group it's different. Is that understood? This is Reina's apartment, so let's start with her.'

The pretty girl on the arm of the chair stood up.

Reina Prinsen Geerligs

'Hello,' she said. 'My name is Reina; Reina Prinsen Geerligs. I'm
nineteen. I was born in the Dutch East Indies. I write poetry and
I write stories ... Anyway, I'm here because I believe in justice.
When the February strikes happened, I got our school to go on
strike, too. I've been distributing the newspaper for quite a while
and I think it's time to start doing a bit more.'

'Now perhaps we could hear from our *colleague* who was
asking about Militair,' Gerrit Kastein said.

Willem Arondeus

'Willem Arondeus,' said the man in the velvet jacket. 'I am a painter. Not a very successful one if you measure these things in monetary terms. If you've been in Rotterdam City Hall, you'll have seen the murals I did there. My father kicked me out because I wanted to be an artist and ... because I liked men. I've been publishing a magazine that defends artistic freedom – *De Vrije Kunstenaar* (*The Free Artist*) – and I've been using my artistic talents to make some pretty convincing forgeries. But that's really the province of my two friends who are here.'

Arondeus waved his hand to beckon a distinguished-looking man at the back of the room.

Gerrit van der Veen

'I'm Gerrit van der Veen,' the man said. 'I met Willem through

The Free Artist. We edit it together. As for forgery, it's a three-way business: Willem, me and Frieda. What do we forge? In the main, identity cards. Principally for Jews. When the Germans started registering them and putting a "J" on their cards, we found ourselves a printer, a fellow named Duwaer, and started churning out fakes. But that was a disaster because we hadn't realised you need a special type of paper to print them on; if you don't have it, the Ordnungspolizei can spot them a mile off. We tried getting hold of blank ID forms and we managed to obtain a few by robbing a warehouse, but that was never going to give us the quantities we needed. In the end we've been making our own paper with the right watermark and the right shading. We've done a couple of thousand so far. We give them to Jews in hiding and to Resistance people who need a new identity. But it's a challenge. We're always needing more – more paper, more ink, more people to distribute the documents. And there's a really big problem that we haven't sorted out yet. The Germans have spent the last two years making ridiculously detailed lists of everyone's names, addresses and religion so even if we produce the most authentic fake IDs in the world, they can still check them against their list and we lose. One good thing about the Germans is that they're methodical. They keep *all* the data in the Amsterdam Registry Office – the *Bevolkingsregister* – so a good bomb underneath it might do the trick!'

Frieda Belinfante

Frieda Belinfante spoke. Her voice was deep, nicotine-stained. 'There are 160,000 Jews in the Netherlands and the vast majority of them did what the Germans told them to do. They filled in all the forms and got themselves registered. We know the Zentralstelle are planning to send these people to the east so time's running out. With the right financial backing, we can produce maybe seventy or eighty thousand ID cards, but it won't happen overnight. As for blowing up the Registry Office, the three of us are not what you'd call well qualified. Arondeus is a painter, Van der Veen's a sculptor and I'm a cellist – bombs are not our forte ... But for Willem and me,' Frieda said, 'there's an added incentive. Once the Germans have dealt with the Jews and the gypsies, they've said their next target will be homosexuals.'

'We have people who know how to use a gun and we can handle explosives,' Gerrit Kastein said. 'I'd like to ask PAM to speak about that.'

PAM Pooters

A dark-haired man in a smart suit got to his feet. 'PAM Pooters. Petrus Antonius Martinus, but everyone calls me PAM. You may know the Friendship Café – *De Vriendschap* – on the corner of Nieuwmarkt and Dijkstraat. That's my parents' place – they're both Trotskyists. They use the café backrooms to store weapons and ammunition. Upstairs and in the cellar it's temporary accommodation for Jews and comrades on the run. My sisters Nel and Mientje and I do armed escorts, moving folk from location to location. We handle the bulk print-runs of *De Waarheid*. Sabotage is important, like blowing up the railway lines to stop the Germans transporting Jews to camps. That's something Militair is already planning. I'm personally ready and willing to do the bombing and I know there are others here tonight who think the same way . . .'

Jan Verleun

'I think that's my cue,' Jan Verleun said. 'I was on the Ijssel Line when the Germans invaded and I've still got their bullets in me. Before the war, I trained to be a priest, but all that changed. PAM and Mientje – the Pooters – taught me that the real way of Christ is communism. So I suggest you think of me as the gun at your service. If the Party – by which I mean Kastein and Pooters – tells me to shoot, then I'll shoot.'

Leo Frijda

'I'm Leo Frijda,' a young man said. 'For me it's self-preservation. My dad was a professor at Amsterdam University. Four years ago, he was master of ceremonies at Queen Wilhelmina's fortieth anniversary. But the Germans fired him and blocked his pension. When I finished school last year, they stopped me going to university. We are Jewish and we're the ones they're coming for. You all could play dumb and sit out the war, but we don't have a choice. I want to fight back!'

The remaining members of the group introduced themselves.

Hans Katan, a communist and a friend of PAM Pooters, volunteered for sabotage duties.

Hans Katan

Sape Kuiper

Eighteen-year old Sape Kuiper said he would go too.

Pim and Anna-Maria said they would do whatever the leadership thought useful.

On the way out they were surprised to be cornered by Uncle Anton.

'You asked me if we know who betrayed Brother Josef,' Anton said. 'Nothing is yet concluded, but I would urge caution about those who did not attend tonight.'

'You mean the Boissevains?' Pim said. 'But they stayed away because they didn't want to be followed here – for our safety. And besides, Jan Boissevain is being held by the Gestapo.'

'Perhaps so,' Anton replied. 'But the Germans arrest their own people to shield them from suspicion. Maybe you didn't know, but the whole Boissevain family used to be fascists. All of them were members of the NSB. Janka and Gideon were picked up trying to sail to England, but the Germans miraculously let them go.'

8

ROUNDUPS

Willy Lages

In the first months of 1942, the Zentralstelle came into its own. When the order was given to move from planning to action, Willy Lages and Ferdinand aus der Fünten were ready.

They picked Zaandam for a trial. On the evening of 14 January, the town's Jews were told they had two days to prepare for removal. They were ordered to report to Zaandam station on the morning of the 17th, with whatever they could carry, including pillows and blankets. All homes would need to be sealed on departure, gas and electricity switched off and keys handed to the police. By special dispensation, Jews married to non-Jews would be allowed to keep their furniture.

It went well. Of the nearly 400 people who answered the Reich's summons, 270 were taken to the barricaded sector of Amsterdam now designated as housing for Jews. Abraham Asscher and David Cohen mobilised representatives of the Jewish Council to help place the incomers with families already in the ghetto.

The remaining hundred or so were shipped to a facility in the province of Drenthe, in the north-east of the country. Westerbork transit camp had been built by the Dutch government in 1939 to house Jews fleeing from Nazi persecution; now it would serve the Nazis as a holding station for those en route to the gas chambers. Between 1942 and 1944 Westerbork's meticulous records would list the names of 97,776 Jewish inmates, of whom 54,930 would be despatched to Auschwitz, 34,313 to Sobibor, 4,771 to Theresienstadt and 3,762 to Bergen-Belsen. Fewer than 5,000 would return.

Arrival of a transport at Camp Westerbork, 1942

* * *

Leo Frijda got his wish. In the bomb-making workshop of Militair Contact, Gerrit Kastein helped him assemble the explosives he would need for his mission.

The evacuation of Jews from Zaandam had been followed by similar roundups in other cities. A Resistance-friendly contact in Seyss-Inquart's office in the Binnenhof reported that transports to the east would begin within weeks. If CS-6 were going to stop them, it would need to act.

The objective designated by the Resistance Council was the rail line that ran north from Westerbork to Assen then to Groningen where it veered eastwards via the border town of Bad Nieuweschans into northern Germany and on to Poland. As Frijda was about to leave, Gerrit Kastein announced that he would be accompanied by a fellow operative, Arend Westerveld.

Frijda and Westerveld selected a left-hand curve at the bottom of an incline. An approaching train would be gathering speed, so the sharpness of the bend would increase the damage from a derailment. In accordance with Kastein's instructions, they first dismantled the bolts securing the iron rail to the sleepers and levered it to the centre of the track. The bomb was placed in a culvert beneath the line, connected to a fuse that Kastein had told them would take between five and ten minutes to burn down. As soon as Frijda and Westerveld heard the train in the distance, they were to light it and disappear.

It worked. A German military freight train consisting of two locomotives and thirty wagons jumped the rails. The bomb exploded as the occupants were detraining.

It took three weeks for the line to be reopened, three weeks in which no transport from Westerbork would be possible.

* * *

Pope Innocent III's pronouncement of 1215 requiring Jews in public places to wear a distinguishing mark had remained in force until the seventeenth century, when the practice fell into disuse.

The Third Reich revived it. On 29 April 1942 Hanns Rauter informed the leaders of Holland's Jewish Council of new legislation. From now on, 'all Jews appearing in a public place must wear a Jewish star ... bearing the black inscription *Jood*. The star shall be clearly visible, affixed to the outer clothing over the left breast.' A 'public place' was defined as 'anywhere a Jew may meet a person from outside his own household'. Severe penalties were stipulated for non-compliance.

Abraham Asscher and David Cohen protested. It was, Cohen complained, 'a dreadful measure ... a terrible day in the history of Dutch Jewry'. He asked why the colour of the star had to be yellow – a 'humiliation' – and requested a delay in implementing the legislation. Rauter didn't listen. The Reichskommissariat delivered 569,355 cloth stars to the Jewish Council with instructions to distribute them all within three days. Each person, on production of his or her ration card, was to be issued with four stars for which there would be a mandatory charge of 5 cents per star. Any Jew found without a star was to be handed over to the Security Police. Non-Jewish citizens were instructed to turn in Jewish neighbours who broke the rules.

'He who wears this mark is an enemy of our race'

The imposition of the yellow star placed a visible target on the breast of the enemy. Rauter and Lages were easing the way for the deportations to come and murder was to be accompanied by robbery. A series of further decrees closed Jewish bank accounts and drew up a list of property to be handed over to the authorities, beginning with jewellery, *objets d'art* and precious metals, extending eventually to cars, carriages, horses and bicycles.

Exempted for the moment were personal wedding rings, four pieces of cutlery per person and gold teeth.

* * *

The attack carried out by Leo Frijda and Arend Westerveld was one of a growing number on railway lines and signal boxes.

Reichskommissar Arthur Seyss-Inquart denounced them as the work of 'wild, hardened criminals' and instructed municipal mayors to organise round-the-clock surveillance patrols. When attacks continued, Seyss-Inquart ordered the Dutch Railway Authority to set up an official Railway Guard, uniformed and armed, with responsibility for keeping the tracks safe.

Hanns Rauter took more direct measures. On 4 May, hundreds of prominent Dutch citizens – politicians, journalists, professors, clerics, musicians, lawyers and writers – opened their front doors to discover detachments of Ordnungspolizei with orders for their arrest. Four hundred and sixty of them were incarcerated in the former Beekvliet monastery in the North Brabant town of Sint-Michielsgestel. If sabotage were to continue, Rauter announced, an unspecified number of hostages would be shot dead.

For Arend Westerveld, death came quicker. On an overnight shift at an underground printing press, he found himself surrounded by SS troops. The German commander shouted through the door that he had been betrayed, called on him to surrender, then stormed the building. Westerveld used five revolver bullets for his attackers and the final one for himself.

* * *

Marlies's father came with yellow stars for her and for her brother, Hans. The farmer's wife made them a bowl of soup and left them to talk. Marlies could see her father was struggling to be cheerful.

'It seems your mother and I are going to be moving,' he said. 'They are finding us somewhere in downtown Amsterdam, so we'll be much closer to all the amenities. We've given our valuables and the family photographs to our neighbours to look after. But our furniture has to be sent to Germany. There are trains leaving every day with banners on them saying, "This is a gift of love from the Netherlands to Germany." It makes your mother quite angry – she says the German people will think the Dutch are on their side. She says the Nazis tell so many lies!'

'If you and Mum are going to Amsterdam, then I shall come with you,' Marlies said. 'You know how much I want to be with you.'

'Thank you, love,' her father said. 'But really, it's best for everyone if you and Hans can stay here on the farm.'

* * *

When Jan Boissevain came home, he told his family that he had fooled the Germans.

'Even the best financial experts would struggle to untangle the false trails Wally and I have laid,' he said. 'And the forgeries we made to replace the bonds in the Central Bank are so professional I'm certain no one will see through them.'

* * *

The betrayal of Arend Westerveld was a shock. Meetings now were called at the last minute and in unheralded locations. A record was kept of everyone who knew the time and place; the Germans had raided other meetings and informers were legion.

Nieuwmarkt, Amsterdam

In the room above the Pooters' Vriendschap Café on Nieuwmarkt, Gerrit Kastein called for order. All those who had been at the Koninginneweg meeting were present, plus Janka and Gideon Boissevain. Leo Frijda was absent.

'We shall use all means to root out traitors,' Kastein said. 'The Party has decided to step up the sabotage effort so I need volunteers for further bombings. I have nominated Leo Frijda – he has to prove he was not to blame for what happened to Westerveld.'

Kastein took Anna-Maria aside. 'We need you for something else,' he said. 'The mission that we picked you for from the moment we brought you on board. Have patience.'

* * *

Paul Citroen came to the farm with his drawings for Marlies, and his love.

'I wanted you to know that we're missing you,' he said. 'Actually, that *I* am missing you . . . I'm going into hiding. And I think you should do the same.'

He had found a cellar in the house of a fellow artist. He would be overjoyed if Marlies would join him. He had already asked his friend and secured his agreement.

Marlies said no.

'My brother Hans is so young and vulnerable he would barely survive without me. My parents have been told they have to move to the ghetto. I may have to go to look after them.'

* * *

Arthur Seyss-Inquart

'*Welkom, Meneer. Kom binnen. Doe alsof je thuis bent!*' Seyss-Inquart was in civilian clothes and practising his Dutch. Ruud Wilders sensed it was a good sign.

'I wish to congratulate you,' Seyss-Inquart said, reverting to German. 'Your efforts on behalf of the Reich are appreciated. And now I have a new challenge for you.'

He motioned Wilders to sit.

'I am assigning you to the office of the Sicherheitsdienst. I want you to work with Polizeiführer Rauter and SS-Sturmbannführer Joseph Schreieder. The relocation of the Jews to the ghetto and then to Westerbork is proceeding too slowly. Too many exemptions are being made and I need a trusted Dutch speaker who can vet them properly.'

Seyss-Inquart paused.

'Even more important is the work you will be doing for me. You must use your new position to be my eyes and ears. I want you to keep a close watch on Herr Rauter and Herr Schreieder.'

* * *

His wife could tell that Commandant Schol was upset.

'It's all quite unpleasant,' Jac said. 'I know Westerbork isn't a holiday camp, but one of the guards has just beaten a woman to death. The fellow says she was insolent to him so he kicked her. She wouldn't be quiet so he kept on kicking.'

'Oh, Jac,' his wife said. 'Don't torment yourself. It isn't your fault. And besides, the Jews are going to the east so they're going to die anyway.'

Commandant Jac Schol and his wife

* * *

The 460 involuntary inhabitants of the Beekvliet monastery settled into a grim routine. The SS colonel in charge told them they were *Todeskandidaten*, candidates for death, their survival contingent on the good behaviour of their fellow citizens.

If Dutch society had the sense to work with the authorities no harm would come to them; but if the so-called Resistance were to continue its campaign of sabotage and murder, they would be executed, in numbers determined by the Reichskommissar.

Piet Sanders, a lawyer from Schiedam, found the weeks between his arrest in May 1942 and the fatal events of that summer surprisingly educational. The men interned at Beekvliet had been selected for their prominence in the worlds of politics, science and the arts, so it was natural that there would be lectures and seminars.

Sanders attended the poet Anton van Duinkerken's talks about the history of his native Flanders and the essayist Simon Vestdijk's recasting of their own predicament as a pastiche of Franz Kafka's *The Trial*. He befriended a Rotterdam police superintendent, Christoffel Bennekers, who gave a wry account of why he thought he had been selected as a hostage. Bennekers had spent the 1930s tracking down communists in the Netherlands and would have continued to do so on behalf of the Nazis. But when his SS supervisors deposited ten copies of Hitler's *Mein Kampf* in the police headquarters library, Bennekers had arranged for ten fellow officers to take them out on loan and forget to return them. His ruse had been discovered by his boss who subsequently put his name on the list.

Police superintendent Christoffel Bennekers

The monastery's country setting, with its imposing buildings, tennis courts and surrounding forests, reminded Sanders of a Rotary club. Its inmates were left free to live as they wanted, with only the uncertainty over their future to trouble the idyll.

* * *

Ruud Wilders moved to his new office. Polizeiführer Rauter told his staff to keep an eye on him. Seyss-Inquart had said his duties would be simple but they weren't. The pile of letters never went down, however much Wilders worked on it.

'I humbly request your indulgence,' was the endlessly repeated formula. 'For the following reasons I beg you to grant my family an exemption from the order to relocate ...'

The 'reasons' included arguments about the applicants' heritage – that they were not really Jews, that they had converted to Catholicism, that they were married to Protestants – and about the value of the work they were doing for the Reich. The Jewish Council was authorised to endorse the identity cards of exempted individuals with a special mark that became known as the Bolle Stamp, after the name of the Council's Secretary.

Max Bolle, General Secretary of the Jewish Council

The Germans' objective was to deport the Jews with maximum efficiency and minimum fuss. Promising exemptions kept hope alive and while hope lived, people stayed silent for fear of being put on the wrong list. It was a charade. The saved were saved *pro tem*, then consigned like everyone else to the knock on the door, the swearing and cursing, the manhandling, the manhunts, the endless, grinding, bestial inhumanity that led to Westerbork and then to Poland and the camps. All the Bolle exemptions would eventually be rescinded. Almost everyone, including Max Bolle himself, would go to the gas chambers.

* * *

Commandant Schol knew he was on borrowed time. He had been in charge at Westerbork for two years, appointed by the newly installed Reichskommissariat in the summer of 1940. Under his leadership, Westerbork had become a tight ship; discipline had been strengthened and security increased. Schol had enlisted the Royal Dutch Constabulary to guard the camp perimeter, instituted twice-daily rollcalls and insisted on strict censorship of incoming and outgoing letters. In what he considered his masterstroke, he had established an internal police force made up of Jewish inmates. Each barrack had a squad of willing young men, incentivised by a distinctive green uniform and the promise of at least temporary immunity for them and their families. All were eager to prove their loyalty, some by ferocious brutality to their less fortunate fellows. It had been one of Schol's Jewish policemen who had kicked the woman to death.

In light of his record Jac Schol felt it unfair that an SS report had accused him of excessive leniency. The report, which was now on Seyss-Inquart's desk, concluded that the Jews in Westerbork were 'too comfortable' and called for Commandant Schol to be replaced.

* * *

Franz and Johanna Friedheim locked their front door, handed over the keys to the local Dutch police and reported to the Amsterdam ghetto. At improvised reception points on street corners, representatives of the Jewish Council were stamping people's papers, ticking off the names in the daily lists that Willy Lages and Ferdinand aus der Fünten sent them from the Zentralstelle.

It took the Friedheims a while to locate the address they had been assigned to, 36 Nicolaas Witsenkade, in the ghetto's southwest corner. When they got there, they found four families already occupying a three-room apartment.

* * *

Jac Schol was fired on 1 July 1942. The new commandant of Westerbork made it his business to tighten things up.

Erich Deppner had been working in counter-intelligence in the Netherlands since the beginning of the previous year, rooting out the places where Jews tried to hide, working closely with Willy Lages and Ferdinand aus der Fünten at the Zentralstelle and reporting directly to Hanns Albin Rauter.

Three months earlier Rauter had sent Deppner to the camp at Amersfoort to deal with a group of 100 Soviet prisoners. Most of them were Uzbeks, captured on the Eastern Front and brought to Holland to show the local population what Slavic *Untermenschen* looked like. Starvation and beatings had killed many; those who remained were emaciated.

Deppner took personal charge of their executions, joining the firing party to administer the *coups de grâce*.

Erich Deppner

9

Deportations to the East

The timing of Erich Deppner's appointment to run the Westerbork camp was not accidental. Ten days earlier Adolf Eichmann had spoken to Franz Rademacher, the German Foreign Office's policy director for the Jewish Question, and informed him that the Führer was ready to proceed with mass deportations. An initial tranche of 40,000 Dutch Jews was to be transported by special trains to Auschwitz for what would be presented to them as 'labour service'.

Rademacher had advised Eichmann to take account of the 'psychological implications' of such a large-scale operation in a country that had previously baulked at Jewish persecution. There were, said Rademacher, around 25,000 stateless Jews in the Netherlands, immigrants from Germany, Poland and elsewhere. Starting with them might be easier than with Dutch Jews.

The order was transmitted to Willy Lages and Ferdinand aus der Fünten. On 26 June Fünten summoned representatives of the Jewish Council to his office. The Council's deputy leader, David Cohen, who sensed there was 'something ghastly' in the air, listened in silence as Fünten read a prepared speech.

'We have received the order from Berlin,' Fünten said, 'for police-controlled labour contingents of Jewish men and women, aged between sixteen and forty, to be sent to Germany. The task of the Jewish Council will be to furnish to the Reichskommissariat all those individuals who meet the criteria. Dutch Jews as well as Jews of foreign extraction must be included and all must be registered on forms that will be supplied to you. I am granting you twenty-four hours to analyse the scope of the work and report to me on the maximum daily numbers you can handle.' The operation, Fünten explained, would involve three stages: Jews still at large across the country would be brought to the Amsterdam ghetto, those in the ghetto would be moved to Westerbork, and those already at Westerbork would be transported to the east.

Cohen objected. 'You know, of course, that this runs directly counter to all tenets of international law?' Fünten replied, 'It is we who decide what is and is not international law.' When Cohen said he would make a note of that remark, Fünten corrected himself. 'What I mean is that we decide who has to go on labour service. After all, it is we who are the victors.'

Cohen picked up his briefcase and made to leave, saying that the Jewish Council was not prepared to assist in such a task; but a look of triumph appeared in Fünten's eyes and Cohen changed his mind. Much better, he thought, to be included and informed – perhaps with some hope of attenuating the coming horrors – than to allow the Nazis to carry out their plans unconstrained.

* * *

The farmer gave Marlies and Hans leave of absence to visit their parents. The ghetto was crowded, it was a struggle to find the apartment where the Friedheims were billeted and when they got there, conversation was difficult. A sense of impending catastrophe hung over them. They talked about the past because it was easier than talking about the future.

'My family have been German since the seventeenth century,' Mrs Friedheim said, 'and your dad's family almost as long ...' From her handbag she pulled out a photograph and passed it to Marlies. 'Look. Dad fought for Germany in the last war. Here he is in his uniform. We are as German as anybody.'

'Well, Johanna,' Mr Friedheim said, 'Things have changed. It all went wrong after 1914 and we had to start our lives over again.'

'But we always knew that you could come and work for my family's furniture business,' Mrs Friedheim said. 'They took you in and you rose to the top.'

'Yes,' Mr Friedheim said. 'I impressed your father – I was a match for his favourite daughter. We had a good life even though we were the only Jews in the district.'

* * *

The dog days of July were spent in negotiation. Ferdinand aus der Fünten opened with a demand that 600 Jews per day be delivered by the Jewish Council, but Asscher and Cohen responded that 'our technical advisers consider this number impossible' and made a counter-offer of 350. After a show of reluctance Fünten accepted the lower figure, but specified it should be 'for the first eight days only' after which delivery targets would be raised: Berlin was insisting that a minimum of 4,000 Jews from the Netherlands be supplied by the end of the month.

Asscher and Cohen raised the issue of who should decide who goes and who stays. Because the Jewish Council was assisting with the provision of candidates for the transports, they argued, it should also have the right to decide on exemptions. It went without saying that members of the Council themselves would be granted dispensations.

* * *

Kastein and CS-6 were as good as their word. Railways, factories and repair shops used by the Germans were subjected to a campaign of sabotage that grew more ferocious as the summer of 1942 wore on. When notices warning of reprisals if the Resistance did not desist were posted on walls and lampposts, Gerrit Kastein sought advice from the Party. A message from the co-ordination council of Militair Contact informed him that there should be no let-up. Inflicting defeat on the forces of fascism outweighed all other considerations.

The Resistance's next attack, on a freight train in Rotterdam carrying German soldiers, caused little damage and only one death, but Hanns Rauter's patience was at an end. He announced that those responsible would be given a week to surrender after which twenty-five hostages from the men being held at the Beekvliet Monastery would be executed.

The Beekvliet commandant called a camp assembly to announce the names of those who had been selected and the date and time they would be shot. Piet Sanders' name was among them. He wrote a farewell letter to his wife and dictated the terms of his will.

On the eve of the appointed date, the commandant informed the men that no Resistance group had admitted responsibility for the Rotterdam attack, so the sentences would be carried out in the morning. In an act of mercy, however, the Reichskommissariat had reduced the number of death sentences from twenty-five to five.

At dawn, soldiers entered the barracks where the twenty-five Todeskandidaten were being held and Piet Sanders watched as five of his fellow prisoners were forced to their feet and led away. Police superintendent Christoffel Bennekers; Willem Ruys, a banker; Robert Baelde, a social worker; Count Otto Ernst Gelder, a judge; and Baron Alexander Schimmelpenninck, a landowner, were taken to the forest at Goirle near Tilburg and shot.

* * *

The men at the top sought relaxation, away from their duties on behalf of the Reich. Willy Lages told his deputy, Ferdinand aus der Fünten, and the Westerbork commandant, Erich Deppner, that there was no shame in enjoying the rewards of their hard work.

Social evenings were a chance to unwind with food and wine in the company of attractive women. The Westerbork complex was large enough to provide the privacy they required, a welcome respite from the unpleasant scenes they had to witness during the day.

Fünten and several of the others had wives and families – posed photographs of domestic happiness were good material for Nazi magazines – but it was wartime, and nobody could object to powerful men with tough jobs taking the occasional mistress. It helped to ensure a harmonious work environment.

Presiding over the happy brotherhood was Willy Lages, who cared for his subordinates like a beneficent father.

In reports to Berlin, Lages wrote that Erich Deppner was 'hardworking, conscientious and of high intelligence, with a doctorate in law and a thorough understanding of international legal principles, dedicated to the advancement of the Reich and ready to carry out the Führer's instructions without hesitation ... Married, with five beautiful children.'

Fünten, according to Lages, was 'a good, simple soul, very sensitive, with a heart of gold; warm and caring towards his fellow men. Under other circumstances, he would probably have been a kindly schoolmaster or a philanthropist.'

* * *

The Germans were worried about possible Jewish resistance. Ferdinand aus der Fünten sent a message to Abraham Asscher at the Jewish Council, expressing alarm at rumours that the Council 'was calling for a strike against the deportations', and warning that SS-Gruppenführer Rauter would take 'very strong measures indeed' if such rumours proved to be true. Asscher responded with a prompt denial. 'We protest most vehemently against the very idea that the Jewish Council, set up by the German authorities, should take its responsibilities so lightly as to even contemplate such action.' Fünten, in reply, reiterated that the Jews assigned to the transports were destined solely for labour duties and that talk of any other purpose was misguided.

It is hard to say how convincing the Council members found this. Asscher sent Fünten a series of conditions that seemed designed to salve his own conscience. 'It is expressly stipulated,' he wrote, 'that the work camps must be in Germany, that the police accompanying the transports must be for the protection of those travelling, and that our people must be allowed religious guidance at all times.'

Fünten gave the assurances, but some suspected the true purpose of the deportations. Fritz Angress, a nineteen-year-old German Jew, whose family had emigrated to Holland in 1937, had found work in the Zentralstelle assisting with the bureaucracy of Jewish registration and helping to escort Jews on their way to Westerbork. Fritz happened to pass Fünten's office as he was telling his staff about the real destination of the transports and the imminence of the roundups. Alarmed, he approached his Gestapo superior, Oberscharführer Erich Stube, to say he was feeling unwell and asked permission to go home. Stube's agreement, given with a knowing grin, allowed Fritz to warn his mother and brother in time for them to move to the hiding place where they spent the rest of the war.

* * *

When the first call-up notices were issued in mid-July, recipients were told they were being taken to work in Germany, that conditions would be good and their labour appreciated by the Reich. Many convinced themselves it was true. The Germans need labourers, they told each other, so it must be in their interest to treat us well.

Jewish Council headquarters, Amsterdam, 1942

Others were less sanguine. Crowds gathered at the headquarters of the Jewish Council at 58 Nieuwe Keizersgracht, demanding the life-saving imprimatur of a Bolle Stamp exemption. Doors were broken, staff were attacked and the police had to be called. Once inside, people queued for hours, pleading, cajoling, imploring, then shouting and gesticulating. All had a reason why they should be exempted – they were ill, they were key workers, needed in Holland, they had fought for Germany in the last war, they had a letter of recommendation from an important person …

'A Jew is a Jew, legs or no legs …'

The stamps became an obsession; the men with the power to issue them became arbiters of life and death. The SD made frequent changes to the criteria for exemption. People would apply and be accepted, only for their stamp to be revoked. A man from Utrecht who had lost both his legs in the fighting in 1940 wrote asking to be declared unsuitable for labour service, but a German official scribbled on his letter, 'A Jew is a Jew, legs or no legs' and passed him fit.

* * *

Gerrit Kastein sensed he was being followed. The war in Spain and now the years of underground struggle had sharpened his awareness of danger. He glanced over his shoulder but saw no one.

'Kastein!'

The voice, unexpectedly, came from beside him. Uncle Anton signalled him to stop.

'A meeting. Tomorrow. 6 p.m.'

Gerrit nodded. 'At the composer's house?'

'No,' Anton said. 'I don't trust the Canadians. Come to 25 Herengracht in the canal district. King Kong wants something done.'

* * *

When it appeared that insufficient numbers of Jews were responding to the Reich's call, Hanns Rauter encouraged them. Detachments of SS men were sent to the Amsterdam ghetto, where they seized 700 people on the streets, marching them at gunpoint to the Gestapo headquarters at 99 Euterpestraat. Asscher and Cohen were then summoned by the assistant head of the Sicherheitsdienst, Hauptsturmführer Hans Blumenthal. Too many Jews were refusing to report for labour service, Blumenthal told them, and too many had gone into hiding. If the Jewish Council did not meet the quotas demanded by the Reich, the 700 prisoners would be sent to a concentration camp where their fate would not be pleasant.

To underline the point, the captured Jews were marched up and down in the Euterpestraat courtyard, while SD women poured abuse on them from upper-storey windows and members of the Ordnungspolizei took souvenir photos. When a young Jewish girl burst into tears after being wrenched away from the pram she was pushing, there was much hilarity among the onlookers.

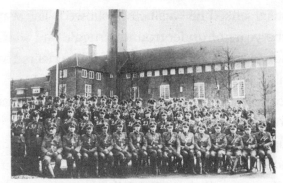

*SD personnel at 99 Euterpestraat, the former girls' high
school that became the headquarters of the Gestapo*

Asscher and Cohen demanded a meeting with Fünten, who
received them with an unexpected apology. All the hostages
would be released, Fünten said, apart from half a dozen who
had been identified as criminal elements, responsible for
encouraging resistance to the call-ups. As evidence he read
them a passage from the latest copy of *De Waarheid*.

> To the Dutch police we say, Think of your professional and
> human responsibility! Refuse to arrest the Jews! Make a show
> of carrying out your orders, while allowing them to escape
> into hiding! You must know that every man, every woman
> and every child you arrest will be killed and you will be their
> murderer. To the Dutch railwaymen we say, Remember that
> every slave transport you agree to drive is taking its cargo
> straight to the slaughterhouse!

'How can we allow such things to be written?' Fünten said.
'Surely you must understand.' Then, having made his point, he
allowed himself a moment of compassion. Cohen reported that
Fünten was 'in a state of great, and it seemed to me, genuine
agitation'.

He told us that the raid had been organised solely because too few Jews were reporting for transportation and the trains simply had to be filled. But, looking at me, he added, 'Believe me, Herr Cohen, it is the last thing I wanted.' I took both his hands in mine and said, 'Then, Herr Hauptsturmführer, please don't do it!' He turned to the window and I could see he was hiding his tears. He turned back again and said, 'Herr Cohen, I have no alternative!'

* * *

'We have attacked trains and factories and the Germans have responded by murdering innocent hostages,' Kastein told the meeting. 'We need to teach the Nazis that they cannot act with impunity; we need to show them they can never be safe in our country. The Rembrandt Theatre, where they watch their news-reels and movies glorifying the Reich, is somewhere they feel at home: so, we will bomb it and show them they are vulnerable. PAM Pooters has volunteered, but I also need a female. Most of the men who go to the Rembrandt are in uniform and the guards search the bags of those who aren't. But a pretty woman can get in with a handbag and a smile.'

Mientje Pooters said she would go with her brother. She and PAM went to collect the explosives, incendiary devices in ciga-rette packets and matchboxes, with celluloid strips in sulphuric acid and potassium chlorate. The explosives team told them to take a knife to cut open the padded cinema seats and push the boxes into them. There would be a delay of a few hours before they exploded and the seat material was highly flammable.

In 1942 the Rembrandt Theatre had screened films including *Quex of the Hitler Youth*, *Stars of the Fatherland* and *Campaign in the East*. PAM and Mientje bought tickets for the late showing of *Die Goldene Stadt – The Golden City –* and held hands in the back row. By the time the fire broke out, they were safe at home.

Rembrandt Theatre bombing, 1942

The pro-German paper *De Telegraaf* splashed the news:

> Conflagration! Theatre in ashes! Building destroyed!
>
> The alarm was raised in the dead of night. At 3 a.m., the cinema's façade collapsed, sending bricks flying into the street. The front elevation and foyer were destroyed; burst pipes spewed water into the wreckage. This was no accident! The Amsterdam police, together with the Sicherheitsdienst, are investigating the likelihood of a terrorist attack. Meanwhile, an unending stream of Amsterdamers pass through Rembrandtplein every day to see the charred remains.

* * *

The influx of Jews from outlying towns had filled the ghetto to capacity. The three-room apartment where Franz and Johanna Friedheim were living now housed fourteen people. When the letters arrived, half of the flat's inhabitants found themselves called up for labour duty while the others, including the Friedheims, received nothing.

There was a debate about who got lucky. Mr Aarons said he was glad that he and his family were on the list because it 'would at least get his children out of this insanitary ghetto' and give him the chance of a new start in Germany. He was a master tailor and the Germans were certain to appreciate his skills.

When the Aaronses reported next morning to the registration point at Amsterdam Centraal train station, the clerk could not find their names in the roster. Instead of leaving, Mr Aarons argued. It was wrong, he said, to receive an invitation and then be turned away. The clerk shrugged and waved them onto the platform, where the contents of people's suitcases were being checked. Twelve hours later, Mr and Mrs Aarons, their two daughters and 958 others boarded two special trains laid on by the management of Dutch Railways. The first left for Westerbork at 2.16 a.m. and the second followed twenty minutes later.

Ferdinand aus der Fünten reported the operation's success. Everything was going smoothly, he told Hanns Rauter; there was no reason to anticipate any obstacles to the implementation of future transports. But Rauter was not happy. Why, when each train had the capacity for 700 passengers, had only 962 Jews been despatched?

Fünten replied that he had followed Rauter's instructions to submit the list of deportees to the Jewish Council, which had deleted the names of 'indispensable' persons; and then there were quite a lot of Jews who had failed to answer their summonses.

'From now on,' Rauter said, 'you must meet the quotas set for you. If you fail, I will be blamed by Berlin – and you will feel my wrath.'

Hanns Rauter

* * *

PAM and Mientje Pooters acknowledged the congratulations of their colleagues. Gerrit Kastein called for quiet.

PAM Pooters

'Bombing the Rembrandt will shake the enemy's sense of entitlement,' he said. 'But we have been targeting property – trains and buildings – while the Germans have been taking lives. They've been taking Jewish lives and they've been taking Resistance lives. The decision has been made that we will now target certain prominent individuals. I don't mean shooting in self-defence; I mean deliberate, calculated assassination. I can assure you that the targets we select will have merited their fate. The Party has identified the perpetrators of repression; our task is to put an end to them. The work is different from what we have been doing and I will understand if some of you have qualms, but please be certain that the task is both justified and vital.'

There was silence.

'The first target is Anton Mussert, a Dutchman who has betrayed his nation to give support and comfort to the enemy. Mussert has used his position to persuade people that it is morally permissible to work with the Germans, to aid and abet their war of aggression and their murderous attacks on communists and Jews. It has allowed Berlin to portray the Netherlands as a willing ally in the Nazi cause. It has to stop. Militair Contact has decided that Mussert must die. I need two volunteers to shoot him.'

Willem Arondeus broke the silence.

'I'm sure the man is a monster,' Arondeus said. 'But he hasn't had a trial. Are we going to take upon ourselves the roles of prosecution, judge and executioner?'

'This is war, Willem,' Kastein said. 'Would you deny us the right to kill an enemy who kills our comrades? Or are you saying that you yourself are unwilling to do so?'

'I am certainly saying the second. As for the first . . .'

'I'll do it!' Jan Verleun was on his feet. 'If the Party tells me to, I will pull the trigger.'

* * *

Ferdinand aus der Fünten would not have his career stymied by recalcitrant Jews. He ordered the number of weekly summonses to be doubled and told his staff to follow up on all those who did not respond. There was an initial improvement in the size of the transports, followed by a marked falling off in the late summer and autumn.

Berlin sent a senior representative from the Foreign Office, Otto Bene, to investigate. Bene found cause for concern. 'The position has changed for the worse,' he cabled. 'The Jews seem to have become wise to the true meaning of "labour conscription" and growing numbers have ceased to report for weekly transport . . . Their suspicions have been increased by the absence of letters from earlier deportees and by the thoughtless language of some of our own representatives. Generalkommissar Fritz Schmidt, for instance, has stated publicly that the Reich's aim is the total destruction of the Jews, which is not helpful for operational purposes.'

Bene reported that Lages, Fünten and Deppner, the men charged with implementing the transports, were feeling under pressure. Fünten, in particular, had begun to drink to excess. Even more worrying were signs of discord at the highest levels. The rivalry between Reichskommissar Seyss-Inquart and SS-Polizeiführer Rauter was hardly a secret, but now it seemed that Generalkommissar Schmidt was harbouring personal ambitions which were creating friction within the Reichskommissariat. Schmidt's outspoken views had sparked a conflict with Hanns Rauter that could be to no one's benefit.

Generalkommissar Fritz Schmidt

* * *

Gerrit Kastein asked Anna-Maria to stay behind at the end of the meeting. Militair Contact was now ready to explain the duties she had been recruited for. Because her stage performances continued to attract the advances of Germans in the audience, Kastein said, she was well placed to assist in the Resistance's targeting operations. Her role would be to entice her admirers to a designated location where an execution party would be waiting.

* * *

Hanns Rauter invited Ferdinand aus der Fünten for a chat. Issuing invitations to individual Jews wasn't working, Rauter said; there needed to be fresh thinking. Berlin had no interest in the names of those deported, Himmler and the Führer just wanted to see the numbers.

'Initiative!' Rauter shouted. 'We need you to use your initiative. How hard is it to go out and round up a thousand Jews? You have all the manpower you need and you can start with the ghetto, where they are sitting targets. Send in the SS. You can fill the trains in no time. And we have other weapons: the register of Jews contains all of their names, their ages and their addresses. Everything you need is on record in the Amsterdam Registry Office – the identity of every Jew in Holland and exactly where to find them.'

* * *

Pim was determined to dissuade Anna-Maria from accepting. He knew the Resistance had experimented with honeytrap operations and he knew the dangers they entailed.

'Moffenmeiden': *Dutch women with German troops*

'I would have done it,' Anna-Maria told him, 'but things have changed. I'm pregnant.'

* * *

In the autumn and winter of 1942, the policy of issuing individual call-up papers was replaced by indiscriminate roundups. The SS mounted raids in Amsterdam and other cities, seizing hundreds of Jews from their homes and from the streets. The charade was over, panic spread. The Jewish Council, which had previously reassured people that the Germans had 'no intention of sending anyone to the remote parts of the east', pleaded in vain for the call-up method to be given another chance. In October, the underground newspaper *Vrij Nederland* described the horror that gripped the Jewish community:

> At the stroke of eight, as darkness falls, the dread ordeal of waiting begins once again for our Jewish fellow citizens. Each footstep is a threat, each car an approaching doom, each bell a sentence. The squad cars are out, the SS and the Dutch Jew hunters ready for their deadly night's work. Every evening doors are flung open, and women, children, old people, the sickly and the rest are dragged out like so many fish from a pond, defenceless, without hope, without help, without appeal. Night after night. By the hundred, dragged away, always to one and the same destination: death. When the morning comes, those left behind do the rounds of their friends and relations to see who is left.

* * *

Uncle Anton went to see his boss. He told King Kong that the Communist Party was pressing for the assassination of high-profile Nazis and Dutch collaborators.

King Kong thought for a moment. 'What is our view on this?'

'There is some disquiet among operatives,' Anton said. 'Some debate about the rights and wrongs of extrajudicial killing. I can't see it lasting very long – the Party will order other people to do the shooting – but the moral qualms might delay things. CS-6 is also recruiting for active honeytrap operations. A couple of girls have had to withdraw, but Kastein has got at least three signed up and ready to go.'

* * *

The last weeks of 1942 saw the ghetto depleted. The other inhabitants of the apartment disappeared, one by one, until Franz and Johanna Friedheim were alone in the three rooms that had seemed so tiny and now appeared too large. The roundup methods had changed, but Nazi bureaucracy ground on. A letter from the Zentralstelle, addressed to Marlies and her brother Hans at the farm in Hollandsche Rading, informed them that according to the records of the Central Registry Office, they were classified as members of the Jewish religion. In light of this, their work assignment had been terminated and they were required to make their way to join their parents in Amsterdam.

The reunion was emotional. The Friedheim family was back together, but there now seemed every chance that all four of them would be swallowed up by the insatiable maw of violence and hatred that lay somewhere in the future and somewhere in the east.

* * *

The Resistance Council sent a representative to inspect Anna-Maria's house. He introduced himself by his Resistance name, Oom Sjaak – *Uncle Jacky* – but Anna-Maria recognised him at once.

Hans Kreisel was a rally driver and adventurer, whose exploits had figured in the pages of the Dutch press. Anna-Maria's husband, Pim, had known him when they were youngsters in Rotterdam. Anna-Maria had been exempted from active duty for the length of her pregnancy, Kreisel said, but that didn't mean she couldn't be useful. Terbregge was a quiet suburb, there was no German garrison and Pim and Anna-Maria had a house with plenty of room. For the immediate future, their contribution would be to take in Resistance members on the run, downed Allied pilots and Jews seeking shelter from persecution. Their home would be a safe house and when the baby was born, it could be useful cover for when the Germans came calling.

Terbregge, 1942

* * *

Ferdinand aus der Fünten was meeting the quotas that Berlin demanded of Hanns Rauter and that Rauter, in turn, demanded of him. But it came at a cost. Fünten, the 'sensitive philanthropist', found the work distressing. He complained to members of the Jewish Council about the strain it was placing on him; he was drunk from early morning until he returned at night to his wife or his mistress.

Jacob Presser

The Jewish Dutch historian Jacob Presser, who would write a detailed account of the ghetto clearance, was detained in one of Fünten's roundups and taken to join the hundreds of others being held in the Amsterdam Schouwburg, the former Jewish theatre that had been converted into a clearing point for those awaiting deportation.

> There was great chaos in the Schouwburg, with people crying and babies screaming, and far too few toilets for the hundreds who were crammed in there. Aus der Fünten was constantly drunk. We had plenty of opportunity to watch him at work. Had he been a sadist, he could have done no worse, dividing his victims to left and right – to salvation or to death ... He was smoking one cigarette after another, leaning nonchalantly against the wall ... He made people file before him, looked at them, inspected their papers and then decided, without a single word, simply by waving his hand to the right or the left ... It was known that Fünten stopped work at 5 p.m. and that all those who had not been processed by then would automatically be sent to Westerbork and from there to Poland. As the afternoon wore on, the tension became unbearable.

Schouwburg Theatre, Amsterdam

Fünten made a point of splitting husbands and wives and if one of them complained, he would wave them both to the right – two for Poland instead of just one. When David Cohen of the Jewish Council objected to the randomness of his decisions, Fünten threw down a pile of identity documents and said Cohen should pick out twenty of his friends, whose lives he could save.

I sat beside Aus der Fünten, who was drunk, and he made the victims file past us. I knew most of them personally and I was forced to make the choice. I couldn't stop thinking of those I had to turn down … Leo Calff, a valued member of the Council's Finance Committee, was brought before us and I exempted him. But he had his three beautiful children with him, two sons and a young daughter, and Fünten said they could not be exempted. I protested, but Fünten was adamant. Leo said he wanted to go with his children, but they begged him to stay to look after their mother and he finally agreed to do so. I would have told Aus der Fünten there and then that I could not go on with the ghastly business, had I not seen so many other men with young children whom I could simply not abandon.

10

WOMEN'S WORK

Hannie Schaft was an attractive twenty-two-year-old law student with golden red hair. And she was a communist. For Gerrit Kastein, both qualities were useful.

Hannie had made contact with CS-6 after more Dutch hostages were executed following the shooting in Haarlem of a Wehrmacht corporal, Alois Bamberger. She said she wanted to kill Germans. She had been active in the Resistance for over a year, she told Kastein, stealing identity cards at swimming pools, theatres, concert halls and cafés, where there were unguarded wardrobes or changing rooms, in order to provide false identities for Jewish people in hiding. Now she wanted to do more.

The Resistance Council gave her basic weapons training and an initial assignment. She was ordered to ambush and shoot an SD officer, who was known to cycle along a certain street at the same time every morning. Hannie did as she was told. She waited for the man to appear and took the shot, but when she pulled the trigger, the gun fired a blank. The supposed SD man was Frans van der Wiel, a senior Resistance commander, and the shooting was Hannie's trial of competence and reliability. The fury she felt at being tested increased her determination to shoot for real.

* * *

The SS came for Franz and Johanna Friedheim in the winter of 1942. Willy Lages and Ferdinand aus der Fünten had been told to extend the Jew hunting round the clock; thousands were seized and extra trains laid on. In a report to Reichsführer Heinrich Himmler, Hanns Rauter boasted that he had caught 13,000 Jews in a single week; Westerbork was now so crowded that thousands were sleeping on the ground:

> The operation is going according to plan. Results would have been even better if the Dutch police had refrained from tipping people off, and I have had to remove one of our own officials who saw fit to object on 'humanitarian grounds'. But there have been no public protests. The Dutch population simply stand and watch. The liquidation of the ghetto is now in the hands of the Sicherheitsdienst and the Ordnungspolizei. As you can see, Herr Reichsführer, I am well satisfied with the course of events.

Rauter's satisfaction was the product of cruelty. On the streets of Amsterdam, husbands were snatched from their wives, women from their children, children from their parents. Jacob Presser saw one of his pupils dragged into an SS prison van, while the boy's mother screamed from her balcony.

Waiting to leave from Amsterdam Centraal station, Franz and Johanna heard their fellow travellers' words of encouragement – perhaps the Dutch railwaymen would refuse to man the trains, British bombers would come and smash the station, the Allied invasion would begin, the communists would appear from nowhere to rescue us ... Hope faded as the train pulled into Westerbork, then flickered anew as passengers were greeted by smiling faces – Dutch policemen, members of the Maréchaussée, young Jews dressed in smart green uniforms.

The SS were present, too, but in the background. The Germans wanted Westerbork to appear benign, to maintain the residual hope of survival that keeps people quiet. Life there had the trappings of normality – a school, a restaurant, a camp orchestra; medical help; weddings, circumcision, even synagogue services; entertainment and sport.

Rollcall, Camp Westerbork

Every Tuesday, normality froze. Each week for two years, from the summer of 1942 to the summer of 1944, Westerbork's inmates were assembled on the parade ground for rollcall and selection. Berlin laid down the numbers, but it was the camp's

Jewish Council that picked the names. As Tuesday approached, panic grew. Hearing your name read out meant transport to the east – few now believed the comforting tales of 'work in Germany' – to Auschwitz, Birkenau, Sobibor and Bergen-Belsen. The fear of being selected led to bribes and corruption; some members of the Jewish administration could be swayed by money or the offer of sexual favours. Those whose names were not called cried with relief. Another seven days of life; a week of grace until Tuesday came around once more.

The loading of the trains was brutal. In his time at Westerbork, Erich Deppner used violence to fill the trucks and meet the quotas. He sent children without their parents and parents without their children; if numbers were short, he told the SS to grab single women and push them on board. The result was chaos, verging on riots. Himmler congratulated Deppner on his 'good work', but it was clear that other methods were needed.

Loading the transports, Westerbork

When a new commandant, Albert Gemmeker, was installed, he took a wilier approach. A Jewish detachment was formed, the *Fliegende Kolonne*, whose task was to reassure the departing prisoners as they were shepherded to the waiting trains. Each cattle truck had a barrel of drinking water and an empty barrel for use as a toilet. There were no seats or mattresses, no straw on the floor and people were packed so tightly that it was impossible to sit or lie down. Dutch Railways ran the trains as far as Nieuweschans, where employees of the Deutsche Reichsbahn took over. With the transports frequently held in sidings to make way for military trains or avoid Allied bombardments, the journey was long and painful. It was into this well of inhumanity that Franz and Johanna Friedheim disappeared for ever.

Johanna Friedheim and Franz Theodor Friedheim.
Both died on 30 April 1943 in Sobibor, Poland

* * *

It was Hans Kreisel who brought them the pilots; young Englishmen and Americans shot down on bombing runs to and from the Ruhr, disoriented, scared and vulnerable. Anna-Maria tended their injuries and made them broth from the vegetables in her Terbregge garden. She put mattresses and blankets in the attic and concealed the entrance behind a bookshelf. Most stayed a night or two before being collected by guides from the Resistance, who would smuggle them across the river, under the noses of German patrols, then on to the first stage of the underground escape line that led to Brussels, Paris and, with luck, via Spain to safety in England. The airmen were provided with false papers, travelling with their minders on overnight trains, halting at the Brussels safe house on rue Franklin, then lodging in the basement of the École normale supérieure or one of several Paris hotels run by trusted French families.

The founder of the Dutch–Paris line, the Dutch textile merchant Jean Weidner, was inspired by his Seventh Day Adventist faith, but its operators included men and women from all backgrounds – Communist Party activists, civil servants, a rabbi's son and a Catholic abbot. Hundreds of them, in four countries, their identities concealed from each other, would hand over their human cargoes to the next *passeur* and never learn what became of them. It was probably for the best: of the 1,000 or so *Engelandvaarders* who travelled on the Holland–Paris route, less than half would reach Britain. The Abwehr had infiltrated the escape lines and the punishment for helping Allied airmen was execution.

* * *

Hannie Schaft had proved her commitment to the cause. She was instructed by the Resistance Council to make contact with two other operatives, sisters by the names of Truus and Freddie Oversteegen. Truus, who was eighteen, and Freddie, sixteen, had taken part in a sabotage operation in Haarlem and were lying low, working as nurses at a hospital in Enschede. They gave Hannie a frosty reception. A growing number of Resistance groups had been penetrated by German agents and the Council had neglected to give Hannie a password. Truus and Freddie readied their revolvers; Hannie clutched a gun in her bag. They sat in silence, fingers on triggers, staring each other down, until Truus burst out laughing. Hannie laid her pistol on the table and the others followed suit. 'Okay,' Truus said. 'How about a drink?'

It was the start of a relationship that would see the three women work together almost to the end of the war, carrying out deeds of unparalleled bravery that would secure their reputation as heroines of the Resistance.

Freddie and Truus Oversteegen

* * *

Christmas 1942 was a time of professional satisfaction for Willy Lages, Ferdinand aus der Fünten, Albert Gemmeker and all the hardworking staff of Westerbork and the Zentralstelle für Judische Auswanderung. Their reward for a year of selfless effort on behalf of the Reich was a message of congratulations from the Führer, triumphantly displayed on the noticeboard of the Westerbork officers' mess, and a Christmas dinner of good food and good cheer. When presents were opened at the end of the meal, there was applause and laughter as colleagues' generosity was toasted by the happy recipients. Willy Lages made a speech in which he raised a glass to some very welcome news. A few days earlier, Lages said, the 50,000th Jew had been deported from the Netherlands; the Zentralstelle was keeping pace with, even exceeding, the targets set by Berlin.

Commandant's Christmas dinner, Camp Westerbork, 1942

Five days later, on 30 December, there was more bonhomie. It was David Cohen's sixtieth birthday and the Jewish Council closed its offices to celebrate its deputy leader. The *Jewish Weekly* reported that Professor Cohen received the plaudits and thanks of the grateful Jewish community. The Amsterdam Chief Rabbi, Simon Dasberg, compared him to Moses, expressing the hope that Cohen and his colleagues would 'lead us past Sinai into the Promised Land' and the deportees would soon return from their banishment.

Jewish Council, Amsterdam

Presenting Cohen with a specially bound first edition of *The Handbook of the Jewish Council*, Dasberg said its contents were 'testimony to the creative genius and great organisational talent of the man whose birthday we celebrate'. Other gifts included an armchair and an album of photographs illustrating the Council's work. Photo number 28, titled 'Departure of one contingent', showed a car laden with suitcases cheerily labelled 'To Westerbork'.

* * *

The new year brought more pain, more death and the growth of a new life. Anna-Maria was examined by her family doctor, who told her she was strong and healthy, and that her baby had every chance of being so, too.

Arrests had reduced the number of operatives manning the escape lines, with the result that fugitives were spending longer in the Dutch safe houses. A British airman stayed with Pim and Anna-Maria for nearly a month, becoming a guest and then a friend. Terence Thompson, the rear gunner of an Avro Lancaster shot down on its return from bombing the Krupp Armament Works in Essen, seemed little more than a boy. He told them it had been his first mission; Anna-Maria suspected he had lied about his age to get into the RAF.

The Resistance stipulated that pilots should reveal nothing about themselves and should not enquire about their hosts, but Terry was gregarious and the three of them became close.

When a Resistance operative finally arrived to take him away, the parting was hard. The guide did not minimise the dangers that lay ahead, not least in the river crossings they were about to undertake, and Anna-Maria could see that Terry was scared. Before he stepped into the night, he put his arms around her, gave her a kiss and blushed crimson. 'I'm so sorry,' he said. 'It's just ... I'm afraid this might be the last kiss I ever have.'

It wasn't. Anna-Maria herself would give him another. But not for seventy-five years.

* * *

Twenty-two-year-old Marlies and twenty-four-year-old Hans Friedheim would follow their parents' calvary from Amsterdam to Westerbork. Sitting in her bungalow in the South Australian sunshine, seventy years later and half a world away, Marlies remained haunted by the memory of it.

We were told that we were being summoned to go and work in Germany under police control. It was all very official. They got our names from the Dutch Central Registry Office; that's how they knew who was Jewish and who was not. The summons said that all we had to do was just go to Germany and work hard and we would be okay. We tried to believe it, but in the back of our minds we knew the Germans had much worse in store ... Some people went into hiding, but you never knew what might happen if you did that. They used to warn people that if you go into hiding and we find you, your punishment will be twice as bad so we didn't know what to do. I had a boyfriend at that time who was already in hiding, and he was begging me to go into hiding, too. He had a place for me, with false papers, and everything was ready.

But when I spoke to my mother about it, she said she was reconciled to going on the transport. She said, 'If all Jews have to go, then I shall go with them.' I couldn't leave my parents. I went to see my father and we sat on a park bench. My nerves were so shattered that I couldn't stop crying. My father was crying too. He took me to the house where my boyfriend was hiding and they tried to persuade me to go into hiding with him. But I wanted to be with my parents ...

Later, after my mother and father had been taken away ...
sorry ... I'm sorry for crying ... Later, I remember how we
also were taken to Westerbork. I remember looking out of the
train window ... I'm sorry for crying ... sorry. We arrived and
the SS received us and we were there with all the other Jews.
And when they put us in the barracks, it was the time of my
greatest fear. I knew a girl who was already in the camp. She
was a friend of mine who'd been among the first to be summoned ... and the first ones were given jobs administering
the camp. So, I tried to find her, to ask her if she could possibly
get a job for me and for Hans, too.

Marlies Friedheim, aged 82

My friend managed to find me a position, delousing children from head lice. There was nothing for my brother, but
the next day he got himself a job in the kitchen. We were
segregated into men's and women's camps, so we could
see each other for only five minutes a day, through the
fence. But it is so lucky that we were able to prolong our
stay, because that is what helped us avoid the transports.
Sometime later, I went to see my brother through the fence
and he shouted to me, 'Marlies! I'm free!' The SS commander had got a telegram saying Hans was being recalled

to the farm. And when I got back to my barracks, I got the same telegram!

I found out later what had happened ... There were very lovely people who cared a lot for us – the Jansen family and Cornelis Griffioen, the farmer, and his wife – and when we were taken to Westerbork, they said, 'We refuse to let these children go!' Mr Jansen wrote a petition to try to save us. He got all the farmers to say that they could not manage without us, that the farm would collapse without our labour. He took the letters to the SS headquarters in Amsterdam, but they cursed him and kicked him out with their boots and said, 'If you're not careful, you can go with them!' He came back in tears.

But Mr Jansen didn't give up ... He sent word for us to try to stay at Westerbork for as long as we possibly could. Nobody knew how long you might be there before being sent to the east, but if you could delay it you might at least have a chance.

Mr Jansen tried and tried again; and this time, he succeeded – he got us reprieved! We got an order to go back to Amsterdam. We had to register with the SS so that we could be recalled to the camp, but the piece of paper I got that day is the most precious piece of paper I have ever had. It is the paper that allowed me to leave Westerbork and I still have it with me ... here it is, the paper that saved my life!

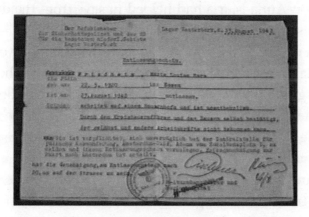

* * *

Many people came to Anna-Maria in those years, seeking help and a place to hide. There were other pilots, Resistance men on the run and Jews in search of shelter, so-called *onderduikers*, submariners who would dive beneath the surface of public life into basements, attics and closets.

Pim and Anna-Maria put them in the room upstairs with mattresses and blankets. Some stayed for days, others for months or even years. The house became known as a haven; people would turn up out of the blue. There were so many arrivals that it was impossible to hide what was happening; but the neighbours, whose son Anna-Maria had helped to save from the drunken German soldier, kept her secret.

When people left, it was rare to learn what became of them. Anna-Maria discovered only decades later that Terry Thompson and his guide had walked the forty miles from Terbregge to Roosendaal, crossing the Rhine, the Meuse and the Scheldt by raft at night. Then they picked up the steam train to the Belgian border, jumping off before the final stop to avoid customs checks and making a detour through woodland paths, continuing by tram to Antwerp and train to Brussels.

There Terry was taken in by David Verloop, a young Dutch lawyer who ran the Belgian section of the Dutch–Paris line and would eventually be betrayed to the Gestapo. Verloop and Jo Jacobstahl accompanied Terry on the overnight train to Paris, checking into the Hôtel Montholon near the Gare du Nord, until the French *passeur* arrived to take him down to the Pyrenees and over the frontier to Spain. An agreement with the Francoist government allowed Allied airmen to travel via Gibraltar to England, and Terry returned to his squadron. He would fly thirty-two more sorties before the end of the war, but the memory of the young Dutchwoman he kissed on the night he set out for freedom remained with him.

* * *

Meetings resumed at Corellistraat. Uncle Anton said nothing further about his suspicions of the Boissevains. The spate of betrayals had abated and the hunt for traitors lost some of its urgency. In any event, Janka and Gideon had distinguished themselves in raids to seize materials for CS-6's production of fake identity documents – official stamps, printed templates and watermarked paper – that left little doubt of their courage and commitment.

Gerrit Kastein brought the meeting an update from King

Kong about the proposal to assassinate Anton Mussert. Almost as if someone had warned him, Kastein said, Mussert had ratcheted up his personal protection. He now had bodyguards with him round the clock; he appeared in public only rarely and with no advance notification. Militair Contact had decided that trying to kill him would be hopeless.

* * *

Marlies and Hans were welcomed back to the farm. In the absence of their parents, and the uncertainty surrounding the fate of those taken for labour service, the Jansens and the Griffioens became their family, watching over them with love and affection. Much as they wished to keep the youngsters with them, they decided the danger was too great. Marlies and Hans had had one reprieve from the transports; if they were picked up again, it was unlikely they could be saved. Mr Jansen said the time had come when they would have to go into hiding.

* * *

Pim and Anna-Maria agreed with the decision to abort the attack on Anton Mussert. There seemed little point in sacrificing Resistance lives in an operation that was doomed to fail, and the Germans would inevitably exact a high price on the Dutch people. When the Czechs assassinated Reinhard Heydrich the previous spring, Hitler had demanded the execution of 10,000 civilians. Whole villages had been razed and their inhabitants murdered.

'The only thing I find puzzling,' Pim said, 'was why Mussert chose that moment to step up his protection. Kastein said it was as if he had been warned. Perhaps I'm being overly suspicious, but I wonder if he *was* warned.'

* * *

Truus was the leader. Freddie was too young and Hannie too impulsive, verging on the reckless. Their initial assignments involved the planting of explosives and attacks on railway lines, but the Resistance needed rarer skills and the girls had them. They were tasked with trailing German officials, frequenting bars and restaurants where Nazi officers gathered, taking note of loose conversations that flowed with the wine and the schnapps. Hannie, for the hell of it, would end the evening by stealing revolvers from the uniform jackets draped over the backs of chairs. Her lack of fear seemed absolute, an absence of concern for self-preservation that made her bold and resolute, buoyed by a conviction of personal invulnerability. Her courage, her beauty and her fluent German would see her assigned to the most perilous operations.

When London asked for updated information about German defences on the Dutch coast, Hannie was sent to liaise with Kees Dutilh and his fellow operatives on the North Holland Peninsula. She went to Ijmuiden, the town at the entrance to the North Sea Canal that the Germans had transformed into a fortress, demolishing hundreds of homes to build gun emplacements and bunkers to ward off threats from the sea. The civilian population had been expelled and the port area was off-limits, but Hannie used her charm to strike up friendships with German soldiers, leading them on to discuss their duties, the size of their garrison, the nature of the installations they were guarding, new minefields and bunkers, all of which could subsequently be bombed by the RAF. She learned that the naval base had become the centre for the construction and housing of Germany's miniature submarines and for a fleet of torpedo boats designed to sink Allied shipping. She picked up rumours of a deadly new weapon that Nazi engineers were developing, a flying bomb that could target London. The Resistance Council noted the success that Hannie, Truus and Freddie were achieving and decided they were ready for the mission that would define their war.

Hannie Schaft

* * *

Marlies and Hans had been back for nearly a month and Mr Jansen was getting worried. He had asked the Griffioens if there might be somewhere in an outbuilding or a grain store that could serve as a hiding place, but they knew the farm would be the first place the Germans would come looking. None of the immediate neighbours were willing to take on the responsibility and Mr Jansen was reluctant to ask too widely for fear of informers. In the end he spoke to an acquaintance who had a contact in the Resistance and was told that enquiries would be made about a possible safe house.

* * *

Pim saw that Anna-Maria was preoccupied. Like her, he had been turning over the names of those who knew about the plan to kill Mussert. Like her, he was at a loss to think of any who might have betrayed it.

'There were so few people who knew,' Pim said. 'And all of

them completely trustworthy. I know Uncle Anton mentioned the Boissevains, but they've proved their reliability in spades.'

'I've been thinking about something Anton said to us after Brother Josef was executed,' Anna-Maria said. 'It was about a suspected V-Mann they'd been tailing in and out of the Binnenhof – called De Wilde or something. I just have a sense that he is someone we know ...'

* * *

Jan Verleun had come up with another target.

'The guy's name is Pieter Kaay,' Verleun said. 'He is Dutch, thirty-eight years old, and he's the Chief Lieutenant of Police in Enschede. Here's his photograph from the police yearbook.'

He passed round a grainy image.

'Kaay has been responsible for the deaths of many Jews including children. He has raided households where Jewish families have been sheltering. He has sent the fugitives to Westerbork and their protectors to Euterpestraat. For all of this, he has been paid by the Sicherheitsdienst. But that is not the end of it. With the Enschede Police Commissioner, Antonie Berends, Kaay has tortured members of the Resistance. They seized two of our people and beat them so brutally that they gave away the names of thirty comrades, who are now in custody, facing execution. We know that Kaay lives at 14 Sweelinckstraat in Enschede. I say we go and shoot him.'

Sape Kuiper raised his hand and Reina Prinsen Geerligs nodded her agreement.

'I will go with Sape,' Reina said. 'In a world without rules, we must make our own.'

* * *

Anna-Maria gave birth to a baby daughter. The midwife said she was so beautiful she could be a painting in the Rijksmuseum. When she asked what the baby's Christian name would be, Anna-Maria said, 'She will be called Hanneke. And she will have all the love she needs and deserves, however much the world tries to prevent it.'

* * *

Jan Verleun took Reina and Sape to the forest. With targets suspended from a pine branch, he showed them how the gun pulled slightly to the right and how to compensate for it before firing.

'That's for a distance shot,' Verleun said. 'But in this case you'll be much closer. You need to be within touching range; you need to see his face and hear his voice.'

Reina Prinsen Geerligs and Sape Kuiper

Reina and Sape went to a café to discuss things. To the rest of the customers they were young lovers gazing into each other's eyes.

'How strange,' Reina said. 'You're nineteen; I'm nineteen. We should be meeting at a dance, not a shooting range.'

'I think we should stick to the operation,' Sape said. 'We knock on the door, we speak politely. We make sure we've got the right guy, then we shoot him.'

'I've got it,' Reina said.

Sape softened.

'I didn't mean to sound brusque,' he said. 'I'm nervous. Can anyone say how they will feel when it comes to pulling the trigger ... ?'

'The man is evil,' Reina said, 'He will kill others if we don't kill him. That's the way we get through this.'

* * *

It was Hans Kreisel who brought her to the house. Anna-Maria looked at the frightened girl on her doorstep and gave her a hug.

'I just feel so lost,' Marlies Friedheim said. 'And so alone. My parents have gone to Westerbork and from there, God knows where. My brother, Hans, is hiding with his old English teacher on the other side of Amsterdam. And you ...' Marlies fought back her tears. 'You are being so kind to me . . . I can never thank you enough . . .'

* * *

Reina and Sape left their bikes at the end of Sweelinckstraat. Number 14 was one of a row of 1930s semi-detached houses of the type built in many Dutch towns. Both of them knew it would be hard to escape if they were pursued.

The door was opened by a middle-aged woman.

'Hello, my dear,' she said, smiling at Reina. 'How can I help you?'

'We're here to see Lieutenant Kaay,' Reina said.

'Come in. It's chilly.'

She called upstairs, 'Piet, there's a lovely young couple here to see you.'

The sound of footsteps on the upper landing set Sape's heart racing. From the front door, he saw the heavy boots and black police trousers as the man descended the stairs. He pulled the gun from his pocket as Kaay came into sight and in the same moment saw – he had a baby in his arms.

* * *

Anna-Maria van der Vaart was twenty-three and Marlies Friedheim twenty-two. Their meeting on the doorstep that day began a friendship that would outlive the barbarous era they were born to. For the next three years, Marlies sheltered in the attic of the house in Terbregge, sharing the space, the blankets, the mattresses and the food with others who came and went, cared for and protected by the young family downstairs.

Marlies had promised her parents she would stay with them. She had pledged never to leave her brother and she felt she had failed on both counts. Anna-Maria told her it was not her fault; sometimes life is just more powerful than anything we can pit against it. There was no way of getting news about her parents, Anna-Maria said, but she would go herself to visit Corrie du Fijan and Sophie Blommers, the former schoolteachers who were sheltering her brother Hans.

* * *

'What would you have done?'

'I would have taken the shot,' Jan Verleun said. 'But I am not you. And we all make our own decisions.'

Verleun's hardness had been forged in the army and in the discipline of the Party; he had determined that compassion was weakness.

'But what about the baby?' Sape asked.

'A discussion for another time. More important now is how you left things.'

'Reina told them we'd come to the wrong house,' Sape said. 'That we were looking for a Mr van de Kaay and we'd confused him with Pieter Kaay ...'

'And did he believe you? Did he seem suspicious?'

'I'm not sure,' Reina said. 'I think his wife liked us and maybe that helped convince him. He gave us directions to the house of some Van de Kaay on the other side of Enschede. But that was miles away. I don't think he really bought our story.'

'I'm ashamed,' Sape said quietly. 'The Party told me to shoot and I didn't do it.'

* * *

Marlies became attached to young Hanneke. She helped to care for Anna-Maria's baby, sharing in the joy of shaping a new existence, a new being who responded with love to those who loved her. Seventy years on, Marlies remembered the happiness.

> I was the luckiest person in the world. They were the loveliest family anyone could imagine. We got on so well. I was able to help Anna-Maria in the house and with the baby. In the three years I stayed there, we never had an argument; that's quite something with all the tension and anxiety of those days. For me, things were hard. I suffered because of the dreadful thought – an awful thought – that I had left my parents and my brother behind. I worried about them all the time, I felt it was my fault that I hadn't saved them. Some of the emotions I had for my family were transferred to Anna-Maria's baby. I think that is why I loved her so much. She was innocent and new; she hadn't been damaged by the world. She was the hope we all clung to.
>
> Anna-Maria and Pim tried to keep me cheerful. Whenever I felt like crying, they handed me the baby because they knew I couldn't cry in front of the baby. That was clever of them. They never took any payment from me. Nothing. They did everything out of kindness. Anna-Maria said to me she was so happy at being a mother that she wanted to share her happiness with someone else – with me. She was putting herself and her family in danger. I knew it and she knew it, too. But we were young and somehow you don't think about it. Later, when she came to see me here in Australia, I asked her, 'Were you never afraid?' and she said, 'There were times in the

middle of the night when I had doubts; there were some tears and worries about what I had done.' But she never showed it at the time. She never showed it.

Marlies Friedheim with Hanneke

* * *

Jan Verleun consulted the Party and was instructed to resume the operation against Pieter Kaay. Willem Arondeus wanted to know what would happen this time: what would they do if Kaay were to appear again with his baby in his arms? Verleun replied that such decisions are taken collectively and once they are taken, they become the expression of a common will. Arondeus cut him off.

'Don't say it, Jan. For God's sake, don't start all that stuff about Party discipline and how we must submit to the will of the leadership—'

'That's not what I was saying,' Verleun replied. 'I was going to say that Kaay deserves to die, but his baby doesn't. Reina and Sape made that judgement and they had the right to make it. I would have done things differently but not for the sake of Party discipline. I would have shot Pieter Kaay – and his child – because it was for the greater good ...'

'The greater good? But who on earth has the right to decide

what a baby's life is worth? Are you going to make that judgement? Because, as sure as hell, I'm not!'

Verleun shrugged. 'History is a river,' he said, 'and we are pebbles in it. Single pebbles get swept away, but enough pebbles together might nudge the river's course. The change we make might be so small that at first it's not even noticeable and only after years, maybe even centuries, will mankind see that we have shifted history's flow to a better place. We matter only as we contribute to the collective endeavour. And to do that we can't afford to be squeamish.'

'My God,' said Arondeus. 'You really believe all that, don't you?'

'Yes, I do. And you?'

'I believe in me. I believe in now, not some hazy future. I believe in the pebbles. Someone has to do some living – otherwise there's no point in changing the world.'

'So why do you put your life at risk for the cause?'

'Because otherwise,' Arondeus said, 'I would not be able to live with myself.'

* * *

Willem Arondeus would have been a pacifist, save that pacifism was impossible when thousands were being murdered. He and others like him had found different ways to resist. Since the February strikes of 1941, Willem, Gerrit van der Veen and Frieda Belinfante had worked to manufacture false identity documents that would save Jews, Allied airmen and Resistance fighters from arrest. Willem and Gerrit had a background in fine arts, which was helpful in the design and printing, but there were other challenges that meant production levels were failing to keep pace with demand. There was a pressing need for more of the watermarked paper the

Nazis used for their documents, for the ink they printed them with and the stamps they used to endorse them. The concerns weighed on Willem, as did the thought of the records the Germans had compiled of the country's 160,000 Jews in the Amsterdam Registry Office. So long as they remained intact, the SS would be able to identify and hunt down the tens of thousands who remained.

* * *

The Enschede police log of Pieter Kaay's last hours on earth recorded that he went late at night to raid the house of a suspected Jew protector at number 496 Broekheurnerweg. The door was answered by a Mrs Marieke Weener, who had been asleep and was visibly shaken to see the black uniforms of the Dutch police demanding access to her home. Kaay asked if it was correct that the Weeners were hiding a Jewish boy whose parents had recently been transported to Westerbork, and who was himself legally subject to deportation. Mrs Weener denied it, but Kaay and his deputy, Jan van Limburg, forced their way inside and discovered the Jewish child asleep in the cellar. Mrs Weener's husband was not at home, so Kaay elected to question her about the identity of the men who had brought her the child. Mrs Weener replied that she did not know who they were and, seeing the boy being carried away to the police van outside, cursed Kaay and Van Limburg in the following terms: 'You just wait. You will get what is coming to you.' Because of the subject's uncooperative attitude, Lieutenant Kaay ordered her to get dressed and escorted her to the police station where she was booked into custody at 1 a.m. Mrs Weener was subsequently delivered to the Sicherheitsdienst, who transferred her to Euterpestraat for further interrogation.

Pieter Kaay, meanwhile, returned home and slept until the

following morning, when he returned to duty. Proceeding by bicycle to Enschede police headquarters on Haaksbergerstraat, Kaay was turning right onto Kuipersdijk at around 07.50, when he was approached from behind by another cyclist travelling at high speed. As the cyclist drew level, he shot Kaay twice in the chest, killing him instantly. Kaay's body was discovered on the roadway outside 123 Kuipersdijk, where the Technical Investigation Service of the Dutch police later photographed the scene.

11

FORGING FREEDOM

As the deportations of the Jews accelerated, so did the efforts to save them. By 1943, there were more than 100 people working in the Resistance's forgery operations, financed by money from Wally van Hall and Jan Boissevain's National Support Fund. Willem Arondeus, Gerrit van der Veen and Frieda Belinfante formed the Persoonsbewijzen Centrale which became the largest forgery organisation of the war, though it struggled to produce the tens of thousands of documents that were needed. The Germans introduced more and more of them: identity cards to be able to move around; permits to use a bicycle; attestations of residency; vouchers to buy food. The Resistance found itself running to keep up.

Underground forgery operations

To make things worse, the authorities periodically changed the design of the documents or appended additional stamps. However meticulous the forgers were about matching the quality and colour of the paper, the typefaces and the thickness of the lines dividing the printed data, it was almost impossible to copy an official stamp without somehow obtaining an example of the original. The need to do so led to increasingly bold acts of larceny.

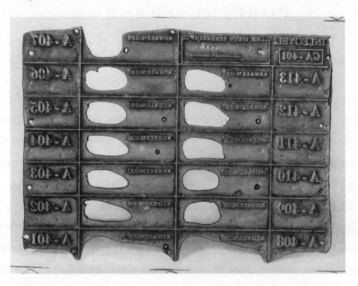

When the Germans produced seals with updated serial numbers in early 1943, Willem Arondeus and Gerrit van der Veen set out to obtain a set. They went to the central pass office of the public administration buildings in The Hague, where Arondeus engaged the guard in conversation while Van der Veen slipped away along a second-floor corridor. He found himself looking into an internal courtyard, full of cars bearing the ochre registration plates of the German military, with a locked gate that gave onto the street. The windows of the pass office opened into the courtyard.

Willem Arondeus   *Gerrit van der Veen*

Willem and Gerrit noted that when the noon-time buzzer sounded for lunch, the staff locked their doors and went out to eat. There was a period in which the stamp office could reliably be expected to be empty, but with no access to it from inside the building. Instead, Willem said, they would get in from the outside. He asked for two volunteers to pose as window cleaners, and Leo Frijda and Hans Katan – both Jewish – stepped forward. They got into the courtyard by climbing onto dustbins outside the gate and Gerrit passed two ladders to them over the wall. Jan Verleun later gave his sister a rather colourful account of what happened:

> The two men sprang out of the getaway vehicle, their white overalls held together by professional window cleaner belts with hooks for chamois leathers and sponges. The ladders proved difficult to balance, especially as one man had overalls that were far too short, the second had trousers that tripped him up and both were carrying brimming buckets of water. They eventually propped their ladders against the second-floor windows which, like the week before, had been left open to air the rooms during lunch hour. Chamois leathers flapped and sponges danced; they would have won a window cleaners' speed contest if it weren't for all the water they spilled. The smaller of the two men hooked his bucket on the ladder and slipped inside. Before the other one could do the same,

our lookout in the street started whistling Figaro's aria from *The Barber of Seville*, which was the signal that someone was approaching and the 'window cleaner' should start washing a window.

Eventually, the whistling changed to the Triumphal March from *Aida* and our man disappeared into the office, slipped the stamps into his pockets and climbed back out again.

The getaway vehicle was a truck from the depot of the Ministry of Food Supply, driven by PAM Pooters, who worked there as a distribution manager. It had the words 'Food Supply' on it in big letters and a very large swastika. Within moments of our fellows climbing back over the gate, the ladders were loaded onto the truck, the window cleaners and the girl who had acted as lookout were pulled inside and they drove off at high speed. Unfortunately, they had forgotten to empty their buckets and the whole lot of them got soaked.

They didn't want to park the truck outside 6 Corellistraat – it would have alerted the Germans to come and take a look – so they stopped round the corner in Beethovenstraat and all walked back, shivering and wet. Mrs Boissevain got them out of their wet clothes and found them dry things to wear – much classier than the stuff they'd been in! – then cooked up lunch in the kitchen to celebrate the success of the mission. Every detail of it was discussed over and again, until one of the men got tired and asked Janka Boissevain to put on a gramophone record. They sat in silence as Bach's Fugue in D filled the air with the unconquerable beauty of the human spirit. When the record finished, one of them said, 'Come on; we have work to do. If anyone thinks we've won the war by landing a few punches, they've got another thing coming.'

* * *

The investigation into the death of Pieter Kaay was carried out by the Dutch constabulary in conjunction with the German security police, the Sicherheitspolizei. The shops on Kuipersdijk had been open at 7.50 a.m., when Kaay was shot, and several witnesses came forward. A grocer's assistant recalled seeing a man on a bicycle, waiting for Kaay to arrive, and a woman standing on the opposite street corner, seemingly acting as a lookout. Both were young; the witness thought they were probably teenagers. In an attempt to jog memories, the police's Technical Investigation Service staged a reconstruction, with photographs showing the young man and woman waiting for Kaay to come into sight.

A passer-by on Kuipersdijk, who had seen the incident, remembered that the assassin sped away into Madoerastraat, but could not add any further detail. An interview with Pieter Kaay's widow proved more helpful, as she was able to describe a young couple who had come to the house prior to her husband's killing. The SiPo report concluded that it had been a scouting expedition:

> The offenders were aware of the victim's residential address. They had explored the situation beforehand and they knew the time at which Kaay would cycle to the police station. On the morning in question, they chose an observation point from which the assassin, sitting on his bicycle, could be warned of Kaay's approach and easily intercept him. Kaay collected his mail from outside his house, then set off for work before being fatally shot with a 9mm pistol. It is highly probable that the couple who visited Kaay's house were the man and woman who committed the murder.

* * *

Hannie Schaft did her best to teach Truus and Freddie German. They remembered the basics from their schooldays, but now they needed expressions that schoolmistresses hadn't taught them. There were plenty of Dutch women who had relationships with German soldiers – they were known as *Moffenmeiden*, or Kraut girls – and it didn't take much to join them. Gerrit Kastein had explained that the Resistance Council had a list of individuals – German officers and officials, Dutch collaborators and members of the NSB – whom it wanted eliminated. The task of Hannie, Truus and Freddie would be to flirt with the target and propose a rendezvous with the prospect of sexual favours in a remote location, where he could be shot.

They discussed the assignment with varying degrees of enthusiasm. Freddie was little more than a child, Truus a tomboy who had never worn makeup, but Hannie was a natural. She took care of her appearance when she went on active service because, she said, she wanted 'to die beautifully' if she were caught.

Hannie, Truus and Freddie

At the Heerenhek bar in Haarlem a Resistance guide pointed out an SS officer who he said was a senior specialist in the Sicherheitsdienst's operation to intercept wireless traffic between London and the Dutch underground. The man's efforts had resulted in the capture and execution of several wireless operators and was threatening to disrupt communications with Britain. Truus and Freddie were to sit at the bar and make eye contact with him when he came to order a drink.

To their surprise, it worked. The man invited Truus to join

him at his table where he propositioned her. Truus found him repulsive. He was more than twice her age, stank of alcohol and cigarettes, and insisted on boasting about each of the medals on his chest. She felt nauseous but stuck to her task. 'My uncle owns a private woodland,' Truus said. 'It's just ten minutes from here, on Wagenweg. Why don't we go for a stroll?'

Heerenhek café, Haarlem

The two of them left the café together. Freddie, who was waiting outside, ran to their Resistance contact. They had agreed that Truus would take the man to the Andriessen estate at 244 Wagenweg where she would lead him down to the ornamental pond in the grounds. When they got there, and with his hands already fumbling under her clothes, he was addressed by an angry voice from the bushes. 'Don't you know this is private property! What the hell do you think you're doing with my niece!'

Truus was ready to burst into laughter, but the German was adjusting his uniform and beginning to apologise when two shots rang out and he fell to the ground.

* * *

There was some disagreement within the Nazi leadership about the efficacy of executions. When further hostages were shot in response to Resistance attacks, Hanns Rauter reassured Berlin that the policy was producing results. 'Every single Dutch citizen,' Rauter wrote, 'now trembles at the thought that some act of sabotage might be committed somewhere in the country.' But the commander of the German military forces, Wehrmacht General Friedrich Christiansen, worried that the executions were polarising public opinion, forcing the previously uncommitted to take sides, fomenting 'an unprecedented rejection and hatred of Germany'.

General Friedrich Christiansen (centre)

Christiansen lost the argument. In the spring of 1943, he announced that severe measures had become necessary to counter the disruption caused by the Resistance. All members of the Dutch army who had been captured and paroled in 1940 were to be immediately reinterned and sent to work as forced labourers in Germany. The announcement caused anger. There were more than 250,000 former POWs and the punishment affected nearly every household in the Netherlands. Strikes broke out: half a million people in factories and businesses downed tools. When the Germans declared martial law and fired on the strikers, 170 people were killed and hundreds injured. Thousands of protestors were arrested, many of them subsequently sent to concentration camps. The predictable consequence was that large numbers of former soldiers went on the run or joined the Resistance.

The man who organised the strike at the Hoogovens steel plant in Ijmuiden already had ties with the communist underground. Jan Bonekamp was the son of political activists and had spent the early years of the occupation distributing illegal literature and raising funds.

Briefly detained after the strikes collapsed, he managed to bluff his way out of captivity and told his wife he needed to disappear. He would never return. A chance meeting later that year would lead Jan Bonekamp to play an important role in the life of a woman whose Resistance exploits would become the stuff of legend.

Jan Bonekamp

* * *

Despite the efforts of the Dutch police and the SiPo, Pieter Kaay's killers were still at large by the time of his funeral. The Enschede police department escorted his cortege to the Ooster Cemetery in full dress uniform. The inscription on the wreath from his family distilled their grief: 'In deepest sorrow: to a dear husband and beloved father of two young children, cut down before his time by fatal events.'

Funeral of Pieter Kaay

Kaay's tombstone was engraved with a tribute from his police colleagues: 'He stood like a rock in the surf.' During the night, unknown hands added, 'But he lay like a fool in the gutter.'

* * *

Hannie, Truus and Freddie were quick learners. Their sting operations became more professional. Posing as ladies of the night, they were sent to lure soldiers guarding German military premises away from their posts, allowing the Resistance to burn the buildings down. On occasions when the assassination party did not turn up at the site of the proposed tryst, they shot the target themselves.

They kept their secrets, forbidden to tell even close family about their work, with the result that at times they received abuse for 'sleeping with the enemy'. When they became known in one town, they would move to another. In Overveen, near Haarlem, they preyed on German soldiers using the Stoops Bad swimming pool. They had been told that Willy Lages sometimes swam there, but their paths did not cross.

Stoops Bad swimming pool, Overveen

A member of the communist Resistance in Haarlem, Joseph Gerritsen, had been apprehended by the SS, interrogated and then released. In the months that followed, a spate of arrests of CP activists had led to suspicions that an informer was at work and the Party believed it was Gerritsen. The local commander, Frans van der Wiel, told Freddie to make a date with the suspect by the Burgwal Canal. When she accused him of treachery, Gerritsen pulled a gun from his pocket and aimed it at her, but Van der Wiel had removed the bullets and Freddie shot the man dead. Freddie told her sister she was tormented by what she had done. 'It is hard,' Truus said. 'But such people are not comrades. We are not shooting a person; we are liquidating a murderer.'

Truus Oversteegen

* * *

Two weeks after Pieter Kaay's funeral, Reina Prinsen Geerligs
left for a meeting at 79 Cornelis Krusemanstraat in Amsterdam.
The apartment was a CS-6 safe house and she had been told to
deliver a message to a Resistance contact there. She rang the bell
at the downstairs entrance, heard the buzzer to open the door
and went inside where a detachment of SS men was waiting to
arrest her.

Reina was taken to the House of Detention, two blocks away
on Amstelveenseweg. She was interrogated but was not physically abused. Her captors told her she had been betrayed so
there was no point in denying her Resistance activities. She confessed to the murder of Pieter Kaay, but evidently did not give
away the others who took part in it. On the wall of her cell, she
scratched a phrase from Bernardin de St Pierre's novel, *Paul et
Virginie*: 'Faithful, though the world may end.' By tapping on the
heating pipes, she was able to communicate with neighbouring
cells and discovered that other CS-6 operatives had also been
arrested. One of them, Rose Lopes de Leao Laguna, survived
to report Reina's last message: 'I am proud of what I have done.'

Reina was joined in prison by an alarming number of CS-6

women, including Cornelia Kossen, also known as Nell Hissink van den Brink, apparently betrayed by the same informer in the ranks. After months of captivity, they were deported to the Sachsenhausen concentration camp in Germany, where they were executed on the day after their arrival. The Resistance let it be known that the women walked towards the firing squad singing and with their heads held high. It was a powerful image, hard to disprove.

Reina Prinsen Geerligs, arrest photo

12

THE FIGHT INTENSIFIES

The Soviet victory at Stalingrad in early 1943 signalled a turning of the tide in the war. It strengthened the morale of the communist Resistance and emboldened its adherents. The Resistance had previously carried out killings to rid itself of traitors and V-Mann infiltrators; now there would be proactive assassinations, the public execution-style elimination of prominent Nazis to strike fear into the occupiers. The threat of reprisals against Dutch civilians had constrained them in the past but no longer. The Resistance Council and the Party decreed that brutality must be met with brutality.

Gerrit Kastein explained things at a meeting in Corellistraat. There would be a cost, Kastein said; the Germans had increased the numbers of Todeskandidaten they were holding and some of them would suffer. But this was war, and compassion was a luxury. The first target nominated by the Party was General Hendrik Seyffardt.

'Seyffardt has used his standing and his reputation to convince thousands of young Dutchmen to fight for the Germans,' Kastein said. 'He has served as head of the SS-Vrijwilligers Legioen – the Volunteer SS Legion of the Netherlands – for over a year.

It mustn't continue. Militair Contact has provided Seyffardt's address: he lives at 36 Van Neckstraat in Scheveningen. I will lead the assassination party and Jan Verleun will come with me.'

* * *

Marlies Friedheim saw the newspapers. She understood what was happening beyond the confines of the Terbregge house. She knew the Germans were intensifying the deportations and she heard the stories of Jews in hiding rooted out by SS search parties or betrayed by neighbours fired by anti-Semitism, eager to curry favour or simply manoeuvring to take over a next-door apartment. She stayed inside. Most of the time, she was in the concealed attic; but when things were quiet, Anna-Maria said it was fine to come down. They would sit and talk in the kitchen or nurse the baby; sometimes Marlies would catch the fresh air in the garden, but always on alert for danger. All who stayed in Terbregge were required to practise hurrying to the attic; two minutes was the most they could take to get upstairs and cover the door. In case Marlies were ever glimpsed by outsiders, Pim and Anna-Maria had let it be known that they had a niece whose parents were in the Dutch territory of Indonesia; the girl had supposedly been in Holland for her studies when the war came and had not been able to return. Marlies's looks could easily be the features of the colonies.

> We had difficult moments. Every time the Germans banged on the door in the middle of the night, I was certain they were coming for me. But Anna-Maria was clever. She would go to the door with Hanneke in her arms and when the Germans said they were going to search the house, she would say, 'All right; just a moment . . .' and hand them the baby. They were human, too, and holding the child stirred their emotions.

They were away from their home; they were missing their own families.

Anna-Maria would come back with a glass of milk for them and speak German to them, so most of the time they weren't as horrible as they might have been. At the very least, it gave us time to hide.

Once, German soldiers came to inspect the balconies of the house. We were on the outskirts of Rotterdam and they were looking for places they could put guns in case the Allies invaded. Usually, Anna-Maria was able to warn me and the others to get into the attic. But one time, Anna-Maria and Pim were out and I answered the door – I don't know why; normally I would never have done such a thing – and a German officer was there. He'd come because they'd found a purse with Anna-Maria's name in it. I was shaking like a leaf. It was just at the time when the Nazis were rounding up Jews and sending us to the camps. I spoke to the officer in German – it was my native language, but I managed to disguise how fluent I was – and he asked where I'd learned it. I said, 'Well, we have good schools here in Holland and I always used to go on holiday to Germany.' The officer accepted my story. But the next day he came again and asked for me directly by name . . . because he wanted to invite me out! I made an excuse; I said I was terribly busy and didn't have time. In retrospect, it seems funny; back then it was terrifying.

* * *

Berlin was pressing for the deportations to be sped up; unfavourable comparisons were being made with the results achieved in Poland. Arthur Seyss-Inquart ordered Willy Lages to boost the numbers by mopping up the remaining easy targets. Lages passed on the instruction to Ferdinand aus der Fünten, who began with the hospitals. Having cleared the Dutch Israelite Hospital and the Jewish Infirmary, he turned his attention to the Jewish psychiatric institution at Apeldoornsche Bosch.

Jewish psychiatric hospital, Apeldoornsche Bosch

Fünten had the site surrounded by SS troops and summoned the hospital director, Jacques Lobstein. He told Lobstein that he was being relieved of his duties and that all his inmates were being 'transferred to hospitals in Germany' on special trains that were waiting at Apeldoorn station. Lobstein protested that many of the patients were not fit to travel, but Fünten replied, 'For us, they are all transportable.' When Lobstein argued, he and his staff were locked in the canteen.

Jacques Lobstein

Having taken charge of the premises, Fünten demanded access to the hospital safe, from which he removed the sum of 42,821 guilders. Phone lines were cut and incoming calls were intercepted by a German officer. When he asked Fünten how he should reply to relatives ringing to enquire about their loved ones, Fünten shrugged. 'Tell them they've gone to heaven.' Eight hundred and sixty-nine adults and ninety-four children were assembled to be taken by lorry to the station.

Twenty of the hospital staff volunteered to accompany their charges and Fünten ordered a further thirty to go with them. There were brutal scenes. Frightened, bewildered patients in nightdresses and pyjamas, many unable to stand, some in straitjackets, were driven out of their rooms by soldiers wielding clubs and loaded onto the back of the lorries, before others were thrown on top of them and the tailgates forcibly closed.

At the station things got worse. People were pushed out onto the platform in sub-zero temperatures screaming and crying, struggling to understand what was happening to them. More than one of them fell onto the rails between the platform and the train. Those who clung to the door frames of the cattle cars had their fingers crushed as the doors were slammed shut.

Left behind at the hospital, the chief nurse, David de Groot, who had worked there since 1919, complained bitterly to Fünten. He demanded to know why no medicines had been taken with the patients and why innocent children were being tortured in such a way, but he was told to be quiet, or he too would be deported. When he continued to argue, an SS man hit him in the face with a belt. Later that day the Dutch police were called to De Groot's house.

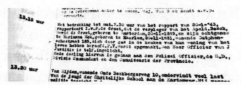

Police report, Apeldoorn. 22 January 1943. 1.15 p.m. 'David de Groot,
born 20-11-1889, and his wife Marianna Mok, born 20-11-1881,
discovered in the kitchen of their home at 185 Zutphensestraat,
having taken their own lives by the inhalation of gas.'

* * *

Jan Verleun and Gerrit Kastein put on a suit and tie. They laughed when they saw each other. The last time they'd been so smart was when Jan had been training for the priesthood and Gerrit was a consultant neurologist before the war. They took the train to The Hague then the tram to the seaside suburb of Scheveningen, two unremarkable businessmen carrying heavy briefcases. Seyffardt answered the door himself. The plan had been to confirm his identity by posing as volunteers for the Dutch SS Legion, but Verleun recognised him and opened fire immediately. Two bullets to the chest sent Seyffardt to the ground. As he fell, his assailants turned back along Van Neckstraat and retraced their steps to 6 Corellistraat.

Seyffardt was not dead. Despite his injuries, he crawled to the telephone and summoned help. His rescuers took him to the Bronovo Hospital in Scheveningen where he gave a description of the two men who had shot him. Aware he was dying, Seyffardt accepted that the attack had been a military operation and asked that no reprisals be taken.

The Germans ignored his request. When Hanns Rauter rang Himmler to tell him about the shooting, Himmler ordered the immediate execution of fifty hostages. Seyss-Inquart feared that fifty executions would unnecessarily inflame public opinion, but nonetheless gave the go-ahead for mass arrests. Shortly after

Hendrik Seyffardt died the following morning, the SS rounded up 1,800 men between the ages of eighteen and twenty-five on the grounds that they fitted the General's description of his murderers, and took them to the Vught concentration camp near 's-Hertogenbosch.

The collaborationist newspaper *Volk en Vaderland* gave a heroic account of Seyffardt's final moments. 'Two individuals appeared suddenly in the darkness, confronting him and demanding to know if he was General Seyffardt. Without a moment's hesitation, in a voice both loud and true, he replied, "Yes. I am he," at which two shots rang out and the General collapsed. Seriously wounded and with an extraordinary show of determination, he found the strength to communicate his injuries by telephone, expressing the noble wish that no hostages should be shot for his sake. Hendrik Seyffardt was a soldier to the last. He had the great privilege to fall in battle at an age when others die in their beds. The honourable nature of his death fills us with emotion and helps to temper our grief.'

Most of the Resistance papers welcomed Seyffardt's assassination, but there were dissenting voices. The underground journal *Trouw* questioned the morality of it. 'This killing was not an act of legitimate defence against an attack. It seems, rather, to have been the result of a sentence pronounced on a traitor. But can there be any legitimacy for the court that issued that sentence? This was a cure that is worse than the disease. Political murder and the abuse of legality should be left to the Nazis, not used by us.'

* * *

On the fifth day following Seyffardt's death, the central court-yard of the Binnenhof was transformed into an extravagant stage set, with banners, flowers and music. His catafalque, draped in the flag of the Dutch SS Legion and crowned by his ceremonial sword, was flanked by columns of flame and a guard of honour from the SS, the WA and the NSB.

Troops filed past Seyffardt's coffin, military planes circled overhead and grieving colleagues read heartfelt tributes. 'General Seyffardt,' Anton Mussert declared, 'we have come here not just to commemorate your life, but also to make a vow to you in the face of death. I pledge to you here and now that we shall continue to reject communism, to eradicate it root and branch, to pursue the great struggle of our allies, Germany and Italy, which is our struggle, too.'

Funeral of General Hendrik Seyffardt

Seyss-Inquart placed a wreath on behalf of the Führer and lauded Seyffardt as 'a true Dutch patriot who worked selflessly on behalf of his people in the cause of our common European, Germanic community'.

The 'Horst Wessel Song' was sung. Seyffardt's coffin was placed on a gun carriage drawn by six horses. Accompanied by Seyss-Inquart, Mussert, Christiansen and Rauter, it was paraded through the Amsterdam streets to the crematorium in Velsen.

Film cameras recorded the ceremony and followed the coffin on its journey. Newsreels appeared in cinemas the following day, with stirring music and a heroic commentary that made clear who Holland's heroes were.

* * *

The perception of Party control was exaggerated. Like its parent body in Moscow, the Communist Party of the Netherlands worked on the basis of centralised decision making; in normal times, it would refer its important initiatives to the Kremlin. But these were not normal times.

Gerrit Kastein had spent the war doing what he was told; he had waited for instructions and relied on the Party to make decisions. After Seyffardt, things were different. The Nazi atrocities, the executions and repressions, had swept away the Resistance's residual scruples. For Kastein, killing Seyffardt was a personal Rubicon, the crossing of which emboldened him. Was there, perhaps, something more? An awareness that he was now a target, that the Nazi machine would come for him and his time was limited? He could have gone to ground to flee from the manhunt, but chose instead to throw himself into further action, as if he were hurrying to do what he could before his time ran out.

Kastein told Uncle Anton he had another mission he wanted to undertake. The campaign of lies about Hendrik Seyffardt's death, the vitriol poured on the Resistance and the longstanding abuse of public information to convince so many Dutchmen that their duty was to join the Nazi cause were orchestrated by one man. Hermann Reydon, the Minister for Information, was the NSB's chief propagandist, Holland's equivalent of Joseph Goebbels, the inflictor of incalculable damage on the nation's morale. Kastein was proposing to kill him.

Anton listened to what Kastein had to say. He said merely that he would consult King Kong. He asked Kastein if he still had the pistol used in the Seyffardt operation and Kastein said he did: he had the pistol and ample ammunition.

Kastein waited and heard nothing. Two days had passed since the death of Hendrik Seyffardt. He could wait no longer.

As church bells rang for the late morning Sunday service, a well-dressed man with an open briefcase in the crook of his left arm knocked on the door of a smart Haarlem address. It was opened by a grey-haired lady in a two-piece woollen dress, who smiled and asked if she could be of assistance. Kastein asked if she was Mrs Reydon and, when she said she was, he slipped the gun out of his bag. Mrs Reydon made the unfortunate decision to scream.

Kastein shot her through the heart and waited for footsteps in the hall. As Hermann Reydon ran to his wife's aid, Kastein shot him too, twice in the chest, then turned and walked towards St Bavo's Church and Haarlem train station.

Hermann Reydon

* * *

Anton Mussert broke the news to the nation. An upstanding Dutch matron, a dear wife and mother, had been murdered by barbarians who have nothing in common with the values of civilised society. Wilhelmina Reydon had innocently answered a knock at her door on a peaceful Sunday morning and for that she had been savagely gunned down. Her husband, the distinguished NSB minister Hermann Reydon, was fighting for his life after running to the aid of his stricken wife and himself falling prey to the assassin's bullets. The timing of the attack on the Reydons, just two days after the murder of General Seyffardt, was proof, Mussert said, that Jewish-communist circles were mounting a violent, concerted campaign of terror against the Dutch people. The assassins were undoubtedly in the pay of the emigrant clique in London who claimed to be the true government of the Netherlands but did nothing other than murder and destroy. The nation could be assured that such crimes would not be allowed to stand. The NSB and the Sicherheitsdienst were already on the trail of the murderers.

* * *

The attacks on Seyffardt and Reydon were a cause of anxiety for many who worked for the Reichskommissariat. It seemed safe to assume that the most senior figures – from Seyss-Inquart and Rauter down – were well enough protected not to have to fear assassination. But other German officials and their Dutch comrades, the NSB men who had thrown in their lot with the Nazis and reaped the benefits of rising through the ranks, felt themselves at risk. The resources of the SD and WA were temporarily diverted to reassess the security of their own leaders, with the result that for a brief period, the pace of the action against the Jews slackened. Marlies took advantage.

Not long before, my boyfriend, who was hiding elsewhere, had been picked up by the SS. They took him to the Schouwburg, the building that used to be the Jewish Theatre, where they kept people they were going to deport. He was about to be sent to Westerbork, but he got lucky. While he was being held there, the Resistance came to the theatre and staged a raid to free the Jews inside.

The Resistance found my boyfriend a new place to hide, but I was worried about him and I wanted to see him. The problem was getting there. I removed my yellow star, of course. I had some identity papers, but I knew they were not very good. Some of the false papers in those days had been made from real documents, so they had the watermark to make them seem genuine. But others were just forged, just printed, and they didn't have a watermark. That is what I had. They may have been good enough to get through a casual check or even a roadblock, but if anyone really examined them – held them up to the light and so forth – they would have seen straight away that they were fake.

All the same, I knew I had to take the risk, it was so important to me. It was arranged that I would meet the person who was taking me to my boyfriend's place at Amsterdam Centraal station and he would be carrying something – I think it was a newspaper, which I also had to carry – so we could recognise each other. It all went very smoothly. There were no patrols or document checks and I saw my boyfriend. I was so happy that on the way back to Terbregge, I was floating on air. But when I got there, Anna-Maria said she had some news. A contact in the Resistance organisation she worked for had sent her a message: my father and my mother were dead.

* * *

Uncle Anton summoned Kastein. Kastein sensed he was angry. Anton asked how many bullets had been used in the Reydon shootings and how many remained; he spoke about the need for discipline and respect for the Resistance Council, then shrugged as if there were little point in continuing.

Uncle Anton

'All right,' Anton said. 'We need to get the gun taken out of circulation. Do you know Piet Wapperom from De Vonk?'

Gerrit said he did. Wapperom was a veteran communist who had been with the Resistance from the beginning and had the job of liaising between the different groups.

'You need to be at De Kroon in Delft tomorrow,' Anton said. 'Wapperom will be there at 10 a.m. and will relieve you of the weapon. Is that understood?'

Café De Kroon, Delft

* * *

Gerrit Kastein walked twice past the café, glancing in at the window, checking that the contact was in the bar and that the SS weren't. He saw Wapperom sitting at a corner table and asked if the seat beside him was free. Wapperom failed to answer. Gerrit realised things weren't right and was turning back to the door when the uniforms entered and Wapperom grabbed his sleeve. 'I'm sorry, Gerrit. They've got my wife ...' Four members of the Sicherheitsdienst were advancing across the floor; Kastein pulled the pistol from his pocket and fired, hitting Sturmscharführer Martin Kohlen in the leg and Untersturmführer Ernst Knorr in the hand, but the others were upon him, forcing him to the ground, bundling him in handcuffs into the black Mercedes outside.

* * *

Joseph Schreieder's decision had been vindicated. He knew the fellow was a raging egotist, greedy, self-seeking and corrupt, but in terms of results, he had no equal. Of all the informers that Schreieder had infiltrated into the Resistance, V-Mann De Wilde was his most valuable asset. In the two years since he had unmasked Josef Klingen's ECH/3 operation in Heemstede, De Wilde had gained the confidence of Resistance commanders at the highest levels. The intelligence he gathered had helped Schreieder make important arrests and assured his rise to the head of Gestapo Department IV E, the most feared in Holland. He read the interrogation reports with satisfaction.

REPORT BY INTERROGATOR OTTO
LANGE, KRIMINALSEKRETÄR
SICHERHEITSPOLIZEI, THE HAGUE.

Subject Piet Wapperom, arrested and held for interrogation
in Noordsingel Prison; and subject's wife, Catharina (née Van
Gent), idem.

Both subjects longstanding known communist activists.
Both arrested on information from Vertrauensmann [name
redacted].

Male subject prepared for interrogation readiness
[*Vernehmungsfähig*] by suspension from the wrists. Subject
acknowledges membership of CPN and involvement in publication of illegal journal. Says motivated by death of younger
brother in Gross Rosen camp, August 1941.

Subject was informed that fellow operatives Van Kalsbeek,
Ruivenkamp, Middendorp and Van der Laan also arrested.
Details of group's activities established by mutual confronta-
tion, matching to V-Mann data and enhanced interrogation
by Gestapo specialists.

Despite intensive treatment [*verschärfte Vernehmung*], subject refuses to divulge names other than those already known
to us. Subject agrees to co-operate only when informed that
wife Catharina otherwise facing execution.

* * *

The apparatus of Nazi control in wartime Holland was laby-
rinthine. A few thousand full-time employees, in addition to
thousands of casually contracted informers, worked across
three security organisations – the Geheime Staatspolizei
(Gestapo), Sicherheitsdienst (SD) and Kriminalpolizei (Kripo).
The Kripo's task was nominally the fight against 'ordinary'

(non-political) crime, but in practice it co-operated closely with the Gestapo and SD, while the Ordnungspolizei (Order Police) had responsibility for keeping the peace and preventing dissent.

Overlapping responsibilities led to conflict. The Gestapo and the SD were both tasked with 'supervising the political health of the state' and removing 'symptoms of disease and infection' by use of all appropriate means. There were attempts to delineate their responsibilities – the Gestapo's remit was to combat 'Marxism, treason and alien elements', while the SD focused on 'hostile associations, churches and sects, threats to party and state constitution' – but rivalries were plentiful. The hostility between Seyss-Inquart, Hanns Rauter and Fritz Schmidt stemmed from a competition for areas of authority, intensified by the growing importance of the Jewish question, for which all tried to assert responsibility.

The headquarters of the SD and Sicherheitspolizei in The Hague was the organ with the greatest oversight of the sprawling machinery. Its 700 officials and auxiliary staff had eyes on all incoming signals and priority access to human intelligence sources. The SD and Sicherheitspolizei claimed Gerrit Kastein. He was driven from Delft to the Binnenhof, where he was taken to an interrogation room on the second floor of the Kamergebouw Building of Binnenhof 7, shackled to a chair and left to wait.

Gerrit Kastein, arrest photograph

* * *

Joseph Schreieder visited the wounded SD men in the sick bay. Martin Kohlen, his right leg smashed by Kastein's bullet, was under the surgeon's knife, but Ernst Knorr was already patched up, his left hand enveloped in a blood-soaked bandage. When Schreieder offered sympathy, Knorr spat it away. 'Don't give me that crap,' Knorr said. 'Just let me at the bastard. He's cost me four fingers on this hand and I'll do much, much worse to him.'

Schreieder did not doubt him. He had seen what Knorr was capable of. When the first Resistance arrests were made in January 1941, Knorr had broken twenty-six-year-old Sjaak Boezemann's skull then slit his wrists and refused him a tourniquet until he confessed. Boezemann stayed silent, Knorr kept his word and the prisoner died. Nine months later, he had forced a rubber baton so deep into the anus of the communist Herman Holstege that his intestines ruptured and he perished in agony. Knorr's methods rarely persuaded his victims to speak; he seemed motivated by little more than sadism, but he had been promoted to director of the SD's Anti-Communism Unit and he was insisting that Schreieder let him loose on the communist prisoner now in the Binnenhof.

Untersturmführer Ernst Knorr

* * *

Gerrit Kastein did not allow himself the luxury of hope. He was a doctor; he knew what pain can do to a person. When colleagues asked, he always told them the chances of staying silent under torture were minimal. He took little comfort from Joseph Schreieder's reassurances.

'We aren't going to harm you,' Schreieder said. 'I have just stopped a colleague of mine who wants to tear you apart. But you and I know how things stand. We want information from you that you don't want to give. So, what I am offering is a deal; you and I can come to an arrangement that suits us both. No one has to suffer.'

Schreieder offered him a smoke. Kastein nodded his acceptance; Schreieder placed the cigarette between his lips.

Joseph Schreieder

'You and I are alike,' Schreieder said. 'We may believe in different paths to the world's salvation, but we both would sacrifice ourselves to secure it.'

'Perhaps,' Kastein said. 'But our ends will be different. And only one of us can die with honour. I can't accept your deal.'

Schreieder shrugged. 'Honour is a luxury.'

'Evil begins with compromise,' Kastein said. 'Tyranny rejoices in clouding judgement.'

'You communists,' Schreieder laughed. 'Perhaps you can share with us the secret of such moral certitude ...'

'The secret is to know,' Kastein said. 'To know without blinking that there is right and there is wrong. One *tiny* betrayal is as fatal as the rankest treachery; it will rise to the surface and destroy us.'

'So, we close our eyes and die?' Schreieder asked. 'We put dogma before all else? One tiny betrayal ... Perhaps you would like to know which one of your friends betrayed you?'

* * *

Dusk was falling. Left alone in the corner room, Kastein felt the breeze from the open window, heard the sounds of the city – the tram bells, muffled conversations in the street, a distant aeroplane, the retreating chorus of pigeons and sparrows.

They had pinned his arms behind his back and shackled them to the chair. There were ties around his calves but not tight. Shuffling left and right, rocking forward and back, he manoeuvred himself to the window, then, with a final effort, tilted himself onto the ledge and pushed off with his feet.

Second-floor corner window in Binnenhof 7, from which Gerrit Kastein jumped, 19 February 1943

* * *

The fall broke Gerrit's neck, but he was alive when the SD came running; still alive when they rushed him to the Zuidwal Hospital. Joseph Schreieder ordered the medics to save him but to no avail.

Kastein's family were informed of his death on the day of his daughter Ina's seventh birthday. They were permitted to collect his body and have his remains cremated at the Velsen Crematorium where Hendrik Seyffardt had preceded him thirteen days earlier.

Obituary in De Waarheid
To our great sorrow, we announce the sudden death of our beloved husband, father, son, brother and grandson, Dr Gerrit Willem Kastein, physician and neurologist, at the age of 32 years. Cremation to be held on Wednesday 24 February at Velsen Crematorium.

13

A LUCRATIVE BUSINESS

Otto Bene (centre)

Otto Bene wrote to his boss, Joachim von Ribbentrop. Overall, Bene said, the first year of Jewish deportations had gone well. He took the precaution, however, of pointing out that there had been challenges and, as a way of highlighting his own role in overcoming them, appended a digest of the reports he had filed since the transports began.

31 July 1942

With the trains that went today, 6,000 Dutch Jews have been deported so far. The evacuation as such went off smoothly and it is to be expected that the transports leaving in the coming weeks will proceed without hindrance.

13 August 1942

Unfortunately, the Jews seem to have found out what lies behind the 'mobilisation of labour to the east'. Out of 2,000 called up this week, only 400 appeared. They are not to be found in their homes. This is making it difficult to fill the two trains and it remains unclear how the trains are to be filled in the coming weeks.

11 September 1942

It is estimated that about 25,000 Jews in the Netherlands are leading an ambulant existence, inasmuch as they have gone into hiding. The evacuation figures have not been met. We are working on measures to guarantee these figures in future.

16 November 1942

Since my report dated 11 September, the evacuation of the Jews to Auschwitz Camp has gone well. By 15 October, 45,000 Jews had been deported. The Reichskommissar has decreed that all remaining Jews must be evacuated by 1 May 1943. This means the weekly evacuation figure has to be increased from 2,000 to 3,500.

6 January 1943

I am pleased to report that half of the Jews due for immediate evacuation have now been deported.

26 March 1943

The following case shows how readily the Dutch still commit the offence of aiding and abetting Jews, either from pity or from avarice. Eight Aryans laid themselves open to prosecution on account of one Jew, whom they had supported and hidden for weeks ... Around 2,000 Dutch police volunteers are helping us to bring in fugitive Jews.

30 April 1943

Various provincial authorities have reported suicides by Jews. The Dutch population shows little interest in the transports and seems to have become accustomed to them.

24 May 1943

Out of the 140,000 full Jews originally registered in the Netherlands, the 60,000th has now been removed from the national body ... The capture of fugitive Jews in Amsterdam and the provinces is continuing. In some cases, this involves the payment of bounties to Dutchmen.

* * *

The 'capture of fugitive Jews' was a lucrative business. In the spring of 1943, frustration over the large numbers avoiding deportation by going into hiding had prompted Willy Lages to pursue new means of filling the transports. The Zentralstelle already had a taskforce whose job it was to seize the property of Jews who had been sent to the camps. The *Hausraterfassungsstelle* consisted of mainly Dutch employees, charged with entering empty homes, drawing up lists of the items they found there and removing them for storage. There were individual divisions and separate warehouses for carpets, furniture, paintings, antiques, gold, silver, bronze, jewels and miscellaneous bric-a-brac. Each item was recorded on an index card and the cards were collected in a central inventory office, presided over by Willy Lages. Twenty-nine thousand homes would eventually be processed, with hundreds of trains and barges shipping the spoils to Germany

*Inventory of artworks and furniture from the apartment
of the Stiebel family, 130 Olympiaplein, Amsterdam*

Lages wrote memos stressing that the confiscated property belonged to the Reich and that the Zentralstelle was responsible for keeping it safe. But some Hausraterfassungsstelle employees had other ideas. Many of them had been recruited from the Amsterdam unemployment office, with few checks on their suitability, other than being members of the NSB. As the department's workload expanded, prerequisites for new workers shrank. The prospect of dealing with large quantities of valuable goods was particularly appealing to members of the criminal community, with the result that property began to disappear. After one especially blatant theft, Lages gave the Hausraterfassungsstelle staff a dressing down.

'Lages called on us to obey the rules,' one of them recalled. 'He told us to conduct ourselves in a professional and honest manner. He said there would be severe penalties for anyone who broke the law. "If you so much as steal the dust from beneath the Jews' fingernails," Lages said, "you will be arrested."'

In March, Willy Lages summoned the Hausraterfassungsstelle's personnel director, Willem Briedé, and its divisional commander, Wim Henneicke, to offer them a new opportunity. As well as rounding up Jewish property, Lages said, they could now earn extra cash by rounding up Jews. For every fugitive they brought to justice, they would be paid a bonus, *kopgeld* – head money – of seven and a half guilders. The work would be profitable, but it would require dedication and a readiness to use physical force. Twenty-five thousand Jews were missing from the census, presumed to be in hiding; the Hausraterfassungsstelle's job would be to track them down.

Wim Henneicke, leader of the Henneicke Column

Briedé and Henneicke expressed interest. When they explained the job to their men, the majority signed up. Between March

1943 and the end of the year, the Henneicke Column, as it became known, grew to substantial proportions. Its members were empowered to hunt down recalcitrant Jews and did so with zeal, bringing in 8,000 people in nine months.

Captured Jews registered in the Schouwburg Theatre

The captives were delivered to the Schouwburg Theatre where Ferdinand aus der Fünten personally signed chits for the numbers received and bounties paid. The reward money came from the sale of confiscated Jewish property, so the activities of the Henneicke Column, like most other aspects of the Holocaust, were self-financing.

*Receipt signed by Ferdinand aus der Fünten for five Jews received
and 37 and a half guilders paid to 'Kolonne Henneicke'*

Henneicke's men developed even more lucrative practices. They extracted bribes from the Jews they captured, sometimes running into many hundreds of guilders. One furrier agreed to auction off his entire stock if Henneicke would release him, handing over 40,000 guilders, equivalent to a quarter of a million dollars today. Other members of the Column requested – or forcibly extracted – sexual favours. Then, having taken the bribes and services on offer, they turned the Jews in anyway. By the end of 1943, the Henneicke Column had become a company of *nouveaux riches*, their homes stocked with luxury items and their wives decked in expensive jewels.

Henneicke Column operatives checking Jewish identity papers

* * *

Uncle Anton said it was time to root out the traitor who was undermining the organisation and getting its operatives killed. CS-6 had over sixty active members and he was determined to question them all. He had had his doubts about the Boissevains, and the refusal of Arondeus and Belinfante to take part in the armed struggle made them potentially suspect, but he would follow the evidence wherever it led.

When he spoke to Pim at the end of February, Anton's manner

was combative, verging on the aggressive. He demanded to know how Pim and Anna-Maria had managed to avoid German searches of the house. He asked why they had become so close to Hans Kreisel, the former rally driver who had brought them fugitive pilots, at least one of whom had subsequently been intercepted and executed. Pim was taken aback. He asked if Kreisel were suspected of double dealing, but Anton would say nothing.

'I know you are doing your job,' Pim said finally, 'but you're going to antagonise everyone and there still won't be any proof. Are you going to torture people into confessing? Because otherwise, I don't see how this will end.'

Anton did not respond.

'There may be something I can do,' Pim said. 'A friend of my father's works in the Binnenhof. He's employed by Rauter and Schreieder, but I think he's having doubts about the work. What if my father were to ask him to help?'

* * *

The methods used to evacuate the Apeldoornsche Bosch psychiatric hospital caused disquiet. The Reichskommissariat's own internal affairs minister, Karel Johannes Frederiks, complained that the brutal way the clearance was carried out 'will inevitably rouse strong emotions in many parts of the population, especially as it could have been avoided with a little goodwill'. Underground newspapers, including *De Waarheid* and *Vrij Nederland*, wrote of the 'terrible scenes ... the despairing screams of the insane, heard from within the locked cattle cars' and reported that many people died on the three-day journey to the east. When the train was unloaded at Auschwitz, some of the survivors had run from the platform in panic, only to be shot by SS guards. The young nurses who had volunteered to travel with their charges and were themselves exhausted from the journey hurried from patient to patient, offering whatever comfort they could give, then were led away to a separate barracks on the pretext of quarantine rules. Once the nurses were gone, the remaining prisoners were taken not to the gas chambers, but directly to the burial pits where bodies were being incinerated. They were doused in petrol and thrown alive into the flames.

* * *

Pim spoke to his father and Adrianus went to see Ruud Wilders. He found him changed. Wilders refused to admit Adrianus to his Binnenhof office, ushering him outside and round the corner to the Goude Hooft café on Groenmarkt.

Adrianus enquired about Wilders' health and how he was finding working for Rauter and Schreieder, but Wilders was brusque.

'I know you haven't come for a nice chat,' he said. 'Why don't you tell me what you want?'

'There's someone playing a double game, spying for Rauter or Schreieder,' Adrianus said. 'Uncle Anton's taken up mole hunting and ... he thinks it might be you.'

'What in God's name gives him that idea?'

'You work for the Nazis. And Anton says there's a V-Mann coming and going at the Binnenhof, in and out of Schreieder's office, using the name De Wilde.'

'Don't be an idiot!' Wilders said. 'If I were acting as a snitch, do you really think I'd be using a codename that's almost identical with my own? Do you think I'm stupid ... or that Schreieder is?'

'I don't know,' Adrianus said. 'But there's a way you can prove it. Uncle Anton wants you to find out who this De Wilde guy really is.'

* * *

With its patients and staff gone, the Apeldoornsche Bosch hospital was ransacked by the SS. Safes were emptied, equipment stolen and furniture smashed. A detachment of Ordnungsdienst policemen was sent to secure the buildings, but they, too, looted enthusiastically. An official inventory put the cost of the theft and damage at 675,000 guilders.

Apeldoornsche Bosch was one evacuation among many. Seyss-Inquart gave the order for all Jewish clinics, sanatoriums, retirement homes and children's orphanages to be emptied, with their occupants sent to Westerbork. The Resistance decided to act. Children in homes threatened with deportation were declared a priority and efforts were made to move them to safety.

Truus Oversteegen was asked to help. A tip-off about an impending German raid had led to twelve Jewish youngsters being removed from a home near Haarlem, who now needed to be cared for. Truus was given the uniform of a German Red Cross nurse and told to meet the children at Amsterdam Centraal station: a fellow Resistance operative would provide forged papers, stating that they were orphans suffering from an infectious disease en route to a quarantine facility in Dordrecht. The man handed over the children and the documents but did not stay. Truus found herself in sole charge of a dozen boys and girls, aged between three and fifteen, none of them aware that she was a friend, most of them believing she was a Nazi. 'All my tension and fear rose to the surface,' she wrote later. 'My knees were trembling and sweat poured down my face. I wanted to cry, but I knew that would be a fatal mistake.'

Truus located the train and boarded the compartment labelled 'Wehrmacht: Transport of Patients.' She could see the children were terrified – separated from their parents, beset by danger, with an unknown woman taking them to an uncertain destination – but she could not allow herself to comfort them. The eldest boy did not hide his hostility. When a German officer came to check their papers, Truus ordered the children to stand up and make the Nazi salute, but the boy refused and Truus slapped him hard across the face. The boy was in tears; Truus was mortified.

At Dordrecht, she had been told to take the children to a ship moored in the Oude Maas, where a sympathetic boatman would ferry them to a safe house in the country. To reach the boat, Truus had to row her charges across the river and there were German patrols. They hid in the nearby woods, waiting for darkness. Here Truus explained who she really was and where she was taking them. She apologised to the boy she had slapped. She cuddled the youngest child, a three-year-old called Rosa, and kept her calm by telling her stories. When darkness fell, Truus led them across a field and found the rowing boat they were to use to get to the ship. She helped the children in, then waded into the water to push them free of the mud. She was clambering aboard when the searchlights lit, converging on the boat, blinding her with the intensity of their glare. She barely saw the young Jewish boy jump to his feet, but she heard the curses he was yelling and felt the impact of the bullets as they sent him tumbling into the water. The boat capsized. Truus tried to grab the children, but they were being swept away and German soldiers were on the bank now, firing at the bodies in the river. She felt a small hand brush against hers. She grabbed it and swam with her other arm to the far side. The hand belonged to three-year-old Rosa. She and Truus were the only survivors.

* * *

Ruud Wilders took a walk round the Binnenhof Gardens. He had known since May 1940 that, someday, he would have to decide. He had spent nearly three years pretending that the path he chose in the wake of the capitulation was the only right one. He'd told himself that siding with the Reich was a decision made in good faith, that Ruud Cornelius Wilders truly believed it to be the best thing for Holland. Had the decision he took actually proved to be in *anyone's* interest? Had the Germans kept their promise to protect the nation? Had he kept his own promise to act with honesty and integrity? And was the heartache and struggle of the past three years the outcome he had hoped for? Wasn't the fact that he was even asking himself such questions proof conclusive that his choice had been the wrong one?

* * *

Generalkommissar Fritz Schmidt was making a name for himself. His strident support for the total extermination of the Jews put into words what other Nazi leaders were thinking and planning but preferred to keep moot. Because of the failure of the Dutch people to rally to the National Socialist cause, he demanded the Netherlands be forcibly incorporated into the greater German Reich. And he gave unconditional backing to the execution of civilians in response to the activities of the Resistance.

Joseph Goebbels and Fritz Schmidt

Schmidt had been an early adherent to the Nazi cause; he was adept at party politics and knew how to ingratiate himself. When Joseph Goebbels visited The Hague, Schmidt made himself prominent in the welcome committee, attending public events, getting himself photographed in the company of the Reichsminister. The hatred Schmidt aroused in the ranks of the Resistance was matched by the distaste he evoked among his own colleagues.

* * *

Hannie Schaft and Truus and Freddie Oversteegen were becoming known – young women who killed like hardened assassins. For the Resistance, they were a symbol of righteous innocence;

for the Reich, they were criminals. Hannie was spotted at the scene of more than one incident; no one knew her name, but people were beginning to talk about 'the girl with the red hair'. Hitler demanded her immediate arrest.

Truus and Freddie were good cyclists. Truus would pedal while Freddie sat on the back and did the shooting. They threw grenades into cafés where German troops were drinking, but one of the grenades killed a passing child. The sisters' anguish was so profound that for the rest of their lives they could not bring themselves to speak of it. When the Resistance Council asked them to help kidnap the children of Arthur Seyss-Inquart, they consulted Hannie and all three refused.

* * *

It was Adolf Hitler's personal wish that Fritz Schmidt should receive a full state funeral. A packed hall heard orations from his colleagues; speeches continued at his graveside.

Funeral of Fritz Schmidt, 1943

'He was always there for his homeland,' declared the newspaper obituaries. 'And his homeland will never forget her beloved son ... Fritz Schmidt's enthusiasm for the National Socialist cause began in 1929, following a personal encounter with the Führer. In 1938, the NSDAP brought Schmidt to its national headquarters, where he worked closely with the leadership staff of Reichsleiter Martin Bormann. In 1939, the Führer attached the Golden Party Badge to Schmidt's proud chest. In 1940, he was entrusted with the National Socialist reconstruction of the administrative structures of the Netherlands. Generalkommissar Fritz Schmidt met his glorious end in the service of the Reich.'

The newspapers were regrettably unable to provide further details of Schmidt's 'glorious end'. The official version was still being constructed.

Generalkommissar Fritz Schmidt

* * *

Esmée van Eeghen was the daughter of Minette van Lennep, a cousin of Mies Boissevain, and the stepdaughter of Baron Alphert Schimmelpenninck.

Esmée van Eeghen

She had lived a gilded life. Her mother's family was wealthy, her stepfather's role as president of the Dutch Olympic Committee brought the spotlight of media attention and Esmée grew up a fashionable young lady, widely travelled, multilingual, at home in the beau monde. She was tall and attractive, sought after by men but with an unstable side. By her late teens, she was a regular drinker, a chain smoker and a periodic visitor to a Swiss psychiatric clinic.

In 1943, Esmée began working with the communist Resistance leader Krijn van der Helm, helping him to smuggle Jewish children to safe houses in the north of the country. She acted as a courier for the Friesland Resistance, delivering forged identity documents, transporting weapons and eventually taking part in armed robberies and attacks on German installations. She proved her courage by carrying a suitcase full of guns and ammunition by train to Amsterdam, knowing there would be a police check on arrival. In the course of the journey, she flirted with a German officer who gallantly agreed to carry her heavy case through the checkpoint and find her a taxi outside.

Esmée's success with men alerted the Resistance to her potential as an intelligence gatherer. The Party asked her to begin an affair with Wehrmacht officer Oberleutnant Hans Schmälzlein. Esmée discussed it with Krijn. Krijn was married with children, but he and Esmée had become lovers. It was hard to think of her new assignment as purely professional.

Krijn van der Helm

* * *

Normally, Ruud Wilders would access the department's archives in the company of Sturmbannführer Schreieder, but the Sturmbannführer was out of town and his secretary thought it would probably be all right if Herr Wilders were to go in alone. Wilders smiled his thanks. Could she perhaps find him a coffee and one for herself?

A moment was all it took. Wilders knew where his boss kept the files that he didn't want others to see. And he had watched Schreieder turn the combination lock.

* * *

The facts of the case were not in dispute. Together with other officials, Fritz Schmidt had travelled from Amsterdam to take part in a tour of newly built fortifications on the French Atlantic coast. For the return trip from the inspection site to Paris, sleeping cars were provided on a night train. When Schmidt did not show up for breakfast, his compartment was opened and found to be empty. The window had been lowered and the curtain was flapping in the wind. A search party discovered Schmidt's body, dressed in pyjamas, at the side of the track near Chartres.

* * *

A social evening at the garrison in Leeuwarden, held to reward sympathetic local citizens for their kindness towards the Wehrmacht, provided Esmée with an introduction. She recognised Hans Schmälzlein from the photos Krijn had shown her and attracted his attention during the meal. At the speeches that followed, she smiled at him, yawning theatrically, and he smiled back. When he asked her for her phone number, she wrote it down.

* * *

The Reich Ministry of Public Enlightenment and Propaganda considered three possible versions. The first was that the Resistance were to blame: Schmidt's undisguised support for repressive measures, including summary executions, had made him a target. But that suggested that senior Reich officials lacked the protection they needed to keep them safe and it handed the communists an unacceptable propaganda victory. The second possibility was that Schmidt had thrown himself from the moving train in a fit of alcoholic imprudence or psychotic despair. Witnesses travelling with him reported that he had appeared nervous and irritable. A Generalkommissar so depressed about the war that he took his own life did not convey a very desirable message. The third version – the one believed by many insiders – was that Schmidt had fallen foul of party infighting, that he had paid the price for challenging the big boys and been despatched by emissaries of Rauter or Seyss-Inquart. In the end, the press was told to write that it had all been an unfortunate accident.

* * *

Esmée accepted Oberleutnant Schmälzlein's invitation to dinner. Her instructions from Militair Contact were to quiz him about the Wehrmacht's presence in Friesland, including manpower levels and the construction of defensive installations. The Party said it would do what it could to monitor her progress and ensure her safety but there could be no guarantees: the work was dangerous and she should remain vigilant.

Esmée told Krijn that the dinner had gone well. Schmälzlein had not been suspicious; he had given no indication that he regarded their relationship as anything other than that of a young man and a woman who shared the same interests and found each other sympathetic. He had not tried to make her do anything she did not wish to; there had been no suggestion of sexual predation on his part. She had made an appointment to see the Oberleutnant again, this time for lunch at his residence on Emmakade in Leeuwarden.

54 Emmakade, Leeuwarden

* * *

She had been expecting a monster, but discovered a modest, unassuming intellectual. Lunch was served by a young Dutch housekeeper, who seemed fond of her employer. Schmälzlein asked Esmée about herself then spoke of his own childhood in Dresden and his studies at the conservatoire. Had the war not come, he said, he would likely be playing in the string section of the Staatskapelle or introducing young students to the masterpieces of the European Baroque. When Esmée asked what Hans thought of the war, he answered without hesitation that it was an abomination that made him ashamed of his fatherland.

* * *

Ruud Wilders made a phone call to Adrianus Roest. The information he had gleaned would be the redemption of a debt of guilt that had hung over him since their discussion in the church in Dordrecht all those months ago. Ruud said he had found a name. Adrianus said he would arrange a meeting with Uncle Anton.

* * *

Some of the Henneicke Column's most egregious activities involved children. Two of Henneicke's thugs travelled hundreds of miles to seize a three-year-old girl from a safe house on the other side of the country, despatching her to Westerbork and then to Sobibor where she was gassed a week later. Other Column employees knocked a father's teeth out to make him reveal the hiding place of his three children, who were duly arrested and sent to their deaths.

Dutch Jews at Muiderpoort station

When the SS summoned Jews to assemble at Muiderpoort train station, Henneicke's men intercepted them and instructed them to report first to the Schouwburg, so that the Jew hunters could collect their bonuses. Willy Lages discovered what had happened and issued a stern reprimand, but he did not stand in the way of other, more vicious ruses. A favourite ploy was to intimidate arrested Jews into betraying others. A wife whose husband had been picked up might be told that he could be freed if she were to supply the names and addresses of friends who were in hiding. At the start of Easter week 1943, Detective Pieter Schaap raided an apartment on Marco Polostraat and detained two Jewish women. When he asked who had provided their accommodation, they said the flat belonged to Ans van Dijk, the owner of a millinery shop on the same street that had been closed down when Jews were banned from running businesses.

Schaap arrested Van Dijk on Easter Sunday but released her after she agreed to co-operate. Over the next two years, she would find herself trapped in a cycle of fear and betrayal that resulted in the deaths of scores of fellow Jews. Posing as a Resistance member, Ans van Dijk used the promise of false identity cards and safe hiding places to lure people to meetings, where her victims – who eventually included her own brother and his family – would be seized. Her hand was suspected in the betrayal of Anne Frank although her guilt was never proved. For every Jew she delivered she received the standard *kopgeld* of seven and a half guilders.

Ans van Dijk

The daily reports of the Henneicke Column recorded another type of betrayal – Aryans who offered shelter to Jewish families, only to turn them over to the authorities. Hotel owners were routinely coerced into reporting Jewish guests; but there were many more cases in which host families betrayed the people they were supposed to be protecting for the purpose of making money.

By the end of the war more than 73 per cent of Holland's Jews would be deported and killed, by far the highest percentage of any Western European country. Fewer than 5,000 of the 100,000 sent to the east would survive.

* * *

Ruud Wilders put the documents in his inside pocket. The Hague was quiet, the war distant. The trains would be busy, but his Ausweis was stamped and checkpoints held no fear.

His first destination was Dordrecht and St Boniface's Church. He sat in the same pew, half expecting to see Adrianus descend from the organ loft. The church was empty. He approached the altar, traced the stations of the cross, peered into side chapels, seeking out the right place to leave it. Then at midday, he left to catch the train to Amsterdam.

The walk from Amsterdam Centraal to meet Uncle Anton at Corellistraat was the last stage of Wilders' road to redemption. As he turned south from the station into Damrak, he failed to see the figure in the long raincoat with the gun.

* * *

Marlies Friedheim devoted herself to Anna-Maria's baby. Hanneke was becoming a person, responding to faces and voices, making connections with the world that would stay with her in the life ahead. She loved music and Marlies loved making it. Marlies, who had played the violin since she was a girl, had kept her instrument with her and Hanneke would laugh at the Jewish nursery tunes she played from memory, then fall asleep to the sound of Brahms's lullaby and Bach's grazing sheep.

In early 1943, a newcomer took shelter in Terbregge. Erwin Sandor, a Hungarian Jew, was a professional violinist and he offered Marlies lessons. Their playing filled the house, transporting all who heard it, lifting them out of the horrors of the world. Half in jest, the two Jewish musicians serenaded Anna-Maria with Schubert's 'Ave Maria' and then his hymn to the redemptive power of music. 'Oh, you holy art,' Marlies sang, 'that in the darkest times, when life's wild storms do shake me, has filled my heart with love ... a sigh from your sweet lyre, a celestial chord that opens happier heavens, you bear me up to a better world above ... *Du holde Kunst, ich danke dir dafür!*'

* * *

Anton rang Adrianus to ask what had happened and why Wilders hadn't come. Adrianus didn't know. It wasn't until three days later that *Volk en Vaderland* published a brief obituary for a loyal Dutch employee of the Sicherheitsdienst, gunned down by an unknown hand in the dedicated pursuance of his duties for the Reich.

* * *

Esmée van Eeghen of the communist Resistance fell in love with Oberleutnant Hans Schmälzlein of the German Wehrmacht. At his invitation she moved in with him at 54 Emmakade in Leeuwarden.

Esmée made no attempt to conceal their relationship. She told the Party that Hans knew no military secrets – he was not a Nazi, barely even a soldier – and she apologised to Krijn. For her the war was over and life was beginning.

* * *

CS-6 had proved itself the deadliest of the Resistance organisations. Seyffardt and Reydon were its most prominent victims, but the group's gunmen had carried out more than twenty other assassinations since Janka and Gideon Boissevain founded it three years earlier. It had a network of active personnel in Amsterdam and the regions, and its forgery operation, the Persoonsbewijzen Centrale of Willem Arondeus, Gerrit van der Veen and Frieda Belinfante, was the most productive in the country. But CS-6 was failing in one of its aims: the Nazis' deportation of the country's Jews was gathering pace and the provision of fake ID cards was not doing enough to save them.

The Germans' ability to check Jewish identities against the
exhaustive records held in the Amsterdam Registry Office made
the SD's task too easy. Arondeus and Van der Veen decided the
only solution was to destroy them.

* * *

Esmée received a message from Krijn, informing her that her
younger brother had been arrested. David van Eeghen had been
trying to sail to England to join the Free Dutch forces, but the
trawler he was sailing on had been intercepted and David was
in custody.

Esmée sought information about her brother. Hans made
discreet enquiries on her behalf. He discovered that David van
Eeghen had been transferred to the camp at Bergen-Belsen,
where he was being held as a political prisoner. There was
nothing Hans could do to get him released; his enquiries were
already arousing suspicion among his fellow officers.

Esmée shared her sorrows with Hans's housekeeper,
Antoinette Jaakke. The two women had become close and
Antoinette did what she could to comfort her.

14

Destroying the records

Amsterdam Registry Office

The population records in the Registry Office at 36 Plantage Kerklaan contained between 70,000 and 80,000 registration documents with the names, ages, professions and addresses of all the country's remaining Jews. Compiling such detailed information was a testament to the Germans' efficiency; they were using it now, with equal efficiency, to track down and murder men, women and children.

When Willem Arondeus explained the role the records

played in the deportation campaign – and how much damage could be done by destroying them – Jan Verleun responded enthusiastically, but Arondeus motioned him to wait.

'Blowing the place up would mean people dying – innocent people, like the clerks and the secretaries and security men who guard it round the clock. I don't want anything to do with that. If we do things my way, we get what we want and we don't hurt anyone.'

* * *

Arthur Seyss-Inquart and Hanns Rauter decided they no longer needed the Jewish Council. Abraham Asscher, David Cohen and their helpers had done well: the transports were proceeding according to plan, but the Council had negotiated 12,000 exemptions from deportation and that could no longer be tolerated. In the spring of 1943, it was resolved that the Jewish Council should be gradually wound up; in the coming months, the men who had facilitated the deportations would be deported themselves. Ferdinand aus der Fünten notified Asscher that 6,000 of his 'indispensables' must report for labour service in the east. It was up to the Council to decide the names, but it must be done promptly or the Reichskommissariat would be obliged to implement measures 'such as the Jews in the Netherlands had never imagined'.

At an emergency meeting, the Council debated whether they should simply refuse to comply. No one said it outright, but it is evident from the minutes that all were aware of the true meaning of 'labour service'. Several department heads argued that finding 6,000 volunteers was an impossible task, and declared themselves unwilling to choose between their own staff. The drawing of lots was discussed and rejected. Instead, Asscher and Cohen appointed a committee to divide the Council employees into three categories: the absolutely indispensable, those who were doing important work and those who could be spared.

Panic ensued. Names were put on one list, then another. A Council staffer wrote that the whole building was in frenetic motion, 'lit up from top to bottom as if it were a great festival'.

> I can still see the committee people sitting there with huge piles of index cards, as secretaries came rushing in with more and more files and other Council officers pleaded for those already doomed ... One young man, who was carrying cards from one room to another, found his own name in them and ran away in a panic ... As for us, we could think of nothing more heroic to do than stand in a remote corridor, shedding tears over the misery around us and our inability to do anything about it ... Even as the whole building resounded with the cries of distress, I was forced to sit with a German-appointed lawyer, helping him with unpronounceable Hebrew names as he made up new lists of Amsterdam Jews.

Asscher and Cohen agonised. Asked to justify their decision to co-operate with the selection, Cohen claimed the Germans would have deported thousands, with or without the Council's help. He compared himself to a military commander who knows he must sacrifice some of his men 'in order to preserve an elite'.

> I fully appreciated that my decision would not be understood by everyone and that it was bound to create resentment. A leader, however, must not allow himself to be swayed when he places the interests of the whole above the interests of the individual.

When the final lists were drawn, Asscher, Cohen and the members of the Council's executive were all in the category of the elite.

* * *

Willem Arondeus told his partner it was time for them to split. He and Jan had lived together for a decade, but Willem said he was about to embark on an undertaking of great danger.

Jan Tijssen replied that if Willem were in danger, he wanted to be there too. They talked and drank. Midnight came and nothing was resolved.

'All my life,' Willem said, 'I was looking for a love like ours – a friendship of such gentleness and such tenderness, a contentment that I had never known.' He spoke of the unhappiness of feeling trapped in a straight world, the bitterness of alienation from his disapproving parents and the years of self-loathing debauchery.

Jan smiled. 'You mean living above the Mother Pilgrim on Spuistraat and getting complaints from the bar owner about the number of men knocking on your door?'

Willem nodded. 'It sounds fun. But it wasn't. Art saved me – Aubrey Beardsley and Oscar Wilde and the thought that love could just be love, without the guilt. I went to live in the country, miles away ... and I met you!'

Jan remembered the strange hermit, the mysterious artist

living in the cottage in the forest. Willem remembered the lithe delivery boy with slim hips, arriving on his pony trap with supplies of milk and vegetables. 'And you let me ride on your cart,' he said. 'You took me with you to the market in Arnhem ...'

'Yes. And then you took me to the big city,' Jan said. 'You wrote your thesis about that painter, Matthijs Maris. I never understood why you called it *The Tragedy of the Dream.*'

Jan went to the bookshelf and took down a copy of Willem's book.

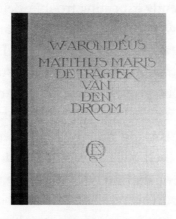

'There's something here I do like, though,' he said.

'It only seems that dreamers run away from life. It only seems they are lacking in courage, that they have no strength of will, that they shrink from responsibility. For in every moment of decision, in every crisis, it is the dreamers who have shown they are ready to make the ultimate sacrifice. They have suffered so much fear and bitterness, they have plunged so deep in the waters of self-doubt, that the prospect of pain no longer frightens them.'

'You are pretending to write about Maris, but I know you're writing about yourself.'

* * *

Despite the best efforts of the Jewish Council, only 1,200 of its former indispensables reported to the registration point at Muiderpoort train station. Abraham Asscher and David Cohen were summoned to appear before a 'grim-faced' Hanns Rauter, who expressed his deep disappointment at the low numbers and explained that he had in consequence ordered a punitive mass roundup for the following day.

Rauter was evidently expecting trouble. Before the raid began, additional guards were posted at the station and along the roads leading to it, but they weren't needed. The Dutch people who had protested against previous operations stayed at home and the Jews themselves proved unexpectedly co-operative. Otto Bene reported that 3,000 people were quickly rounded up, with the majority coming quietly. Many seemed resigned to their fate and had their bags already packed. There were a few glitches, including an air raid warning at 2 p.m., which allowed a party of Jews to run away, and a Jewish doctor who was only narrowly prevented from escaping justice by poisoning himself with cyanide.

David Cohen went to Muiderpoort station to wave goodbye to his ex-colleagues.

> The ghastliness of the scenes enacted by these desperate people devoid of all hope was indescribable. Even on the platform, I pleaded with Lages to exempt this one or that one, but all in vain. I had to watch the last of these wretched men and women leave for their final destination.

Otto Bene reported that ordinary Jews were turning against their leaders. 'People were angry at the ability of prominent members of the Jewish Council to avoid the transports, while they themselves were not so lucky ... Some were heard to demand the immediate dissolution of the Council which, under the cover of neighbourly love, was merely trying to save its own skin.'

When the unfortunate officials selected by Cohen and Asscher were transported to Westerbork, Bene wrote, they were greeted with 'undisguised glee' by earlier arrivals, who expressed their regret that 'the top brass, including the bosses themselves, had not been thrown in with their minions'.

Jewish Council officials and their families at Muiderpoort

* * *

Reports of Esmée van Eeghen's relationship with a German officer reached Militair Contact, which convened a People's Court to judge her. There, talk of love carried little weight. Schmälzlein might be a good German, but he was still a German. The Party court condemned Esmée to death.

* * *

Sjoerd Bakker

Sjoerd Bakker was a tailor and a friend of Willem Arondeus's from his days living above the bar at Mother Pilgrim's. They had never been lovers, but they were close enough for Willem to tell him what he was planning. There would need to be seven uniforms in total, Willem said, two for the officers and another five for the constables. Would Sjoerd be up for making them?

Bakker had a contact, Elmar Berkovich, at the Hollandia Garment Factory in Kattenburg, which had been commandeered to make uniforms for the Wehrmacht. But what about the measurements? Who did Willem have in mind to wear them?

'I'm going to be a captain,' Arondeus said. 'Gerrit van der Veen's a lieutenant, and for the constables we've got Rudi Bloemgarten, Karl Groger, Coos Hartogh, Guus Reitsma and Sam van Musschenbroek. I've got their vital statistics here and we have a CS-6 member, Cornelis Roos, who works in the Amsterdam police department: he can get us samples of the uniforms for you to copy and he'll supply the police caps we'll be wearing.'

'I can do it,' Bakker said. 'But on one condition: I want to come along too.'

* * *

The 3,000-person raid boosted the Zentralstelle's morale, but there were still large numbers of Jews unaccounted for. Official estimates put the total of those in hiding at close to 20,000, with the same number and more still waiting to be traced from the records in the Amsterdam Registry Office. The roundup dented the authority of the Jewish Council and its previously untouchable leaders. Abraham Asscher had a taste of the persecution he had previously been spared.

> As I was cycling home, I was repeatedly stopped by the German police. Just before I arrived at Schubert Street, I began to get fed up with it and told one of them that I had been showing my identity card so many times in a few hundred metres that I was sick and tired of it. He hit me on the nose and it began to bleed. I grabbed him by the throat and punched him several times, until a group of soldiers placed me under arrest and brought me before Aus der Fünten. He told me I would be released, but that I must henceforth keep away from the vicinity in order to avoid a breach of the peace.

Official portrait of Abraham Asscher, 1942

* * *

Krijn van der Helm pleaded for a stay of execution. Esmée had been his lover; Krijn said she was not a turncoat. He took her case to Militair Contact, reminding them of Esmée's previous loyal service and pointing out that Schmälzlein was a simple soldier, not an agent of the SD. The couple were living openly, even speaking of marriage, Krijn said: was that really the way spies and traitors behave?

He secured a meeting with the head of Friesland's communist Resistance, Pieter Wijbenga, but Wijbenga was unsympathetic. He pointed out that after Esmée moved in with Schmälzlein, the SS raided one of their most important weapons stores in the Tamminga warehouses in Leeuwarden: someone must have tipped them off. Krijn countered that there was no evidence of Esmée's involvement in the raid and that the information had likely come from a young fighter, Ben de Vries, who had been wounded, captured by the SS and subsequently tortured. Wijbenga softened. The death sentence on Esmée van Eeghen could not be lifted, he said. But if she agreed to give up her liaison with the German and get out of Leeuwarden immediately, its execution could be suspended pending further enquiries.

Krijn van der Helm

* * *

In the spring of 1943, Anna-Maria was involved in events that would help to shape Holland's future. She remembered it as a turning point, when global outcomes were swayed by individual acts of heroism or cowardice.

Willem Arondeus and Gerrit van der Veen took the lead, co-ordinating the preparations, directing the measures to ensure the operation's secrecy. Sjoerd Bakker's police uniforms were judged perfect, with only minor adjustments needed. The explosives were brought by Henri Halberstadt from supplies stolen from the magazine of the Naarden Fortress during the fighting in May 1940. The architect Koen Limperg drew up detailed plans of the Registry Office building and Martinus Nijhoff, a former military engineer, marked the points where the charges should be placed. Johan Brouwer, who had seen action in the Spanish Civil War, provided Arondeus with an officer's revolver.

They were young, most of them in their twenties or thirties. None of them knew it, but their names would be forever linked in fame and death.

* * *

Hannie and her parents, Pieter and Aafje

Hannie Schaft was still living with her parents in the family home at 60 Van Dortstraat in north Haarlem. Pieter and Aafje

Schaft were members of the Workers' Party. When the war came they gave shelter to Jewish refugees, but they were worried about their daughter. Hannie's Resistance activities were becoming known and her distinctive red hair meant she was readily identifiable. Her parents tried to persuade her to withdraw from active duties, but Hannie refused. Family rows turned to reproaches and acrimony. In the spring of 1943, she announced she was leaving.

Hannie at her parents' house in Haarlem

Frans van der Wiel told Hannie to report to a cigar shop in Haarlem owned by Henk Ypkemeule, a communist Resistance member who could help her find accommodation. It was soon after the wave of national strikes that had been crushed by the Germans and Ypkemeule was harbouring one of the activists who led them. When Hannie entered the shop, behind the counter was Jan Bonekamp, the communist who had organised the strike at the Hoogovens steel plant. He and Hannie would become lovers; within a year, they would be the deadliest couple in the Dutch Resistance.

Hannie Schaft   *Jan Bonekamp*

* * *

Asscher and Cohen knew that time was running out. They would be the last on the list but, like all those who had gone before them, they were human and they dreamed of a reprieve – an Allied invasion that might save them, Hitler's death, a last-minute intervention by the Resistance.

Hanns Rauter had other plans. Buoyed by the successful roundup of the Jewish Council's indispensables, he ordered another mass raid, this time in south Amsterdam. On the eve of the operation, Willy Lages invited the whole of the Zentralstelle staff to a film screening at the Roxy theatre in the canal district. At the end of the movie Lages appeared on stage to congratulate them and to invite 'frontline personnel' back to headquarters on Euterpestraat. The men were given a bowl of soup and issued with orders. The raid would be the biggest yet; it would last for two full days, round the clock. The target was 5,000 Jews.

Bolle stamps and exemption permits issued by the Jewish Council were no longer valid, Lages said. Anyone with non-Jewish papers but who 'looked Jewish' should also be arrested. The homes of all those detained should be searched and Jewish property, including bicycles, motorcycles, radios and pets, confiscated. In light of the Wehrmacht's current challenges on the territory of the Soviet Union, the highest priority should be given to the seizure of furs and other items of winter clothing.

* * *

Willem had spoken to one of the guards inside the Registry Office, secured the necessary medical equipment and notified sympathetic members of the fire department that they should not be in a hurry to respond to any emergency calls. At 11 p.m. on Saturday 27 March, a police patrol knocked on the door of the Amsterdam Population Registry – the *Bevolkingsregister* – on Plantage Kerklaan. Captain Willem Arondeus and Lieutenant Gerrit van der Veen introduced themselves under false names: they had received credible information that explosives had been planted in the building, they said, and they needed to search the premises. When the security guards let them in, the policemen drew their revolvers and demanded their surrender. Those guards who were part of the plot did so without complaint, but others were less sanguine. One of them, Gerrit van Doorn, demanded to know what was going to be done to them.

'The captain was forty-five to fifty years old,' Van Doorn later reported. 'He was of slender build with a tanned complexion, spoke politely, acted decisively and gave the impression of really being an officer. The men all addressed him as captain and it was clear that he was in command ... When I asked him what was going to happen, he said we would be given an injection that would put us to sleep. We didn't need to worry, as the men accompanying him were medical students and we would just have a little nap. They took us into the Registry garden, where the "doctors" produced a syringe and administered a powerful sedative to all eight of us guards. I became drowsy but remained aware of my surroundings. After some time, I was conscious of a series of explosions. The sky above us turned red.'

Bomb damage to the Amsterdam Registry Office

* * *

Shortly after midnight, Willem told his men to disperse and make their way to Koen Limperg's house in the suburb of Bussum. They burned the counterfeit police uniforms in the central heating furnace and buried the weapons in Limperg's garden. Then they opened the champagne. A sober debrief turned into a celebration; everyone had a tale to tell. Gerrit van der Veen had overseen the emptying of the filing cabinets, opening drawers, tipping them forward so they spilled their contents onto the floor. The 'constables' Bloemgarten, Groger, Hartogh, Reitsma and Van Musschenbroek had run back and forth splashing petrol onto the piles of documents, then setting fuses in the locations specified by Martinus Nijhoff. Henri Halberstadt had primed the explosives and begun the count-down that would warn them when it was time to leave.

Early the next morning, Cornelis Roos, the Amsterdam policeman on Willem's team, rang his office, pretending to have heard rumours of an overnight attack. The sergeant who answered was audibly stressed. 'They're not rumours,' he said. 'The place has gone up in flames. God knows why, but the fire department didn't turn up for hours and when they got there, they poured so much water into the building that any files that survived the explosions were turned into papier-mâché!'

* * *

Abraham Asscher complained that his house was besieged by Jews demanding help. His family were being harassed and he could get no rest. 'To my sorrow,' Asscher wrote in his diary, 'I had to tell the petitioners that there was nothing I could do for anyone in the face of these German barbarians.'

He and David Cohen held a series of urgent talks with Ferdinand aus der Fünten, in which their chief demand was a firm guarantee that the Council's top leadership would be exempted once and for all from the threat of transportation. Fünten gave an oral undertaking, backed up by his boss, Willy Lages, but neither of them was prepared to put anything on paper.

Professor Cohen was given permission to visit the Westerbork camp, where he found 'appalling' conditions of overcrowding caused by the sudden influx of occupants picked up in the recent raids. He recorded the efforts he made to help.

Whenever I went on these sorts of missions, I used to slip into my pocket a book called *Die Tröstung Israels*, 'The Consolation of Israel', which contained the prophecies of Isaiah, in Hebrew on one side and in the Buber-Rosenzweig translation on the other. I turned to it in the twilight and began to recite, *'Tröste, tröste, o Jerusalem* – Comfort ye, O comfort ye, Jerusalem!

As a gesture of goodwill, Fünten conceded that Cohen could select ten inmates to be released from the camp. After detailed discussions with fellow Council members, Cohen produced ten names and the lucky nominees were allowed to go. All of them were picked up again soon afterwards. None of them survived the war.

* * *

In the aftermath of the Population Registry attack, Anna-Maria fell prey to fluctuating emotions. Exhilaration and relief at the apparent success of the operation turned to pride and satisfaction as the official media railed at the malevolent perpetrators who had sought to disrupt the machinery of government, then to anxiety as the Germans pledged to track down those responsible. The newspapers carried an announcement from Willy Lages of a 10,000-guilder reward for information leading to arrests.

Marlies followed the unfolding news, encouraged by the thought that the destruction of the *Bevolkingsregister* records might offer protection from the Nazi Jew hunts. She spoke to Erwin Sandor, the Hungarian violinist hiding with her in the attic, and found him eager to celebrate. He told Marlies that a friend of his, a pianist colleague from his Budapest days, was hiding in Kralingen, a couple of miles away, and had invited them both to come and play music. Emboldened by the success of her previous outing to see her boyfriend, Marlies agreed to go.

It was a lovely invitation. Music was a consolation in my life back then and the chance to play with two professionals was hard to turn down. Erwin and I walked from Terbregge, through the Kralingse woods and past the lake. He had been in the attic for six months and I had been there longer, so it was a relief to be out in the open. We got to the friend's place at dusk. He made us coffee and we played a lot of Beethoven and Schubert. It was such an emotional release to be making that beautiful music – it lifted us out of the dark place we were in.

Late in the evening, we heard a noise. There was a blackout in force, so Erwin's friend turned off the lights, peered through the curtain and saw the street was full of SS men. They had parked their trucks at the end of the road and we could see they were going from house to house, smashing down doors and dragging people out.

Erwin's friend said they were rounding up men to go and work as forced labourers in Germany, but they were also looking for Jews. They had started on the other side of the road and we saw people being dragged out of the houses and thrown into the SS trucks. Lots of them were crying and trying to get away. It was horrible. We saw the SS going all the way up the other side of the street, then reaching the end and turning round to come back on our side. Erwin couldn't stand it. He opened the door and ran into the street. He was trying to outrun the Germans, but he disappeared before we could see what happened to him. We didn't know what to do: the SS men were nearly at our house and I was sure we were done for. But, one door before they reached us, we heard the German commander shout, 'That's enough!'

* * *

Willem and Gerrit had picked up several hundred blank identification cards during the raid, to be used in the Persoonsbewijzen Centrale's forgery operations, as well as 50,000 guilders from the Registry Office's safe. The central section of the building, where they had planted explosives, had burned down, but much of the rest of it survived, along with a disappointingly large number of files. Because the record cards were packed so tightly together, many of them were shielded from both the fire and the water from the firefighters' hoses. The damage to the building meant the SD was not able to use it for several weeks, however, and civil servants sympathetic to the Resistance took advantage of the clean-up period to slip false data into the records.

For those who took part in the attack, things began to go wrong. Joop Hoogsteder, a friend of Willem Arondeus and a CS-6 courier, was betrayed to the SD and arrested on 1 April. Under interrogation by Willy Lages and his assistant Günther Klein, Hoogsteder was tortured into revealing the names of his comrades.

* * *

Hannie Schaft and Jan Bonekamp made an unlikely couple. Hannie was the daughter of middle-class academics, with a university education and cultured tastes. Her outlook and conversation were those of an intellectual, while Jan's were unmistakeably proletarian, a truck driver with working-class views, expressed in direct, profanity-laden language. Hannie loved Jan's vigour and commitment; he admired her sophistication and erudition. Both had the immense physical beauty that kindles relationships of overwhelming, sometimes destructive passion.

Jan and Hannie were billeted in a Resistance safe house in Limmen, twenty miles north of Amsterdam, where the Bult family farm served as a staging post for operatives on the run. The farmer's wife, Trijntje, remembered Hannie as attractive, with sumptuous red hair that she combed in front of the mirror, still a girl, on the point of becoming a striking, remarkable woman. She was more wary of Bonekamp. Trijntje thought he was rough and unyielding, determined to the point of obsession, possibly dangerous. The two of them were constantly together, helping out in the fields, sharing a bedroom and disappearing for long periods on secretive errands. 'I saw them go out with revolvers under their coats,' Trijntje recalled, 'and I looked at Hannie and thought, "Child, how reckless you are, how impetuous and daring." But, for all that, I could see she was extraordinarily happy ...'

* * *

The Germans raided the addresses provided by Joop Hoogsteder and made twenty-one arrests. Of those physically present in the Population Registry, only Gerrit van der Veen evaded the manhunt; others, who played supporting roles, went into hiding or waited anxiously for the knock on their door.

Willy Lages sent the captives for interrogation at Weteringschans prison on Kleine-Gartmanplantsoen in Amsterdam. Willem Arondeus confessed immediately that he had led the operation and stated that he alone had persuaded the others to take part in it. When he refused to implicate his comrades, Lages had him shackled by the wrists and ankles to an iron bedframe, unable to move, in a basement cell where the light was kept on night and day. Günther Klein administered the kickings and beatings prescribed under the SD's code of *verschärfte Vernehmung* – enhanced interrogation. Willem remained silent, but a search of his apartment revealed incriminating correspondence and notebooks. For several days after the raid, Cornelis Roos, the Amsterdam policeman on the CS-6 team, had passed on confidential reports of the ongoing police investigation to Rudi Bloemgarten and others, which were also discovered and introduced as evidence.

The trial was held at the end of June in the courtroom above the Weteringschans cells. Arondeus repeated his claim that he alone was to blame, but the judge wasn't interested. After a perfunctory hearing, the SS High Court of Justice pronounced twelve death sentences with only the four medical students escaping the firing squad. The verdicts stated that the perpetrators had 'all been directed by the Communist Party' and that 'five of them were Jewish, or had Jewish blood; and two of them were homosexuals'.

The condemned men were held overnight in the hospital wing of Weteringschans jail, where a fellow prisoner reported that they 'sang, debated and laughed to the very end ... everyone was impressed, including the German guards.' For his last meal, Arondeus requested a slice of meringue cake, made for him by his friend the communist poet Henriette Roland Holst and by Frieda Belinfante, herself on the run from the Germans. To console her comrades, Frieda recounted her last conversation with Willem before his arrest.

> He said to me, 'Do you think we shall live to see the end of this war?' and I said, 'I don't think so.' He said, 'I don't either,' and asked me, 'Do you mind?' I said, 'No, not really.' He thought for a moment, then said, 'Neither do I.'

When Willem's lawyer, Lau Mazirel, brought the cake to him, he asked her to tell the world that he went to his death without self-pity and that his last words were, 'Let it be known, homosexuals are not cowards.' He gave Mazirel his farewell letter.

My comrades and I have known an honourable fate; for us, this has been a time of happiness and death holds no horror. The love and respect we have been shown on all sides, from prisoners and soldiers and guards, have made our destiny light. Life has been good to me in all the things it has brought. I leave it now with a grateful heart. Greet my friends for me. I think of you all with the greatest friendship and love.

At six o'clock the following morning, 1 July, the twelve were taken out of their cells, handcuffed together in pairs. They were driven in police vans to the dunes at Overveen, near Haarlem, where they were executed with submachine guns, still hand-cuffed to each other and without a blindfold.

Monument to the twelve executed Resistance members

* * *

For those who remained at liberty, the days following the Registry Office raid were a time of uncertainty. Someone had betrayed Joop Hoogsteder to the SD, knowing that he would not withstand the German pressure. He was a young boy, timorous and frail and, as Willem's courier, he knew all the details of the operation and the names and addresses of those involved in it. The choice of Hoogsteder had not been accidental; the person who made it had an insider's knowledge of CS-6 and its personnel.

With the Germans continuing their search, Pim and Anna-Maria feared the ring of the doorbell. When it came, it was not what they were expecting. Hans Kreisel, the debonair playboy who had brought them Allied pilots, Jews and Resistance operatives, looked broken. His face was bloodied, one arm hung limp under his jacket. Anna-Maria hurried him inside.

Kreisel refused to speak about what had happened. Anna-Maria dressed his wounds, gave him fresh clothes and put him to bed. He slept for thirty-six hours and when he woke, he said he would need to stay with them. Hans Kreisel moved into the house in Terbregge and became a part of Anna-Maria's life.

He regained his strength in the weeks that followed, helping around the place, tending the vegetables in the garden. Visitors came to see him, bringing documents, writing down his orders and saluting as they left. Pim, who had known him before the war, understood that Kreisel had become a figure of importance in the Resistance.

His arrival brought deliveries of fresh meat, including on one occasion a whole pig. The three of them shared the food and the confidences and emotions of the clandestine life. Hans spoke about his background. His surname was German, he said, because his father was German. The family had come to the Netherlands many years ago, but he and his siblings all spoke German with a native fluency. Under current circumstances, a useful talent.

When the newspapers announced the death sentences imposed on Arondeus and the others, Kreisel was distraught. 'My God,' he said. 'We did what we could ... but it wasn't enough!'

15

THE CANCER OF BETRAYAL

Hannie Schaft and Jan Bonekamp were part of the team that bombed the Velsen-Noord power station in an attempt to disrupt the railway network carrying supplies to the Ijmuiden steel factories. The attack was only partially successful, but the authorities announced extended curfews in Velsen and the neighbouring town of Beverwijk, intensified patrols to hunt down the saboteurs and mandatory death sentences for those involved. Trains running from the northern Netherlands to the Belgian border were targeted by flying squads of armed inspectors led by Hans van de Berg, an NSB officer whose fanatical pursuit of Resistance operatives led to a series of damaging arrests.

The Resistance Council decided that Van de Berg had to be eliminated and Jan Bonekamp volunteered to do it. He trailed the target to his home in Beverwijk where he spent a week observing his movements. Having established that Van de Berg regularly drank in a tavern close to the junction of Baanstraat and Zeestraat, Bonekamp waited for him to emerge late in the evening and shot him twice in the chest.

* * *

Erwin Sandor did not return. Marlies and Anna-Maria scoured the newspapers to see if they could discover his fate, read the execution lists that the Germans pasted on walls and billboards, made enquiries with contacts who worked at Westerbork. Hans Kreisel notified Resistance intelligence to report any sightings. All without success.

Kreisel spoke sparingly about the work he was involved in. But he took Pim and Anna-Maria into his confidence about the mole hunt. The arrests of Arondeus and his comrades had dealt CS-6 a near-fatal blow, Kreisel said; Gerrit van der Veen had avoided the roundup and others, including all of the Boissevain family, Jan Verleun, Leo Frijda, Hans Katan, Sape Kuiper and PAM Pooters, were still active and at large. But if the group were to continue to operate, it was imperative to excise the cancer of betrayal that had dogged it for too long. Kreisel was liaising with Uncle Anton, and through him with King Kong, to discover the traitor.

* * *

Hans van de Berg was buried with state honours in the Duinrust cemetery in Beverwijk. In the days leading up to his funeral, the media made much of his murder, inciting public anger at the killing of an innocent official carrying out his duty to protect the Dutch people. In impassioned speeches at his graveside, NSB leaders and representatives of the Reichskommissariat called for revenge.

Revenge was already underway. At a secret meeting with German and Dutch SS commanders, Hanns Rauter let it be known that terror would henceforth be met with terror: the Resistance was using the tactics of covert assassination, so the authorities would respond in kind. Rauter instructed thirty-three-year-old Standartenführer Henk Feldmeijer, the leader of the Dutch SS and an Iron Cross veteran of the Nazi campaign in Russia, to create a force of like-minded Dutchmen, whose task would be the extrajudicial elimination of Resistance sympathisers.

Henk Feldmeijer

Feldmeijer's death squad would carry out scores of murders, beginning with the men whom Rauter held responsible for the killing of Hans van de Berg: Gerardus Paauw and Lambert Verdoorn, suspected of betraying Van de Berg to the Resistance, were attacked in their offices in Beverwijk. Paauw was hit in the arm, Verdoorn died of his wounds.

The Sonderkommando Feldmeijer and other assassination teams were part of Operation Silbertanne, a campaign of terror that employed some of the most ruthless killers of the occupation. Silbertanne signalled an intensification of the battle between the authorities and the Resistance that had significant consequences for both sides. Several of the CS-6 members arrested following the raid on the Population Registry had been held without trial, their fate uncertain, but now Rauter announced that two of them, Leo Bos and Dirk van Geenen, were to be executed. Already haunted by his failure to rescue Arondeus and his colleagues, Hans Kreisel told Pim and Anna-Maria that he would not allow the same thing to happen again.

* * *

The Allies were gaining ground in Russia and North Africa; landings in southern Italy were just weeks away; in the Netherlands and other European countries, hopes of liberation rose. The Reichskommissariat's response was to step up its repression. Operation Silbertanne was proof that even the pretence of judicial procedures observed in the past no longer applied. The decision to execute the two CS-6 operatives reinforced the impression of an impending showdown.

Information from a guard in Weteringschans prison that Bos and Van Geenen were scheduled for execution within a week made the Resistance hurry. Hans Kreisel told Janka and Gideon to bring the black Mercedes to a garage in the industrial suburb of Zaandam, where an engineer would prepare it for the operation ahead. The surviving members of the Persoonsbewijzen Centrale were commissioned to produce the documentation and the roundels and pennants for the car.

The uniforms were a problem. Anna-Maria suggested a solution. The SS sent its dry cleaning to a company in north Amsterdam and she knew the owner. Might it be worth asking him if he had the right uniforms on the premises?

PAM Pooters, who was still working at the Ministry of Food Supply, quizzed the drivers about deliveries to Weteringschans and discovered that the guardhouse was manned by junior ranks from 10 p.m. until the following morning. Personnel shortages meant the Germans were using Dutch guards and senior officers were scarce.

The operation was fixed for the day before the executions. Anna-Maria had secured two German SS uniforms, a captain's for Hans and a corporal's for Maurits de Jong, who would act as his driver, but neither of them fitted. Anna-Maria barely finished adjusting them in time for the two men's departure and as Hans was climbing into the car, a button flew off his trousers. Panic turned to laughter as she knelt before him and began to tug at his flies. They were still laughing as the Mercedes pulled out of the garage.

* * *

Curfew regulations were enforced by checkpoints and patrols, but the black Mercedes was a standard model SS staff car and the CS-6 forgers had done a good job with the markings. When Maurits, who spoke no German, asked what would happen if they were stopped, Hans said, 'I'll do the talking; you do the driving. And make sure you pull up to the prison like we own it.'

At Weteringschans things began well. The sentry waved them into the courtyard and held the car door open for Hans to step out. The men in the guardroom jumped to their feet as he entered, responding deferentially to his 'Heil Hitler'. But he was an SS officer and he was angry. 'Goddammit,' Hans snapped. 'This place stinks of beer and cigarettes! Don't you know the enemy are all around! And you lot sitting here smoking and drinking like you're on holiday!'

'Yes, sir. Sorry, sir.'

The guard was saying the right thing, but was there suspicion in his eyes? Hans fingered his revolver.

'All right. At ease. I need two of your prisoners . . .' He pulled out the requisition order his colleagues had printed. 'Names of . . . Bos and Van Geenen. Here's the docket.'

The guard took the paper. Hans's mind raced. Would he swallow it?

'Yes, sir.' The guard was picking up the phone. 'I'll just confirm with the Polizeiführer's office . . .'

'Put the phone down!' Hans shouted. The man looked alarmed.

'There's no need for that,' Hans said more evenly. 'I'm taking the prisoners directly to Rauter and you've got five minutes to get them in the back of my car ...'

The guard hesitated. 'That's an order!' Hans snapped.

The guard saluted and nodded to a warder who went to fetch them.

* * *

Trijntje Bult knew in her heart that it was Jan Bonekamp who had shot Van de Berg. He had always lived on his nerves, Trijntje thought, but now he was fevered and restless, agitated to the point of blood lust. When a local policeman called at the farm to quiz the Bults about black market sales of asparagus, Jan had to be restrained from shooting him. Trijntje feared that Hannie was going the same way. She asked Hannie how she coped with the emotional strain of killing people, but Hannie seemed untroubled. 'We don't have a choice. If we didn't do it, good men and women would be betrayed and murdered. It's our job to stop that happening.'

When Trijntje asked Bonekamp if he felt guilty about being away from his wife, he shrugged. 'She'll just have to take it. I asked her to come and fight with me, but that was impossible. I can't sit and do nothing.'

Passions were high. Trijntje feared they would erupt.

* * *

Hans Kreisel rang Anna-Maria an hour after the operation. They were afraid the phone was tapped, so they had agreed he would say simply 'Yes' or 'No'. Hearing him answer in the affirmative calmed her, but she had to wait another two weeks for him to return.

'I needed time,' Hans told her. 'The two guys were

shattered – they'd been expecting to be shot and they weren't thinking straight. But I had to hear everything they could tell me about how they were interrogated and who might have betrayed them.'

'Did they have any clues?' Anna-Maria asked.

'They picked up a few things from the thugs who were torturing them,' Hans said. 'And if I'm right about what it means, it doesn't look good.'

* * *

The decision to suspend the death sentence against Esmée van Eeghen was endorsed by the Frisian Resistance, but the group's leader, Pieter Wijbenga, remained uneasy. He instructed his assistant, Piet Oberman, to deliver the message in person, with a warning to Esmée that if she did not break with her German lover and leave Leeuwarden, the verdict would be reinstated and carried out at once. Krijn van der Helm persuaded Oberman to take him with him. When they got there, Krijn asked for five minutes alone with her. After half an hour waiting outside, Oberman went in and found Krijn at Esmée's feet. According to Oberman, Esmée had told him she was planning to marry her Lieutenant Schmälzlein.

> She said she was going to marry Schmälzlein as soon as possible and go with him to Germany; she loved him; she felt as if they were already man and wife ... I explained to her what had been decided, namely that she must disappear from Friesland and that if she refused, or if she returned, she would be shot. She understood that I was not joking; she had been in the Resistance long enough to know that these are not idle threats. She gave her word that she would comply with our demand and swore she would never betray the Resistance ...

We agreed that Esmée would leave Leeuwarden at ten o'clock the following morning and we sent one of our agents, Tiny Mulder, to make sure she got on the train.

Mulder reported that Hans Schmälzlein arrived on the platform arm-in-arm with Esmée and helped her on board with two large suitcases. She was playing a game in which the stakes are life and death, Mulder said, and it was starting to spin out of her control.

* * *

Operation Silbertanne was deemed a success. Between August 1943 and September 1944, the Sonderkommando Feldmeijer succeeded in murdering more than fifty Dutch civilians. Some of them had tenuous links to the Resistance; many just happened to be in the wrong place. Silbertanne gave individual SD officers the freedom to pick their victims and settle their own scores. In the case of Untersturmführer Ernst Knorr – the man who had arrested Gerrit Kastein – and his Dutch SD colleague Frans Lammers, they were having difficulty tracking down the Resistance killers of one of their colleagues, police lieutenant Sikke Wolters. Knorr and Lammers suspected that Wolters' assassins were being sheltered in the village of Rottum, north of Groningen, so they picked the names of three local residents and instructed Feldmeijer to shoot them. Two of the targets were not at home; but the third, a fifty-nine-year-old cattle farmer by the name of Albert Rinkema, was. At 1.45 a.m. he was woken by knocking at his front door. When he asked, 'Who is there?' he was told, 'The police.' Rinkema opened the door in his night-gown and was shot three times, in the shoulder, the abdomen and the forehead.

Piet Faber   *Klaas Faber*

Among Rinkema's killers was Piet Faber, a former member of the Dutch SS who had served on the Eastern Front and now worked for the Sonderkommando Feldmeijer. Faber and his younger brother Klaas would become Operation Silbertanne's most prolific employees. Their involvement in two particularly brutal killings would secure them a place in Dutch history.

There is some debate about Esmée van Eeghen's movements after she boarded the train out of Leeuwarden. Her initial destination appears to have been her mother Minette's home in Baarn, near Hilversum. According to Minette Schimmelpenninck, Esmée said the Resistance had cleared her of any misconduct and that an investigation had blamed the betrayal of the arms cache in the Tamminga warehouse on the captured Ben de Vries. What was more worrying, Esmée told her mother, was that one of her friends, Riek Stienstra, had been arrested and might be forced to incriminate her to the Gestapo.

Riek Stienstra was the owner of a house in south Leeuwarden that had been used by the Frisian Resistance for its meetings and she knew Esmée well. Following her arrest, Riek had been sent to the Sicherheitspolizei in Groningen, where she was handed over for interrogation to the brutal Ernst Knorr and Frans Lammers. Knorr and Lammers were convinced that she knew the identities of the men who killed Sikke Wolters and, since Wolters had been a close friend of theirs, they were determined to make her talk. When threats and beatings proved ineffective, they tried a different tactic.

It was evident that the SD had already acquired a lot of incriminating information, which made it hard for me to keep denying everything they accused me of. When they ran out of patience with my refusal to talk, they said they were going to try another approach: they were going to bring in Mr de Vries. I was in such a state that I didn't even realise who they were talking about, so when the door of the interrogation room opened and they brought in young Ben de Vries, in manacles and with marks of terrible beatings on his face, I was completely overcome with emotion. We have all been taught not to give any sign of recognising an imprisoned comrade and I did my best; but, to my great dismay, Ben immediately greeted me with the words, 'Hello, Riek.' It was clear what the situation was, because Knorr and Lammers burst into laughter and Ben said to me, 'Riek, girl, you'd better confess to everything. We are lost.'

What went through my mind at that moment is indescribable. I think I cried terribly. I sobbed and sobbed and only when I had calmed down did they recommence the interrogation, with Ben de Vries sitting next to me. There was little point in continuing to deny things; Ben had already told them everything they wanted to know.

Still, I tried to do what I could to protect people, including my friend Esmée van Eeghen. Esmée had said to me that if ever I was captured, I should tell the interrogators that Esmée van Eeghen was working with the Germans and, in particular, with a German officer named Hans. Esmée told me she was completely certain that this German officer would vouch for her and protect her. So, I did so. I stated that Esmée was a German agent and that her double game was the only reason I had myself got involved in the Resistance.

Knorr and Lammers seemed unsurprised to hear this. Lammers just said, 'An officer named Hans, huh? Would that be Schmälzlein by any chance?'

* * *

At the height of the Silbertanne period, in the final months of 1943 and the first part of 1944, the death squads were carrying out individual assassinations at the rate of two a week and public mass executions would soon follow. The Sonderkommando Feldmeijer tried to conceal the identities of its members but some of them, including Piet and Klaas Faber, became known to the Resistance and subject to reprisals. When attempts to kill the Faber brothers failed, the Resistance Council looked for other targets close to them.

Piet and Klaas's father, Pieter Faber, was a fifty-nine-year-old baker in the town of Heemstede, south of Haarlem. He was cycling home from work at 6 p.m. on a Thursday evening when he noticed a young couple standing on the corner of Eerelmanstraat and Tooropkade. As he approached the point where the road draws level with the river, Faber realised that the young man and the young woman were reaching inside their overcoats and then felt a sharp pain in his left leg followed by another in his side.

A young boy, Lex Leffelaar, who was cutting the grass outside his parents' house, saw Faber fall off his bike and watched as the young couple climbed onto theirs and pedalled off south down Tooropkade. Lex called to his mother, who helped the injured man inside and made him comfortable with a pillow under his head. An ambulance took Faber to the Spaarne Hospital on Kleine Houtweg in Haarlem where doctors treated his wounds but did not fear for his life.

Because of his longstanding commitment to the cause of Dutch fascism – and because his two sons were valued members of the Feldmeijer operation – Faber was given the best possible medical treatment. He was visited in hospital by the NSB mayor of Haarlem, who brought him flowers and chocolate, then by Anton Mussert himself. Faber's younger son, Klaas, had served as Mussert's bodyguard and the NSB leader was effusive in his thanks. He pledged that the would-be assassins would be brought to justice and asked Faber to tell him everything he could remember about them. Faber said he had little recollection of the man, but the young woman had struck him because of her nonchalant attitude – he remembered her laughing loudly as he fell from his bicycle – and because she had striking red hair.

* * *

The Dutch SD men Frans Lammers and Sikke Wolters had sworn an oath that if either of them were killed, the other would not rest until he tracked down his assassins. Lammers took personal responsibility for the new lead in the search for his friend's killers: Ben de Vries had confirmed that Esmée van Eeghen and Krijn van der Helm were present at the planning of the murder, and Riek Stienstra had now revealed where Esmée was living.

Frans Lammers

Ernst Knorr told Lammers to begin by investigating Lieutenant Schmälzlein. The first priority was to discover the truth about his relationship with Esmée and whether he had been passing information to the Resistance. When Lammers confronted him, Hans Schmälzlein swore that their affair had been innocent, that Miss van Eeghen had left Leeuwarden and that he did not know where she had gone.

Schmälzlein was told to remain in his office while Lammers went to search his house. Fearing a trap, Lammers ordered Piet Faber to accompany him as an armed bodyguard. The first thing they discovered was that Schmälzlein had many photographs of Esmée, including one that hung above his bed. There were also letters from her, but none of them with an address. Schmälzlein was summoned to the house and Lammers challenged him about his relationship with 'a possible Resistance spy'. Lammers and Faber were about to leave when a young woman stopped them in the entrance hall and whispered to Lammers that she could tell him 'much more' about Esmée than Lieutenant Schmälzlein had been willing to divulge. Lammers agreed to meet her the following morning at her apartment on Prins Hendrikstraat.

Antoinette Jaakke told Lammers that she was Hans

Schmälzlein's housekeeper and had got to know Miss van Eeghen while she had been living in the lieutenant's house. The two women had become confidantes. Esmée had told Antoinette about her work for the communist Resistance; she had shared her heartache when the Party ordered her to leave her lover; and she had confessed her fear of reprisals from both sides – from the Resistance because of her affair with Schmälzlein, and the Germans because of her illegal past. 'She did tell me, though,' Antoinette said, 'that she'd much rather be caught by the Germans, because she knows exactly how to wind them round her little finger.'

When Lammers asked why she was volunteering such detailed information about her friend, Antoinette said, 'Well, it's my duty, isn't it. And you know what else? I can help you find her.'

* * *

Jan Brasser, the Resistance Council's commander in North Holland, had arranged to meet Hannie Schaft and Jan Bonekamp for a debrief after the operation against Pieter Faber. 'I was waiting for them on the Nauernasche bridge,' Brasser recalled, 'when I saw Bonekamp pedalling furiously towards me at top speed. He had his heavy overcoat on, which he wore summer and winter in order to conceal the guns he always carried, and he was gasping for breath. When he got to me, he was yelling, "We got him! We got the bastard!" and before I could say anything, he was already shouting, "Who's next? Who do we do next?" That's how Bonekamp was – always pumped up, always flat out, always wanting to do more.'

The news that Pieter Faber was not dead came as a shock. For Hannie and Jan there was the disappointment of a failed operation, made worse by the possibility that Faber might have given their descriptions to the authorities. Relief came six days later. A black-bordered announcement in *Volk en Vaderland* expressed deep sorrow that a distinguished public servant and loyal member of the NSB had succumbed to peritonitis, brought on by the fatal bullets of cowardly assassins.

* * *

The SD recorded that Antoinette Jaakke showed commendable enthusiasm in her assistance to police lieutenant Lammers, to the point that Lammers himself at times seemed bemused by it.

> Jaakke, Antoinette. Working-class Catholic family, industrial Amsterdam suburb of Jordaan. Eldest of nine. Active in Catholic Youth movement. Salesgirl at Bonneterie department store. Arrested May 1941 on suspicion of illegal activity. Three months detention Scheveningen, released due to pregnancy. Child's father, suspected Resistance operative, disowns her. Child given up to orphanage. Begins liaison with German officer, Oberzahlmeister Paul Pingel, who introduces her to Schmälzlein.
>
> Secures position as Schmälzlein's housekeeper. Develops romantic feelings for him. Resents arrival of Van Eeghen. Regards her as rival for Schmälzlein's affections. Feels inferior to better-educated Van Eeghen.

Antoinette Jaakke's offer to turn Esmée over to the SD was gratefully received. Frans Lammers instructed her to write a letter to Esmée saying she had 'important news about our mutual friend' that could be conveyed only in person. Esmée replied by telegram suggesting a meeting the following Thursday at Amsterdam Centraal station. Lammers arranged for Antoinette to stay overnight at the Hotel de Kroon in Leeuwarden and told her that two SD men would come for her in the morning. Officer Piet Faber and the German Hauptscharführer Helmuth Schäper took Antoinette on the first train from Leeuwarden to Amsterdam, where they watched as she stood waiting for Esmée on the platform. Piet Faber had told her how to designate their target.

> We told Antoinette Jaakke to give her friend a kiss on the cheek, which would identify her and allow us to move in for the kill. We saw her meet a lady whom she embraced, so we knew that must be Esmée. We allowed both ladies to walk outside to a neighbouring café on the water, where they sat down at a table. We then joined them, instructing them to remain silent and informing them that they were under arrest. In order to avoid compromising our informant, we made a show of arresting her, too.

* * *

Piet Faber had fought for the Nazis in Russia and murdered for them in Holland. He was already a fascist before his father's assassination, but after it he became a fanatic, thirsting for revenge. By the end of the war he would have twenty-seven documented killings to his name, with a hundred more in which he was named but never formally indicted. He volunteered for the Haarlem police department's 'Jew squad', sending scores of women and children to their deaths, took part in execution parties in the Westerbork, Exloo and Norg detention camps, and gunned down Resistance fighters in Haarlem, Groningen, Friesland and Drenthe.

There was passion and anger on both sides but in the Resistance, some thoughts of morality persisted. The assassination of the elderly Pieter Faber led to heated exchanges. A letter in *Trouw*, the underground newspaper of the Protestant Resistance, asked, 'Why was it considered necessary to kill this man? He was an NSB member, but so are thousands of others; he did not commit acts of violence or betrayal. Is it not more likely that he was shot because of the crimes of his sons? And if that is the case, can we genuinely look ourselves in the eye and say that we have acted in good faith?'

Truus Oversteegen demurred. 'The man was genuinely dangerous,' she would say later. 'Just like his offspring. It was a family business in terror and there was extensive deliberation at the top of the Resistance before the decision was taken to remove him.' Gerrit van der Veen, himself on the run from the SD's assassins, denounced the killing as 'absolutely unnecessary', but Jan Bonekamp was unmoved. 'One more of them dead means a hundred of us saved,' he told Hannie. 'The sins of the sons are visited on their fathers.'

* * *

The events immediately following Esmée's arrest have been cited as evidence that her true loyalties were, at the least, ambiguous. Piet Faber and Helmuth Schäper did not take their prisoners directly to jail but went instead for a drink at Piet's family home in Haarlem where Mrs Faber treated Esmée in a friendly manner and Esmée commiserated with her on the recent death of her husband. The two SD men then escorted Esmée and Antoinette to a hotel where they spent a convivial evening before travelling together the next day to Groningen. Antoinette Jaakke was dropped off at the train station to make her way home to Leeuwarden, while Esmée was taken to meet Ernst Knorr. After some discussion, Esmée was allowed to phone her mother. She told her that she would be away for a few days and there was no need to worry. She said three friends from Groningen would come to check her room and fetch her some spare clothes. Mrs Schimmelpenninck felt her daughter was anxious, possibly under pressure. When she asked what the matter was, Esmée replied, 'I'm going to do the same as Dave,' which her mother took to be a reference to David van Eeghen's attempt to cross the Channel to England.

For the next month, Esmée was held at the Scholtenshuis, a large nineteenth-century building on the Grote Markt in Groningen that had become the headquarters of the SD, but which had previously been the family home of Esmée's childhood friend, Edzard Bosch van Rosenthal, himself now active in the Resistance. Her arrest triggered alarm. Fear that Esmée might be tortured into revealing the names of her comrades turned to panic as stories emerged that she was co-operating voluntarily. Ernst Knorr's secretary, Jacoba Baptisten, later gave her version of Esmée's relationship with her boss.

She was given a room of her own on the second floor of the Scholtenshuis, with a comfortable bed and a couch, and she was allowed to move freely around the building. She got special food, with bread and milk every day, and as many cigarettes as she wanted. Untersturmführer Knorr took her out for drives in his car, including one trip to Leeuwarden, which Esmée said she wanted to visit, and Hauptscharführer Schäper took her to see a film at the cinema. She was never ill-treated, no physical pressure was applied to her and she voluntarily communicated all the details of her work for the Resistance. Her 'interrogations' were simply a matter of writing down the information she provided and whenever she remembered additional details, she would come to Knorr's room of her own free will to tell him. Esmée offered to go undercover as an agent for the SD and I believe that Knorr planned to accept this, but no final decision was made.

As to whether there was a [sexual] relationship between Esmée and Untersturmführer Knorr, I cannot say for sure; but it is certainly possible.

Jacoba Baptisten – and Frans Lammers, who provided similar testimony – were speaking after the war and were mindful of minimising their own responsibility for the treatment of Resistance prisoners, but it does seem possible that Esmée revealed damaging information. Lammers said she was concerned to protect her friend, Riek Stienstra, and offered to collaborate in return for Stienstra's release. In their first meeting, she told Lammers who had killed his colleague, Sikke Wolters.

There was no need to put pressure on her, as she volunteered the information without hesitation and without the slightest coercion. She showed no loyalty to her former friends. Her evidence allowed the Sicherheitspolizei to arrest five important Resistance fighters and also to learn the name of Piet Oberman, who managed to evade arrest only by using a firearm ... Van Eeghen wanted to be the centre of attention, keen to demonstrate the importance her own role, with little regard for the number of victims she caused among her former colleagues ... She was worldly-wise and very sexually charged, someone who had become accustomed to using her charms to make men follow her wishes, and was trying the same tactic now with the Sicherheitspolizei. I could not understand why the Resistance had put so much trust in her.

Pieter Wijbenga, who long doubted Esmée's reliability, was among those who later refused to condemn her. He believed that her testimony to the SD was calculated to name only those comrades whose identity had already been compromised and that she was not directly responsible for any arrests or executions. 'If Esmée had told them everything she knew,' Wijbenga concluded, 'many more people would certainly have been shot.'

The most serious accusation against Esmée van Eeghen concerned the fate of her former lover, Krijn van der Helm. On the day that Esmée left Leeuwarden, Krijn went into hiding, but Lammers had become convinced that he was behind the murder of his friend, Sikke Wolters, and demanded Esmée's help to find him. He pressured her into writing a letter which Esmée addressed to Krijn's mother's house, almost certainly in the belief that he would not be there. Piet Faber was ordered to deliver it.

I was instructed by Untersturmführer Knorr to drive to Amersfoort to the address on the letter. I was accompanied by Hauptscharführer Helmuth Schäper and by my younger brother Klaas Carel Faber, who also worked for the SD. When we got there, I rang the bell, while Schäper and Klaas kept watch from a distance. The door was opened by an elderly lady, who took the letter inside. When she came back, she asked me to wait in the hall and in walked a gentleman whom I immediately recognised as the man we were looking for, Krijn van der Helm. I had not expected him to be there, so I had to quickly rethink my strategy. I introduced myself by my real name and Van der Helm took me to a conservatory. I could tell he was trying to determine who he was dealing with and he was terribly suspicious. He demanded to see my ID and I gave it to him. He said I could see his ID, too, and made a move as if to reach for it in his back pocket, but I sensed he was going to draw a gun and I was too quick for him. I pointed my gun at him and shouted for him to drop his gun and raise his hands, but he didn't comply and grabbed my gun, so I grabbed his wrist with my left hand to stop him shooting. I was trying to get my own gun free and cocked and when I did so, I shot Van der Helm in the region of the heart. He was still struggling. I shot him several more times until he collapsed, and moments later he was dead. I picked up the subject's weapon, a Walther, and called in Schäper and my brother to search the house. Immediately afterwards, the Ordnungspolizei arrived to cordon off the area. They threw the subject's body onto a truck and drove off with it to Groningen.

16

THE MURDER BUSINESS

The shooting of Pieter Faber had the consequence of turning his sons into unbridled killers. Piet Faber had already embarked on his career of murder, but the younger brother, Klaas, began killing only after his father's death, driven by a desire for vengeance. Hannie Schaft and Jan Bonekamp, who remained unaware of the impact of their actions, were themselves not very different. They, too, killed with a frenzied determination that brooked no argument and paid scant regard to moral niceties. The hunt for Pieter Faber's assassins was widely covered in the press, with the fact that one of the killers was a woman attracting particular opprobrium. 'We denounce the killing of a defenceless man,' wrote the *Haarlemsche Courant*, 'and are indignant that a woman helped to take his life – the very gift that God has given women the privilege to bestow. Has our nation lost so much of its senses in these unruly times that it should fall into such unnatural behaviour?'

Bonekamp's response was to step up his work. There was a bravado about him, a confidence in his own immortality. When the mayor of Wormerveer on the northern fringes of Amsterdam refused to assist the Germans in their recruitment of slave labourers, he was sent to the Amersfoort concentration camp and replaced by an NSB loyalist, Piet de Vries.

De Vries's zeal in delivering his fellow citizens for transport to Germany angered the Resistance. Jan Bonekamp and Jan Brasser broke into the townhall, locked up the staff and knocked on the mayor's door. 'Big man De Vries was sitting behind his big desk,' Brasser recalled. 'But when he saw us, he went white as a sheet. We showed him our guns, told him we had work to do and ordered him to keep his head down.' The two of them began stuffing the town's population records that were used for the slave labour programme into hessian sacks, but De Vries tried to call for help. Bonekamp knocked him to the floor and rolled him up in a large Persian carpet. 'You could see the guy's head poking out at one end and his feet at the other,' Brasser wrote. 'But he couldn't move any more and just had to watch as we stole the records.'

When they found there were too many files to fit in their sacks, they poured petrol over them and set them on fire. Bonekamp and Brasser escaped as the fire spread and the townhall went up in flames, to the delight of those watching outside. De Vries was unharmed but would henceforth be known to everyone as 'Piet the Carpet Man'.

Other assignments ended less amusingly. A Dutch policeman, Willem Ritman, was in charge of the Velsen police department's anti-communist unit and had been responsible for the arrest of several of Jan Bonekamp's comrades.

Willem Ritman

When the Wehrmacht corporal Alois Bamberger was assassinated, Ritman had personally rounded up the ten hostages whom the Nazis would execute as reprisals, including Bonekamp's friends, Piet Weij, Rolf Strengholt and Simon Warmenhoven. The men had been held for a week in De Koepel prison in Haarlem, from where Warmenhoven had smuggled out a series of messages. Their fellow prisoners included the Haarlem chief rabbi, Philip Frank, and two other members of the city's Jewish Council, all of whom Warmenhoven said were particularly badly treated by their jailors. When they were told they would be shot in the morning, the three communists wrote farewell letters expressing their faith in the rightness of their cause. 'Better to die honourably than live with a lie,' Weij wrote. 'I go to my death with my head upheld.' 'I die a righteous death,' Strengholt told his wife Annie and daughter Erna. 'Both of you should know that you can look people straight in the eye.'

Willy Lages reported that the hostages died bravely. He had spoken at length to Rabbi Frank and had been impressed by his calm dignity. Frank had told Lages that he forgave him for his own death but could not forgive him on behalf of the Jewish people. 'The Germans are nothing,' Frank told one of his fellow prisoners. 'All they can do to us Jews is to kill us; but we are protected by a higher, spiritual authority. We must endure our martyrdom and as a rabbi, I must help my people to do that.'

The ten executed hostages

Jan Bonekamp swore to avenge his comrades, but Willem Ritman was well guarded. It was only several months later that Bonekamp and his commander Jan Brasser were able to act. Using a stolen Wehrmacht car with fake number plates, they parked outside the Velsen police headquarters on Wijkerstraatweg and waited for Ritman to emerge. Bonekamp wanted to shoot him himself, but Brasser ordered him to drive the car and another operative, Joop Jongh, pulled the trigger.

In retaliation for Ritman's death and for three other assassinations carried out by Jan Bonekamp and his accomplices, the Germans sent 486 hostages to the Amersfoort concentration camp and from there to camps in Germany. One hundred and forty-nine of them did not survive.

* * *

Krijn van der Helm's heavily pregnant wife was in the house on the day of his murder. She had been resting upstairs, with their son Krijntje beside her, and was woken by the sound of gunshots. She rushed down, but the hallway was full of Germans and she was forcibly restrained from entering the conservatory where her husband's body was lying. A young Jewish refugee, Ruth de Jonge, who had been in hiding with the Van der Helm family since 1942, was mistaken for the maid and was ordered to clean up the blood. The following day, the two women travelled together to Friesland to speak to Pieter Wijbenga. Wijbenga was sympathetic, but he said Krijn had been foolish to hide out in his parents' house as that was the first place the Germans would look. Esmée had evidently taken the decision that Krijn would not be there, Wijbenga said, and so used that address on her letter to him.

Ernst Knorr's secretary, Jacoba Baptisten, was present when Knorr announced the news of Van der Helm's death and witnessed Esmée's reaction. 'She was taken aback,' Baptisten remembered. 'She cried inconsolably for a long, long time.' Others also saw her in jail. When the Resistance operative Jeanne Evenhuis was arrested and taken to the Scholtenshuis, she was left alone in a corridor where Esmée was sitting. It was a trap to see if the two women would recognise each other. Evenhuis asked her what she was doing there, but Esmée blanked her.

'I think you're wrong; I don't know you,' Esmée replied very distantly, and I realised she was protecting me. Later, I was interrogated by the same SD officer who had worked on Esmée, a man named Frans Lammers. Lammers told me I could go if I slept with him, but I refused and the next day I was transported to Borkum, which was an Organization Todt camp for forced labour. I knew that Esmée had contact with the Germans, because I had seen her talking to Germans on the train and I caught her at our house ringing one of them, but she was not a traitor. In all the interrogations they put me through, they never brought up anything that Esmée could have told them about me. They never mentioned any of the shot-down pilots we helped. Esmée knew all about that; she knew how we got them treated and their broken bones operated on in secret. She could have told the Germans about all of those things, but she didn't. I wouldn't be alive today if Esmée had snitched. She could have betrayed us all and got us all killed.

* * *

An element of uncertainty appeared in the actions of the Reichskommissariat. For the first time, it seemed that the occupying forces might not be fully in control of events. The unyielding machinery of repression no longer seemed quite so impregnable. With Allied forces gaining momentum and the Nazi war machine faltering, the Resistance was emboldened. Attacks increased.

Exasperated by the dysfunctional rivalry between Seyss-Inquart and Rauter, Berlin sent in a new man to stiffen resolve. Karl Eberhardt Schöngarth had commanded the Einsatzgruppen death squads in southern Poland, whose members had murdered tens of thousands of Jews; it was he who issued the order legitimising the summary execution of any Jew found outside of the ghetto. Shortly after his arrival he announced that 'Polish conditions' would henceforth apply in the Netherlands; his Order on the Fight against Terrorism and Sabotage removed the need for legal process, devolving the authority to impose death sentences to officers of the SD:

> Whenever it becomes known that any illegal grouping is formed, or when centres of resistance can be identified, these groupings shall be ruthlessly destroyed and their participants eliminated ... All persons deemed guilty of the offences mentioned in this order are to be shot immediately, either during or shortly after their arrest.

Schöngarth appointed Erich Deppner to enforce the new order and to communicate its contents to officials. Deppner requested to be notified of *Sonderbehandlung* (death penalty) decisions by means of a short telex containing the personal details of the offender, the nature of the offence and the outcome of the investigation, including confession or denial. But he made it clear that he would not overturn such decisions and that the new powers should be used as widely as possible.

The Rotterdam office of the Sicherheitspolizei took him at his word. When their officers raided an apartment at 8a

Saftlevenstraat and discovered illegal literature, forged documents and a clandestine radio transmitter, they arrested the owner, Adriaan Struik, then waited in the flat until another Resistance operative, Willem Bulk, came to the door and was also arrested. A third man, Johannes van der Loo, arrived the following morning to inform Mrs Struik that the Resistance was working on a plan to rescue her husband from captivity. He, too, was taken into custody and the commander of the Rotterdam SD, Sturmbannführer Herbert Wölk, confirmed that all three should be executed.

The captives were shot at SD headquarters on Heemraadssingel and Wölk phoned the Rotterdam police to dispose of the bodies. When the police arrived, they found that Johannes van der Loo was still alive. After some discussion among themselves, they took the injured man to the Zuiderziekenhuis Hospital and rang Wölk to tell him what they had done.

Wölk ordered the firing party to reconvene and finish Van der Loo off. Van der Loo was carried to a waiting car and driven to the shooting range in Kralingen. No longer able to stand, he was laid on the ground and despatched with a burst of fire from a machine gun.

Johannes van der Loo

* * *

The inhabitants of the Groningen suburb of Paddepoel were used to the noises of war, but the gunfire in the night sounded alarmingly close. In the morning, Elias Kroeske, a local farmer walking his dog by the Van Starkenborgh Canal, discovered how close. Two bodies, a man and a woman, were floating in the shallow water. Both were young and the woman was strikingly well dressed. The policeman who arrived at the scene noted that she was five feet five, weighed around seven stone and had dark blonde hair. Her designer clothes included blue cotton trousers made by Determeijer of Amsterdam, silk stockings, low cut shoes by Sabatini, a cream jacket over a grey shantung blouse and a white leather belt. She was wearing two gold rings, one with a stone of aquamarine, two gold bracelets and a crescent-shaped gold brooch inlaid with pearls. Nothing had been stolen and both bodies had their documents on them. The man was Luitje Kremer, later revealed to be a member of the Noord-Drenthe communist Resistance, and the woman was Esmée van Eeghen. Her watch had stopped at 10.47 p.m. when she had been killed by thirteen bullets.

Piet Faber, the Sonderkommando hitman who had shot Esmée's former lover Krijn van der Helm twelve days earlier, would give a graphic account of what happened:

> My brother Klaas and I were summoned to the Scholtenshuis, where we were told by Untersturmführer Knorr that Van Eeghen and a certain Kremer, also a political detainee, had to be killed. At nine o'clock, when it got dark, Knorr took us to his car. The prisoners were already there, so we all got in. There were five of us – Knorr, my brother Klaas, Esmée, Kremer and me. We drove north along the Nieuwe Ebbingestraat in the direction of Winsum and when we reached the Groningen city limits, we stopped. Knorr gave some explanation to the prisoners – I don't remember what it was – and asked them to

get out. Knorr got out with Esmée and I got out with Kremer. I told Klaas not to shoot, because I didn't want my brother involved in anything, and at that moment I heard Knorr open fire. He had shot Esmée dead and I did the same to Kremer. The three of us then threw the bodies into the canal. It was Knorr who gave the order for the shooting and I assume that he received the command from someone higher up.

By the time Piet Faber gave his statement, the war was over and Knorr was no longer alive, so pinning the blame solely on him was convenient. But Knorr undoubtedly bore responsibility for what happened to Esmée, as he did for the murder of other Resistance fighters. His loyal secretary, Jacoba Baptisten, claimed he had had no other choice:

> The war was not going well and the atmosphere in the Scholtenshuis was very tense. A policeman from the Ordnungspolizei brought a suitcase into Knorr's office and I recognised it as Esmée's. When I asked the man what had happened to her, he said she had been transferred to Germany and Knorr told me the same thing. But a few days later, I saw a photograph taken by the Dutch police of a woman's body that had been found in a canal and I knew it was Esmée. I said this to Knorr, but he insisted she had gone to Germany . . . He was very fond of Esmée, but his colleagues in the SD decided that she was dangerous and had to be eliminated. It was in his nature as a conscientious and principled officer that he overcame his feelings and did his duty.

* * *

Public executions proliferated. What had begun as a calculated deterrent now seemed the act of a beleaguered regime, prey to anxiety and rage. Sturmbannführer Herbert Wölk decreed that hostages should be shot at the location where their crime against the Reich was committed and that their bodies should be left on view as a warning to others.

Sturmbannführer Herbert Wölk

Two days after a junior officer, Herbert Römer, was assassinated on the corner of Pleinweg and Goereesestraat, Wölk ordered the execution of twenty civilians. Dutch police were made to stand guard over the corpses for twenty-four hours, preventing relatives from retrieving their loved ones' bodies and demonstrating to the population the penalty for resistance.

When a police detective, Jacobus Tetenburg, betrayed a Resistance operative who was later executed, Militair Contact debated whether or not to retaliate. Because Tetenburg was Dutch, they considered that the Germans were unlikely to take reprisals and despatched two shooters to ambush him as he left the Hoflaan police station on his motorcycle.

Assassination of Jacobus Tetenburg

Unknown to the Resistance, Tetenburg's wife was German, and she lobbied Herbert Wölk for revenge. Wölk consulted Hanns Rauter, who ordered the shooting of twenty more hostages.

* * *

The likelihood of reprisals troubled all the Resistance groups. Some of them, notably the Christian organisations, suspended their attacks, but the communists were less squeamish. The CS-6 group of Jan and Gideon Boissevain had been weakened by the betrayals and arrests that followed the raid on the Amsterdam Population Registry, but its remaining members continued to operate.

Sape Kuiper, still only nineteen, stepped into the shoes of the men who were gone. He brought in new recruits, young and inexperienced, all eager to fight. Johan Kalshoven had been a member of CS-6 for less than a month when Kuiper asked him to take part in his first operation. A Dutch police officer, Hermann Blonk, was the leader of an SD task force charged with hunting down Resistance fighters; CS-6 believed he was targeting their operations, and that he was receiving information from an informer within the group.

Kuiper and Kalshoven forced their way into Blonk's home. When Blonk pulled a gun, they shot and wounded him and his wife.

A week later, Kuiper took twenty-seven-year-old Hugo Geul with him on an assassination mission. A Jewish dentist in Amsterdam, H. E. B. de Jonge-Cohen, had been earning bounty money from the Germans by passing on the names and addresses of his Jewish patients. Kuiper and Geul found him in his consulting room and shot him dead.

* * *

Another Boissevain signed up for CS-6. Louis Boissevain was Jan Karel and Gideon's first cousin, a twenty-one-year-old poet whose life had been spent writing and dreaming. He and Leo Frijda had worked together on an underground literary journal, *Lichting*, publishing independent verse, inspired by thoughts of freedom and resistance to tyranny.

Louis Boissevain

Frijda wrote fiery poems decrying the persecution of his fellow Jews, with calls to action that Louis found moving.

> Who then strikes down
> The guiltless Jew, the youngster
> Starting life, but ending in
> A filthy cell, shot by evil hands.
>
> His corpse rots; his ragged soul
> Speeds, a whistling shell,
> Through the night.
> Who dares interrupt his
> Sacred parabola?
>
> I shed a tear and fold the evening 'paper
> With his name in black borders,
> A small ad, a keepsake,
>
> Paid for with his parents' hearts.
>
> No, I shall not walk the line!
> I shall not do what they dictate.
> A life like that of others
>
> Can never be mine!

Louis fired two shots at a collaborationist police commander, E. J. Woerts, without causing serious injury. The SD's informer, V-Mann De Wilde, handed over Louis' address and he was arrested the same day.

* * *

De Wilde approached Kees Dutilh, CS-6's observer on the North Holland coast who had taken Pim and the Boissevain brothers to photograph the German radar. He told Kees he was working for the British, that he had just arrived from London and that he had a secure transmitter with a direct connection to Baker Street. Packs of English cigarettes and detailed stories about his flat in Marylebone seemed proof that De Wilde's offer was genuine. When Dutilh took him to meet his colleagues the SD was waiting to arrest them.

CS-6 operatives were being rounded up; no one was safe. But those who survived pressed on. Folkert Posthuma, a minister in the Mussert government who had supported the Nazis' repressions, was on the group's assassination list and Jan Verleun volunteered to do it. He cycled to Posthuma's country cottage on Schuttestraat in Vorden, leaned his bike against the telegraph pole and cut the wires. Posthuma was in the conservatory and saw Verleun approaching through the garden. He picked up the phone to call for help, but the line was dead. Verleun fired twice through the conservatory window and Posthuma collapsed.

Verleun rode off towards Ruurlo, threw away his revolver at Zieverink's farm and remained at liberty when his victim was buried ten days later.

Funeral of Folkert Posthuma, 1943

* * *

The arrests had begun with the rank and file, but CS-6's leaders were not immune. Joseph Schreieder ordered his informant, V-Mann De Wilde, to establish their whereabouts and sent the Sicherheitspolizei to seize them. Mies Boissevain described her family's capture.

> My family and I were arrested in our home on Corelli Street by an SD detachment under the command of Willem Mollis. My sons were the leaders of the illegal group CS-6 and the women of the house were involved in the distribution of false identity cards. Jan Karel and Frans were at home when the SD came and they were taken straight into custody, but my other son, Gideon, was out. I learned later, when I was already in captivity, that he was arrested that same day and that their cousin Louis was also seized. My husband Jan and the boys were taken to the Weteringschans Prison and the women to the detention centre on Amstelveenseweg, where we were held for two months. After that, my husband and I were transferred to Camp Vught, where we spent almost a year. I was then taken to Ravensbrück and my husband to Buchenwald.
>
> I learned that the SD discovered the bomb-making equipment in the Corelli Street basement and that they hid in my home for three weeks after we were taken away, waiting for other CS-6 members to arrive, who were then also arrested.

Mies and her husband Jan 'Canada' were reunited for the first time following their arrest when they arrived at Camp Vught. They were informed that their sons, Jan Karel and Gideon, as well as their nephew Louis, had been executed. Jan Canada was able to send a letter by underground courier to their daughter Annemie, who was hiding with family friends.

Please deliver to:

Miss A.M. Boissevain, 14 Hacquartstraat, Amsterdam (South)

Dear Annemie,

I just spoke to Mum. It wasn't easy to get to see her, but people helped out. She is being brave. I have managed to get her a job as physio nurse in the prison hospital.

Frans is also with us here and it's much easier for me to see him. Every evening he stands waiting by the fence with his shaven head, looking like a hungry seal, and I give him some bread whenever I have any. I am trying to get him transferred to my barracks, but quarantine rules are making it tricky.

I am still using the little box you gave me with your special message, 'Hi Daddy, Love and kisses from your Annemie,' so I get your kisses every morning, my darling, and every evening.

Now, the news. They hadn't told Mum anything in Amsterdam, so she only heard those terrible things when we were on the train here to Vught. Frans told us the whole story. He was kept with his brothers in Weteringschans and they allowed them to say goodbye to each other. They let them have five minutes together, but they kept them under guard and told them they could only speak in German. Janka said to Frans, 'Up to now you were the youngest son, but now you're the oldest. It's your job to look after Mum.'

Janka faced his death with open eyes. That's what I heard from the man who shared a cell with him and from another who shared a cell with Gideon. Both of the men agreed about the way your brothers behaved. They died with dignity. And they died for a cause.

There was no trial. There was a preliminary interrogation (I can imagine how Gideon took them on with his sharp tongue, telling them things that we would never have dared), then an officer arrived from Berlin who read the transcripts and took the decision on his own about who should be executed. At first there were 20 death sentences, but right on the morning of the executions they sent one man back – the man who had shared Gideon's cell and was already standing in the line-up. The other 19 were taken away and shot on the dunes at Overveen.

Mum is being very brave. This morning she led her fellow prisoners in a fitness session. She will cope better here in the prison camp than she did in jail. She is very pale, but strong in spirit. These last two months have not broken her. Her hair is much greyer. She gets lots of support from the sympathy and friendship of her fellow prisoners, as I do, too.

Now, Annemie, your brother Frans would be very grateful for a pair of warm socks. Do you think you could find him a pair? At the moment, he's walking barefoot in his clogs and it is hurting his feet.

I get lots of comfort from people here. Everyone helps me in their own way to overcome my devastation and grief. Yesterday, I had to crawl under the wire fence to reach Mum, and it was just like that Hans Christian Andersen fable where the maids of honour make a circle round the princess so she can kiss the swineherd.

There are many here who have also lost a son or a brother and they know what I am going through. It is a comfort that everyone understands things in the same way.

Nobody denies your brothers' heroic deaths. You know my deepest feeling? My deepest feeling is that they haven't wasted their lives. You can only truly understand someone's ideas and emotions when you really love them, and that's how it is between me and your brothers. I have to trust that God has a place for our young heroes and that we who remain can come to terms with our terrible loss.

We have rich memories, love. We have the comfort of knowing that there was never any strife or disagreement in our family. All of us wanted the same thing that Janka and Gideon wanted and I believe we will achieve it. We will benefit from their sacrifice. The freedom they died for will be ours; I am as sure of that as I can be.

Be careful, my darlings. Your mum and your dad and your brother will be with you again. Have courage, my love.

Love and hugs from,
Your Dad

17

THE RESISTANCE BETRAYED

The full story of what happened in the Weteringschans prison in the two months that the CS-6 men were held there emerged after the war. Joseph Schreieder's V-Mann De Wilde had done a good job of betraying the group: scores of CS-6 operatives were imprisoned and tortured. Beatings were administered, bones broken, electric shocks inflicted, and intestines ruptured by water pumped into prisoners' rectums. The supposed aim was the extraction of information about CS-6 fighters still at large, but much of it was sadism.

Prisoners who survived would later identify their torturers and the officials who took part in their sham trials, which lasted many hours and ended with the inevitable verdicts of death.

They confirmed Jan Canada's belief that his sons had died bravely and that they had wanted their parents to know it. On the wall of his cell, Jan Karel had scratched the family's motto, adopted during the Boissevains' flight from persecution in seventeenth-century France. *'Ni regret du passé, ni peur de l'avenir'* – No regret for the past, no fear of the future.

* * *

It took several days for the trial and execution of the CS-6 fighters to be reported in the press. The German censors had been considering how to present the welcome news that one of the most powerful Resistance organisations had been liquidated, without giving clues to the person or persons who betrayed it. When the Reichskommissariat gave the go-ahead, newspapers across the Netherlands carried identical, carefully worded accounts, all with the same details and all with the same inconsistencies. Most of CS-6's actions were listed, but some were attributed to operatives who had not been involved in them. The men in the dock, knowing they would die, had taken upon themselves the deeds of comrades still at large.

Leo Frijda, for instance, appears to have accepted responsibility for killing General Seyffardt, together with the already dead Gerrit Kastein, thus protecting Jan Verleun, who remained at liberty. Also notable is the prominence given to CS-6's Jewish and communist members. The Jewish Hans Katan is named as the group's prime leader, along with the communist Kastein, while CS-6's actual founders, the Christian and formerly NSB-inclined Boissevains, are accorded less attention.

De moordenaars van luit.-generaal Seyffardt en dr. Posthuma veroordeeld

Studenten en communisten pleegden moorden, en aanslagen op spoorwegen en gebouwen.

Murderers of General Seyffardt and Dr. Posthuma convicted: students and communists committed murder, attacked railways and buildings

By order of the Police Court of Amsterdam, under the provisions of the decree of 9 January 1943, 'On the Protection of Public Order', the death sentence has been imposed on 19 Dutch members of a terrorist organisation, who murdered prominent members of society and attacked railway lines and installations, thereby inflicting harm on the German occupation authorities. The members of the terror group are nationalists and Jews, under the command of the Communist Party of the Netherlands, who conspired together to commit acts of violence and were supplied with weapons and explosives by the agents of foreign powers.

The court found that the group was led by the communist Dr Gerrit Kastein and by the half-Jew medical student Hans Katan. The half-Jew Katan gave the order to murder General Hendrick Seyffardt, commander of the Dutch Volunteer SS Legion, an act that was carried out by the full-Jew Leo Frijda and the communist Kastein on 5 February 1943. The fatal shot was fired by the communist Kastein, who was also guilty of the murder of the Minister of Public Information, Hermann Reydon, on 9 February 1943. When he was subsequently arrested, the communist Kastein ended his own life by committing suicide.

The half-Jew Hans Katan additionally conspired with the full-Jew Leo Frijda to murder the Dutch citizen Van Blom in Amsterdam on 25 June 1943; to assassinate the former Minister of Agriculture Dr Posthuma in Hengelo; the Minister of Public Information, Hermann Reydon; the police lieutenant Postman; the bicycle dealer Hoff; the

Lieutenant Commander of Police, Pieter Kaay; the dentist De Jonge-Cohen; as well as the attempted murder of the Dutch policeman Blonk and his wife, while he further ordered a series of other murders that did not succeed. The half-Jew Hans Katan was, in addition, the instigator of all the sabotage attacks and bombings carried out by members of the terrorist organisation, personally taking part in some of them. For these crimes, he was sentenced to death.

The fully Jewish medical student Leo Frijda, a founder member of the terrorist organisation, was found guilty of taking part in the murder of General Seyffardt, the Dutch citizen Blom, and the attack on the bicycle dealer Hoff, personally firing the fatal shot. Together with Katan, Frijda took part in sabotage attacks and bombings against railway lines and installations, as well as an arson operation against a cinema in The Hague. For these crimes, he was sentenced to death.

The student Sape Kuiper was found guilty of shooting dead the Dutch dentist De Jonge-Cohen in his consulting room and of firing two shots that injured his wife. Kuiper's accomplice was the student Henri Geul, who was also equipped with a weapon. Geul had recently joined the terrorist organisation and had declared himself ready to take part in all manner of terrorist activity. In the attack on the policeman Blonk and his wife, Sape Kuiper had as his accomplice the student Johannes Kalshoven, who had equally declared himself ready to take part in terrorist activity. Kalshoven fired the shots against Blonk, while Kuiper fired several shots, injuring the wife who had come to her husband's aid, as well as one shot that hit Blonk himself. Both victims were severely wounded. Kuiper and the other members of the terrorist organisation received their orders from hostile forces in England, together with equipment and financial rewards for their illegal deeds.

Kuiper moreover took part in the attack on the bicycle

dealer Hoff and in the arson attack on the Rembrandt Theatre in Amsterdam, during which he placed inflammable devices in the cut-open fabric of the seats. It proved impossible to extinguish the incendiary devices and the cinema burned down. It was later discovered that in the basement of a house in Amsterdam, members of the terrorist organisation, including Kuiper and the Jew Frijda and others, had been preparing and building bombs, arson devices and other means of sabotage that were recovered by the occupation authorities. For these crimes, Kuiper, Geul and Kalshoven were sentenced to death.

Jan Karel Boissevain, a trained engineer, was responsible for the manufacturing of explosives and other incendiary devices in the basement of the abovementioned Amsterdam house. He was also involved in receiving sabotage materials from the agents of foreign powers. In May 1943, Jan Karel Boissevain and others attacked a German passenger train by the application of explosives. Together with other unknown persons, he also attempted to blow up a train carrying German troops, but this failed. A third attempt was successful and the explosives manufactured by Jan Karel Boissevain were used in other deadly attacks. For these crimes, he was sentenced to death.

Gideon Boissevain, brother of Jan Karel Boissevain and a clerk by profession, was declared to be a founding member of the terror organisation, involved moreover in the printing and distribution of false identification documents for Jews and for Dutch citizens living in illegal conditions. Gideon Boissevain and others were involved in sabotaging radio sets that were handed in to the occupying authorities by the implantation of explosive charges that would ignite and burn down the buildings in which the radios were being stored.

Gideon Boissevain and his accomplice Maarten van

Gilse were guilty of providing explosives for two sabotage attempts on railway lines. And Gideon Boissevain conspired with other members of the terror organisation to carry out the murder of an unnamed police officer. He and others were involved in robberies to secure illegal funds for the terrorist organisation, including raids on the banker Lokeren-Campagne in Blaricum, the estate agent Honing in Soest, the house of a woman in Laren and a villa in Lage Vuursche. In three of these cases, they secured access to the properties by claiming to be members of the German Sicherheitspolizei. Gideon Boissevain was also involved in burning down a German Wehrmacht warehouse, the firebombing of an employment exchange in Amsterdam and the notorious raid on the Amsterdam Population Registry of 27 March 1943. For these crimes, Gideon Boissevain and Maarten van Gilse were sentenced to death.

The court sentenced the office worker Anton Koreman to death for the offence of harbouring a weapon that had been used in the raid on the Population Registry of 27 March 1943, although he did not personally take part in the attack. Viktor van Swieten, a mechanic, received the death sentence for the offence of possessing illegal weapons.

The chain of command and ideological instruction from the Communist Party of the Netherlands was ensured by 32-year-old Petrus Pooters. Pooters was a longstanding member of the Communist Party, having been active in communist agitation since his youth, filling various positions in the party command structure. After the judicial dissolution of the CPN, Pooters took it on himself to forge links between communist elements, nationalist groupings and active terror cells, making concerted attempts to recruit students to these secret illegal organisations. For these crimes, he was sentenced to death.

The case against various female members and other

arrested accomplices of the terrorist organisation will be heard separately.

The full list of the executed CS-6 men was carried in official publications and in the underground newspapers. Some of their jail photographs, taken in the final days of their life, appeared. Their faces showed signs of beatings, but also defiance, in the knowledge that this would be the last image by which the world would remember them.

     Gideon Boissevain   *Jan Karel Boissevain*

     Johan Roemer   *PAM Pooters*

* * *

Leo Frijda had written a farewell letter in which he sent his love to his parents, his sister Jetteke and brother Nico.

In a few moments, I shall be put to death. You will read about it in the press. I don't have time to write all the words that I would like to send you, but I want to assure you that I shall die without fear. Nico will remember my poem 'Goya' that was published in 1941. Let him read it to you. It will say a lot.

I am dying not for some abstract ideal, but for myself: I fought because I had to, because that was the meaning that my life was meant to have. The fight was lonely, but it was a loneliness that I chose.

I thank Father and Mother. You gave me my life and my life has given me a lot. I know even as I write these lines that I did not live for nothing. Please do not be sad.

Leo

The poem Frijda mentioned was inspired by Francisco Goya's painting *The Execution of the Third of May 1808*, depicting a firing squad of Napoleonic troops shooting five Spanish rebels.

Don't speak.
They did not speak.
Maybe just a name, whispered,
As their chests awaited
The cold-blooded bullets;
A brief moment of silence,
Then music and another Disgrace for eternity.
Don't speak.
Let us go now.
I have said the words
And made the promise.

His fellow poets understood the hidden triumph in Leo's sacrifice: by convincing his interrogators that it was he who shot Hendrik Seyffardt and Folkert Posthuma, he had deflected the blame from his friend, Jan Verleun. Yge Foppema, a member of Leo's former *Lichting* circle, wrote the secret into his poem 'The Ballad of Leo Frijda'.

> He knew the slanderers
> Would smear him when he was gone.
> The bile of those who betray the people
> Is sour; but sweet is his spirit, his heart, his life.
> You who read these words, who share his faith,
> Whose soul is pure, whose heart pounds at his name,
> Say it now: Leo was one of ours, Leo was us!
> On our soil he poured his blood;
> For our freedom he was quick to die;
> For his comrade, quick to lie.

* * *

Jan Bonekamp and Hannie Schaft discussed the betrayal of the CS-6 group and the execution of so many of its members. Hannie was concerned that her own introduction to the Resistance had been through Gerrit Kastein; might there not be some record of her brief involvement with CS-6 that the Germans' mole inside the group could have had access to? But Jan laughed. 'Don't worry,' he said. 'You and I are immortal! We're just going to keep on going until we kill the lot of them.'

At the request of Jan Brasser, Bonekamp had been shadowing a Zaandam police captain, Willem Ragut, who had been active in rounding up Jews and Resistance fighters. Brasser had warned him that Ragut was heavily armed – in a previous assassination attempt, he had gunned down his assailants – but Bonekamp was unperturbed.

Willem Ragut

He took Hannie to stake out Ragut's home at 77 Westzijde and they rode behind him as he cycled the short distance to police headquarters on Vinkenstraat. On Botenmakersstraat, Hannie overtook the target and was preparing to fire, when a bomb from an RAF Lancaster landed on the neighbouring freight depot. Ragut fell to the ground and seemed to have been wounded, so Jan dismounted to give him the *coup de grâce*. In fact, Hannie's shot had gone wide; Ragut had been blown over by the blast from the bomb but was unhurt. There was an exchange of fire in which the two men shot each other several times. Ragut would die from his injuries, but Jan Bonekamp was also hit. He had a wound to his stomach that made it hard for him to run. He stumbled down an alleyway next to a florist's shop and found sanctuary in the house of Naatje Unk, whom he asked to call a doctor. Mrs Unk sent her daughter to the next-door neighbour, Johan Schipper, who had a telephone; but instead of ringing the hospital, Schipper rang the police. When Captain Jan van der Schaaf of the Zaandam force arrived, he found Bonekamp lying in the kitchen.

Mrs Unk told me that the subject had burst into their house and fallen to the floor. He gave her a pistol and a wallet and told her to make them disappear, but she kept the said items and I duly confiscated them. Bonekamp appeared badly injured. Blood was coming from his stomach and his mouth and he was crying for help. I stood guard until Sergeant Hendrikse arrived and between us we transported the wounded man to the station, where we put him in cell number 2. Our doctor, Willem Levend, examined the prisoner, who asked him, 'Am I going to die?' Dr Levend told him the wound was bad, but he would be taken straight to hospital, and Bonekamp replied, 'All right, then. Send everyone my best.'

An SD detachment arrived to take Jan to the Luftwaffe Clinic in Amsterdam. It was evident that his wound was fatal, but the SD commander ordered the doctors to administer stimulants to keep him alive until he could be interrogated.

Hannie, who had cycled away after discharging her pistol, as they had agreed, sought refuge in the Wagenweg studio of the sculptor Mari Andriessen, a Resistance safe house where Truus Oversteegen was also staying. Truus found her in tears, full of remorse that she had abandoned her partner and determined to go back and rescue him. Truus calmed her down. She asked her about her feelings for Bonekamp and Hannie said, 'I love him.'

The next morning, the two women cycled to the hospital and waited by the entrance. According to Truus, they witnessed Bonekamp being carried on a stretcher to the operating theatre and Hannie was able to whisper to him, 'Oh, Jan ... oh, Jan,' but there was no chance of mounting a rescue. On their return to Wagenweg Hannie collapsed.

18

TRAITORS UNMASKED

Adrianus Roest had found something. He had been sorting through the sheet music in the organ loft at St Boniface's and had come across an envelope slipped between the pages of his Bach chorales. 'Have a look,' Adrianus said, handing it to Pim and Anna-Maria. 'It was tucked into BWV 622, *O Mensch, bewein dein Sünde groß*, which I think is a pretty clear clue to who left it . . .'

The first page was the text of a poem. Anna-Maria recognised it as the work of Hendrik Marsman, who had drowned trying to escape to England in the first months of the war.

> The evening descends; a sinking ship,
> the keel strikes a blind cliff.
>
> O, passion
> of this cold decay, in cool night,
> in cool moon,
>
> 'And thou, who once this life did praise, loud of voice
> sure of throat,

is then the shining of your word
and promise forever lost?'

I've learned in death
the soul shall rise life-sized,

or descend in shadow;
then all the world is thin delusion.

The man said,
'I am tired now;
my enemy, leave me be, I shall resist no more.'

But to the priest who says,
Absolvo te,
he rebels, dashes the cross from his lips and cries:

'Away! do not take from me the last thing I possess.
My sins are mine and all
my sins go with me to my grave!'

Attached to the poem was a copy of a personnel file stamped, 'Highly classified'. Anna-Maria opened it. One look at the photograph told her whose it was.

* * *

Jan Bonekamp surprised the doctors. He had an inner strength, a physical determination that kept death at bay. They operated on his wounds and flushed his veins with morphine. The SD harangued him, demanding information, but Jan refused. When they saw him weakening, they tried another approach. A kindly Dutch nurse leaned over him and said, 'You will die,

my dear, but I can take a message to the person you love.' Jan
thanked her and gave her Hannie's address.

* * *

Adrianus said he was positive the documents had been left by
Ruud Wilders, almost certainly on his way to deliver the origi-
nals to Uncle Anton. The markings on the personnel file showed
it was from the office of Joseph Schreieder and while the photo
was an old one, the face was unmistakeable.

'My God!' Hans Kreisel said when they handed him the file.
'Wilders was taking evidence of the traitor ... to the traitor!'

* * *

The SD surrounded the house at 60 Van Dortstraat. Hanns
Rauter had warned them to expect armed resistance, but they
found only a middle-aged couple. Pieter and Aafje Schaft were
not surprised to be raided by the Germans – they knew Hannie
was on the wanted list – but they were able to say in all honesty
that they had no idea where she was. The SD man in charge of
the operation, Emil Rühl, told them they were under arrest; they
would be held as hostages until their daughter gave herself up.

* * *

'No wonder they had Wilders killed,' Kreisel said. 'This file is a complete record of Schreieder's dealings with his V-Mann "De Wilde" – from the betrayal of Brother Klingen, right up to the entrapment of poor Kees Dutilh. And by far the thickest dossier is about us, CS-6! It's got chapter and verse on the way De Wilde betrayed Gerrit and Willem and Sape and Leo and all the others. And right here, almost the final page, someone has forgotten to delete the guy's real name. V-Mann De Wilde, Uncle Anton, is *Anton van der Waals . . .'*

* * *

Hannie was exhausted, close to a breakdown. Bonekamp's death and the arrest of her parents had brought on a depression so deep that she was incapable of making decisions. The Resistance moved her to stay with Lien and Harm Elsinga on Buitenrustlaan in Haarlem, where Lien found her taciturn and withdrawn. For days Hannie did not leave her room; then she said she would have to go to her parents' house to get fresh clothes and, despite Lien's misgivings, she went. The house was locked so Hannie climbed in through a window. A neighbour who spotted her told her the NSB was keeping watch and she should not come back. With the Elsingas' help she got her distinctive red hair dyed black. Make-up and a pair of thick-lensed glasses transformed her from a beauty to a frump.

* * *

Schreieder's dossier revealed the extent of Anton van der Waals's treachery. In addition to his betrayal of CS-6 and other groups, he had been a key player in the Germans' infiltration of radio communications between the Resistance and London, in a sting operation led by Schreieder, codenamed *Englandspiel* – the England Game.

PERSONNEL: CLASSIFIED

V-Mann de Wilde, d.o.b. 11 October 1912, Rotterdam

Height 1.79m; thin; longish face; pointed chin; dark brown hair (possibly dyed), sometimes combed straight back, sometimes parted; thin nose, with small growth on bridge; small brown eyes, prominent ears, cleanshaven; when walking slowly, inclines his head to the right; when walking fast, takes long strides and inclines his head backwards. A good technician and experienced wireless operator, but also an adventurer. Chief weaknesses are money and women. Inability to separate work from pleasure and work from profit has led to friction with the Department.

Aliases: De Wilde, Kranendonk, Van Lijnden, Uncle Anton. Mother's address: 102 Rijksstraatweg, Wassenaar.

Als zeer belangrijk kan ik in het spionnageverhaal opgeven, een per-
soon, die onder verschillende schuilnamen op allerlei gebied tegen goede be-
taling activiteit aan de dag legde. Hij is mij bekend onder de naam Kranendonk. Hij is afkomstig uit Rotterdam en hij zou voor de oorlog voor de Inlich-
tingendienst van de Rotterdamsche politie als spion onder de communisten
Linker Maasoever hebben gewerkt en als zoodanig good werk hebben gedaan.
Kranendonk werd betaald door de SS Sturmführer Schneider, voor wien Slagter
en Poos toen in hoofdzaak werkzaam waren. Het zijn werken heeft Kranendonk
zooveel geld verdiend, dat hij te Den Haag aan de Staten of Stadhouderslaan
eenige huizen kan koopen. Eenige malen heeft hij een premie van fl.10.000.-
ontvangen, welke gesteld was op het hoofd van de(n) dader(s) van een of an-
dere terroristischen daad. Op zijn werk kom ik later terug.

2.2.iii Operational history

First contact with Department end 1940 or beginning 1941. De Wilde attends office of Abteilung IV and provides intelligence leading to arrest of Dutch assassin of German soldier in Leiden. At conclusion of meeting, De Wilde is referred to SS-Sturmführer Schreieder, who from this date takes responsibility for directing his activities.

3.1.iv List of cases operated by De Wilde

'Brother Joseph', of monastery in Heemstede, active member of illegal resistance. De Wilde responsible for this man's arrest.

Group of spies operating from inn at Rijswijkse Plein, The Hague. De Wilde responsible for six arrests.

Englandspiel operation: De Wilde makes contact with agent Jonkheer de Jonge, sent from London to operate secret wireless transmissions on behalf of illegal resistance. Jonkheer De Jonge and accomplice Leendert Pot subsequently arrested in Rotterdam.

Englandspiel operation: wireless operators Radema and Emmer sent by London and arrested as result of De Wilde gaining their confidence.

De Wilde put on the trail of wireless operators Jordaan and Kloos, sent by London and arrested in Baarn following De Wilde's infiltration of their network.

De Wilde establishes contact with Ordedienst resistance group led by agent Ramon. Ten arrests made as result of De

Wilde's work. Information extracted from arrestees leads to capture of OD leader, General Roel.

Englandspiel operation: De Wilde intercepts two operators sent from London and gains their confidence. Offers to deliver their transmitter to contact in Amsterdam and uncovers illegal group including journalist Van Looy, industrialist Van Tijen, socialist (SDAP) activist Koos Vorrink. These and thirty others arrested as result of De Wilde's work.

Sabotage group of shipbuilding engineers who blew up German minesweeper at Rotterdam infiltrated by De Wilde. Group members arrested and plot to blow up three other minesweepers thwarted.

Englandspiel operation: De Wilde infiltrates 'Wim' Service transmitters. Engineer Juten and other operators arrested.

Several wireless operators entrapped by De Wilde persuaded to work for German authorities; others forced to transmit false messages, with result that British plans to land further agents in Holland are known in advance.

When female agent Beatrix (Terwindt) lands, she is arrested and addresses of her contacts uncovered. De Wilde takes her message and documents to owner of Bally shoe store in The Hague, who is arrested.

De Wilde present at parachute landing of George Jambroes and radio operator Tom Navis. De Wilde leads them and reception personnel to house in Ede, where SD waiting to arrest them. This and other operations enable SD to seize large quantity of airdropped agents and supplies.

Kees Dutilh, student acting as lookout for illegal resistance group, arrested as result of De Wilde's contact with him. Other operatives also arrested.

CS-6:

De Wilde's infiltration of CS-6 resistance group is his greatest operational success. See separate file (attached).

* * *

Truus Oversteegen was shocked by the difference in Hannie. She thought she looked 'thin and ugly now, with dull black hair and a pale, tired face'.

This wasn't the Hannie I had known, but a completely different one. We all knew what the reason was, but none of us could bring ourselves to talk about Jan and the loss she had suffered. Hannie said she was ready to start working again, so we went to see Frans [van der Wiel] to ask what needed to be done. But Hannie said she wanted to do the most dangerous job possible; she wanted something suicidal in the risk it involved. When we came out, I glanced at her and I saw a face I didn't recognise, the hard, stubborn face of the unknown Hannie. I yelled at her, 'Stop! Come on, here's my gun – you take it and put an end to all this right now!' Hannie took the gun and stood there in the street looking lost. I said to her, more quietly, 'We're partisans, Han, and partisans can't let themselves be suicidal. At the very least, they have to think about their comrades and the responsibility they have to their friends.' 'Oh, goddammit!' Hannie said, throwing down my gun and cycling away at high speed. I waited, then cycled after her. In the Haarlemmerhout Park with the leaves falling off the trees, we sat on a bench labelled 'Forbidden to Jews' and hugged each other and sobbed.

* * *

Jan Verleun came. Gerrit van der Veen and Frieda Belinfante were in hiding – since the raid on the Population Registry, Frieda had been living disguised as a man – but they were also consulted, as were Ernst Klijzing, Kas de Graaf, Bob Celosse and the other surviving CS-6 members. All of them agreed that Uncle Anton must be eliminated. Hans Kreisel was delegated to tell King Kong.

'Yes,' said the voice on the line. 'I see. Just one note of caution: the Germans have been known to use ruses like this to frame innocent people. I suggest you call Anton to a meeting. You can confront him and see what his reaction is. Be sure to have armed backup.'

* * *

When Hannie said she was thinking of giving herself up in the hope of saving her parents, Truus shook her head. She would have to shoot her before she let that happen – having Hannie in the hands of the Gestapo would be too big a risk for everyone. Instead, she said, they should make themselves useful. Truus brought clothes and hats from her parents' wardrobes and the two of them spent an afternoon disguising themselves. Truus laughed as they looked in the mirror, but Hannie barely smiled. Once, she had wanted to die beautiful. Now she didn't care.

Truus Oversteegen and Hannie Schaft

In their new guises of delivery boy and dowdy housewife, Truus and Hannie shot the police inspector Willem Zirkzee, the SD informant Gerdo Bakker, the traitorous hairdresser Ko Langendijk and the French collaborator Jeanne Sieval, all within a fortnight.

* * *

He read the warning note that had been left for him and struggled to take in what it meant. He had led a charmed life for so long: throughout all the operations he had undertaken, all the infiltrations he had carried off, all the confidences gained and lives betrayed, the lying, the deceit and murder, thoughts of personal danger had barely entered his head. Like all confidence tricksters, supreme self-belief was Anton van der Waals's stock in trade. But suddenly, the note was there and its message was clear – imminent danger, take action.

* * *

Truus and Hannie's shooting spree had consequences. A week after the assassination of Willem Zirkzee, two covered lorries drove up to the edge of Haarlemmerhout Park, less than a mile from the Wagenweg safe house where his killers were hiding, and fifteen young men in handcuffs were pushed out. Because the SS lieutenant in charge insisted on making passers-by stand and watch, eyewitness accounts have survived. Eight of the Todeskandidaten were lined up and shot by soldiers with machine guns. One man did not die, so the lieutenant called for another burst of fire before ordering the remaining seven to take their place in front of the guns.

In accordance with Eberhardt Schöngarth's Order on the Fight against Terrorism and Sabotage, the fifteen bodies were left to lie where they fell. In an act of great courage, members of the Resistance covered them with Dutch flags.

* * *

Hans Kreisel did what King Kong suggested. He invited Anton van der Waals to a meeting on the western edge of Rembrandtplein where the artist's statue had stood for a hundred years before his Jewish connections made it necessary to remove it. Kreisel let Anton know that the meeting was routine and that they could adjourn afterwards for a beer at De Kroon.

But Anton did not come. Kreisel waited until nightfall, then called off the snipers.

* * *

There was no let up from Truus and Hannie. Frans van der Wiel asked them to deal with three Haarlem police officers, Harm Smit, Fake Krist and Franciscus Willemse, all of whom were known to be helping the Germans. It was decided that the women would each work with a male partner, in order to pose as lovers while they waited outside the victim's house, and Truus got the first assignment. She and Jan Heusdens stood holding hands on the bridge over the Spaarne River until Smit appeared at his front door, then pedalled after him as he cycled to work. Truus took two shots, hitting him with both. Heusdens administered the *coup de grâce*.

Fake Krist was a harder target. He beat off the first attempt against him and came close to shooting one of his assailants, nineteen-year-old Henk de Ronde. When De Ronde returned two weeks later Krist was lying in wait to arrest him. As he was being transferred to Gestapo headquarters on Euterpestraat, he tried to escape and was shot dead. 'Such devastating news,' Truus wrote. 'Henk was just a boy, who wanted to be brave because his father was a hero. He was desperate to show his dad that he was a man, too – and now he is gone.'

* * *

The no-show confirmed what they already knew: Anton van der Waals was a traitor who had gained the confidence of the CS-6 leadership in order to betray them. But behind that certainty was a more terrifying uncertainty.

'Anton was the mole,' Hans Kreisel said. 'And all the time we spent asking him to help us track down the mole played into his hands. But who the hell tipped him off that we had seen through him? Who was it who warned him not to come to the meeting on Rembrandtplein?'

* * *

In the weeks after Henk de Ronde's death, Truus and Hannie kept watch on Fake Krist's movements. He had a bodyguard with him now, but the women were bent on revenge. They caught up with him near St Bavo's Church and followed him to the bridge at Westergracht. They were about to fire when Krist toppled from his bicycle and fell to the ground: another Resistance group had shot him from the upper storey of an adjacent building. Within minutes the area was surrounded by police who ordered people out of the eight closest houses and burned them down.

Assassination of Fake Krist

* * *

Anton van der Waals disappeared. Hans Kreisel asked King Kong for help and King Kong alerted the Resistance Council, but weeks went by without any sign of him. There were other names in the dossier obtained by Ruud Wilders, though, including that of the intermediary Schreieder had used to run his agents in the field. Herbert Oehlschlägel had been Van der Waals's point man, passing on the information that allowed the SD to arrest CS-6's operatives and personally taking part in their interrogation. The dossier suggested that he had been involved in the torture of Irma Seelig, the Jewish girlfriend of Leo Frijda.

On the corner of Beethovenstraat and Apollolaan, just 200 yards from CS-6's now empty Corellistraat headquarters, Oehlschlägel was intercepted by two armed men. A third man reached out from behind, pressing a chloroform-soaked rag over his face. Oehlschlägel tried to break free. His assailants hissed, 'Don't struggle – it's your friend Anton we want,' but Oehlschlägel was not for negotiating. He lashed out at the person behind him and, as he did so, was shot in the head.

Joseph Schreieder complained bitterly to Willy Lages, who consulted with Hanns Rauter before ordering the destruction of the properties adjacent to the site of Oehlschlägel's killing and the execution of twenty-nine Todeskandidaten.

Destroyed houses on Apollolaan

* * *

Hannie and Truus had dealt with two of the three policemen on their list and now they were going to deal with Franciscus Willemse. With Cor Rusman acting as her boyfriend, Hannie waited outside Willemse's house on Schoterstraat and when he appeared she shot him in the arm. She was about to shoot again, but her gun jammed and Willemse fired back, hitting her in the thigh. Cor leapt onto his bike and scooped her onto the crossbar, sprinting away before Willemse could do any more damage.

The doctor who treated her said she had been lucky: the bullet had passed through her flesh without hitting a bone or an artery. When she got back to the Elsinga house on Buitenrustlaan, there was more good news. Hannie's parents had been released.

* * *

From the moment Anna-Maria and Hans Kreisel met, when he arrived battered and injured at the Terbregge house, a bond had grown between them. They had worked together on perilous operations; but her fears for his safety had never been as acute as they were now. All the CS-6 survivors were consumed by apprehension – Anton van der Waals had been alerted to his unmasking by someone who was still at work and who remained a threat to their lives – and Kreisel was in more danger than anyone. It was he who agreed to take the stolen personnel file to *De Waarheid* and he who vouched for the threat Van der Waals posed. On the strength of his word, the paper's editors agreed to print the warning that would alert the Resistance to Anton van der Waals's treachery.

The first publication was rudimentary, little more than a grainy mugshot included in a handwritten list of potential suspects. As the certainty of Van der Waals's guilt was confirmed, the warnings became more strident, the list of his crimes more detailed.

The Resistance Council added his name to the definitive Signals Sheet, the *Signalementenblad*, whose stated aim was 'the immediate liquidation of the most dangerous traitors and the shielding of Resistance groups from betrayal'.

* * *

Hannie let herself go. She no longer cared for her appearance. Her black-dyed hair was growing out and the old flame-red returning. She wanted to go and see her parents, but Frans van der Wiel said the SD had the house under surveillance; a visit would be suicidal. Truus at times thought Hannie had a death wish and the Germans certainly wished her dead. They had found a photograph of her in Jan Bonekamp's pocket which they published in *Volk en Vaderland* with an urgent appeal for information about her whereabouts.

* * *

Three weeks after Anton van der Waals's name figured in the *Signalementenblad*, an announcement appeared in *Volk en Vaderland*.

Politieke moord te Rotterdam

10.000 GULDEN BELOONING

In de avonduren van 19 Juli 1943 — tegen 23 uur — werd in de Zestienhovensestraat in 't Noordelijk deel van Rotterdam de Nederlandsche staatsburger Anthonius van der Waals, geboren op 11 October 1912 in Rotterdam, door verscheidene schoten ernstig gewond. De gewonde is tijdens het vervoer naar het ziekenhuis aan zijn verwondingen bezweken.

De daders wisten zonder herkend te zijn te ontkomen. Op den doode werd een persoonsbewijs gevonden, uitgeschreven ten name van Antoon de Wilde. Het vermoeden bestaat, dat het slachtoffer zich soms van den naam Antoon de Wilde bediend heeft.

De bevolking wordt aangespoord om mede te werken aan het opsporingswerk. Voor ter zake dienende aanwijzingen, die leiden tot het vinden van de daders, wordt een belooning van 10.000 gulden uitgeloofd.

De leider van de Sicherheitspolizei en van de S. D.
Rotterdam
W. G. WöLK,
SS-Sturmbannführer

POLITICAL MURDER IN ROTTERDAM
10,000 GUILDERS REWARD

In the evening hours of 19 July at around 11 p.m., in Zestienhovenstraat in northern Rotterdam, the Dutch citizen Anthonius van der Waals, born 11 October 1912 in Rotterdam, was seriously wounded by several shots and succumbed to his injuries while being transported to hospital. The perpetrators made good their escape without being recognised. An identity card in the name of Anton de Wilde was found on the dead man and it is believed that the victim sometimes went by that name. A public appeal is being made for assistance in the investigation of the crime. A reward of 10,000 guilders is offered for information that leads to the arrest of the perpetrators.

Sicherheitspolizei Commander and head of the
Rotterdam SD, Sturmbannführer Wölk

* * *

Hannie Schaft had never been circumspect. Her early actions, mixing with the enemy in bars and restaurants, stealing guns from officers' jackets, entering restricted areas and seeking out intelligence from German soldiers, had grown into the reckless bravado of her operations with Jan Bonekamp. But now there was something else, an almost deliberate refusal to take precautions, a lack of concern for personal safety that spoke of deeper troubles.

The Gijzenbrug Bridge was one of the most fortified checkpoints in Haarlem. It stood at the northern entrance to the city, a strategic cross route that the Germans manned round the clock. There had recently been an incident in which Resistance fighters fleeing from a robbery had been flagged down on the bridge and opened fire, killing a Wehrmacht NCO. The Resistance men escaped but were quickly arrested and were now in jail, awaiting execution. Not content with shooting the direct participants, Hanns Rauter had announced that eight Todeskandidaten would also be selected to face the firing squad.

Hannie knew the Gijzenbrug was a danger point that should be avoided, but she chose to cross it. When the German sentry asked her to open her bag, she tipped out a revolver and several copies of De Waarheid. It was then that he noticed her red hair.

* * *

The Rotterdam Police Commissioner, Johannes Boelstra, read the newspaper report of the shooting on Zestienhovenstraat and asked his men if they had attended the crime scene. None of them had any knowledge of it. Boelstra's enquiries produced a warning from the Sicherheitspolizei commander: the matter was sensitive, Herbert Wölk wrote, and would remain under the sole jurisdiction of the SD. If the police were asked for information about the case, they should reply only that the dead man, Van der Waals, was probably an undercover agent of the occupying powers who had been unmasked and murdered by the illegal underground; the populace of Rotterdam played no part in it. Boelstra asked if this meant no reprisals were required and Wölk replied in the affirmative.

* * *

CS-6 had been badly weakened; its forgery division, the Persoonsbewijzen Centrale, had lost many of its key workers, but Gerrit van der Veen and Frieda Belinfante were alive and determined to stay in business. Before he was betrayed and executed for his part in the raid on the Population Registry, Willem Arondeus had identified another target. The Algemeene Landsdrukkerij, the State Printing Office on Fluwelen Burgwal in The Hague, was where the Germans produced the blank forms for Holland's national identity cards. Stealing enough of them would facilitate the provision of false documents for Jews and Resistance workers on the run.

Gerrit consulted his fellow forgers. Frits Boverhuis was a printer who knew the layout of the Landsdrukkerij from his official visits there and was able to draw detailed plans of the building, including the lift to the basement strongroom where the ID forms were kept.

Gerhard Badrian, a German Jew and art photographer who had fled to the Netherlands in the 1930s, volunteered to take the role of an SS officer who would demand access to the premises on the pretext of a security inspection. Shortly before the Landsdrukkerij was due to close for the weekend, Badrian marched into the front lobby in full uniform and introduced himself as SS Captain Georg Fischer, accompanied by civilian 'inspectors' Gerrit van der Veen, Frans Meijer, Cor Verbiest and Henri van Gogh. Badrian told the director he had received evidence of malpractice involving the misuse of official documents and demanded access to the strongroom to check the identity cards. The director took them downstairs where he was tied up and gagged, while the intruders bundled rolls of ID forms, in printed sheets of 10 by 20, into sacks. When they had gathered around 10,000 of them, they gave the director a choice: he could agree to cover up the theft and go home to his wife or he could cut up rough, in which case things would not end so happily. The man opted for a quiet life and the robbers made their getaway.

Gerhard Badrian

* * *

Jan Verleun was also active. When two CS-6 operatives, Marius Esman and Nico Bruinsma, were arrested following a failed bomb attack, Verleun, Ernst Klijzing and eight others stormed the Utrecht police station where the men were being held, throwing open the cells and freeing their comrades. They forced the policemen they were holding at gunpoint to take off their uniforms which they then put on, marching out of the building as a twelve- man patrol before boarding a train that took them to The Hague.

* * *

Suspicion had become endemic. Treachery and double dealing had undermined trust; few were the comrades who could be relied upon with confidence. When Hans Kreisel received the request for a meeting, he hesitated. The man said that he was the official wedding photographer at the townhall in Hilversum, he was sympathetic towards the Resistance and had potentially important information to pass on. Kreisel did not reply. Only when he had made enquiries and found that the story checked out did he agree to meet.

The photographer began by apologising. 'I might be wasting your time. But I was reading the *Signalementenblad* and I thought, well ... this could be important.'

As soon as he laid his photographs on the table Kreisel saw he was right.

* * *

The men Jan Verleun rescued were told to go into hiding: the Germans knew their identities and would be searching for them; their use to the Resistance had come to an end. Marius Esman and Nico Bruinsma both survived the war; Esman would live into his eighties and see in the twenty-first century.

Jan Verleun was not so lucky. Irma Seelig, Leo Frijda's former girlfriend who had been arrested and released by the SD, asked him to meet her in a bar on the fashionable Overtoom street in Amsterdam. When he got there the SD were waiting.

Ernst Klijzing, who had also taken part in the rescue from the Utrecht police station, was arrested as he drove his motorcycle through the centre of Alkmaar. Both men had been betrayed.

* * *

Hans Kreisel showed the wedding photos to Pim and Anna-Maria. Anton had lost weight, grown a moustache and changed his hair, but they all agreed it was him.

'The audacity is breathtaking,' Pim said. 'The man is a traitor, a murderer. His mugshot is in all the underground journals. Yet here he is in wedding photos!'

'Van der Waals is a psychopath,' Kreisel said. 'But he's smart. The woman Anton married is called Corrie den Held and her sister Kitty is Joseph Schreieder's mistress – here they both are, at the ceremony. He marries Corrie and Schreieder can't throw him to the dogs.'

'So, his death notice was fake,' Anna-Maria said. 'They're doing everything to protect Van der Waals.'

* * *

The Allied forces were advancing; the Reich was under threat. In Holland, the authorities responded by eliminating their prisoners. Jan Verleun was shot in the Waalsdorpervlakte dunes near The Hague. Ernst Klijzing was executed with thirteen others, including Frits Boverhuis, who had helped Gerrit van der Veen rob the State Printing Office. Kees Dutilh was shot in the basement of Fort Rhijnauwen in Utrecht. And in Weteringschans prison, the eight Todeskandidaten awaiting execution for the killing of the NCO on the Gijzenbrug Bridge were told to write their farewell letters. Among them was Walraven van Hall, the cousin of Jan Canada Boissevain, who had stolen millions from the Dutch National Bank to finance the Resistance. A ten-year-old boy, Jan Heerze, was on the Gijzenbrug when Wally and the others were killed.

About twenty German soldiers stopped the traffic and told us all to stand in a line. Three trucks arrived and a lot of SS men jumped out. They waited with their guns ready, until the other trucks opened their doors and a man was pushed down onto the street; then another man, and another. I couldn't see how many. The Germans made them stand together and I heard an officer shouting orders. When they started firing, I closed my eyes. The noise was horrible. They ordered us to walk past the bodies. They were lying there twisted and bloody. I counted eight of them.

With Jan Verleun and so many others gone, the leadership of CS-6 passed to Kas de Graaf and his deputy, Bob Celosse.

* * *

On the day of her arrest, Hannie Schaft was taken first to the Ripperda Cavalry Barracks on Kleverlaan in Haarlem and then to De Koepel prison. To establish her identity the guards rinsed her scalp to wash out the black dye. By the time she was handed over to Emil Rühl, the SD man who had led the hunt to track her down, she was once again *the girl with the red hair*.

Rühl took Hannie to the House of Detention on Amstelveenseweg in Amsterdam where she was subjected to intensive questioning by him and by Willy Lages. She confessed to enough of her Resistance operations to satisfy her interrogators, without implicating her comrades. Her prison photographs show her looking nervous and afraid – she is gripping her thumbs in her fingers – but apparently not physically harmed.

* * *

Anton van der Waals had been Joseph Schreieder's most important V-Mann, but they had never liked each other. Schreieder found him manipulative, more interested in lining his own pockets than furthering the Nazi cause. Van der Waals's courting of Corrie den Held struck him as a cynical manoeuvre to protect his own back now that his cover had been blown and his value as an asset compromised. At Van der Waals's insistence, Schreieder had provided him with false papers in the name of Piet van de Velde and a flat on Benoordenhoutseweg in The Hague, but the man was becoming a liability.

Corrie's brother Simon also worked as a V-Mann and he, Schreieder and Van der Waals had operated some profitable sidelines. Simon had specialised in arresting black-marketeers, whose illegal goods they would confiscate and sell on, dividing the proceeds between them. But an argument over money led to a falling out. Simon den Held had been grassed up after he offered to get an arrested man released for a bribe, and he suspected Van der Waals of being the snitch. When Schreieder called him in for questioning, Den Held alleged that Van der Waals had asked him to come to a houseboat on the Westeinderplassen lake, south of Amsterdam, where he had made him help dismember a corpse. According to Den Held, Van der Waals had murdered the man, a certain H. W. Mossinkoff, because he had threatened to turn him over to the Resistance. Mossinkoff had been chopped up, his body parts wrapped in weighted parcels and dumped in the lake.

* * *

Hans Kreisel rang King Kong to say that 'our friend' had finally been sighted and had left an address in the townhall wedding register. The address would likely turn out to be false, Hans said, but he would nonetheless like to send a visiting party with a special present. King Kong said it would be a nice gesture.

* * *

Hannie Schaft was put in a cell measuring six feet by six, with an iron bedframe, a jug of water and a barrel to use as a toilet. She was kept apart from the other inmates and forbidden to talk to the German guards. Interrogations began at midnight and lasted until sunrise. Worn down and isolated, Hannie stopped eating. Another prisoner, Ada van Rossem, heard from a warder that the Germans feared she would die. For Emil Rühl, speaking after the war, Hannie Schaft was a criminal who deserved the treatment she got.

> To us, she was a killer. She was a terrorist who shot and murdered our colleagues and friends. She had hunted us, so it was simple – we hunted her. We had a special division at Euterpestraat that specialised in combating communist subversion and she was the top of our list. We regarded her as dangerous and sadistic. She never gave any warning; she just shot without mercy. When we caught her, it was a case of *Kein Gerechtigkeit aber Vergeltung* – Retribution over justice.

* * *

Anton van der Waals was furious. He told Joseph Schreieder he had nearly been killed. When Schreieder asked him why he had been so foolish as to put his real address in the townhall wedding register, Van der Waals exploded. 'Do you think I'm an idiot? Of course it wasn't me! They asked Corrie where she lived and she just wrote it down. Someone must have scoured the records then sent a hit squad to murder us. It was lucky for me that we were tipped off and got out in time – and lucky for you, too. What would your precious Kitty think if you let her sister and brother-in-law get killed because you couldn't be bothered protecting us? What are you going to do to keep us safe?'

* * *

Truus Oversteegen did not give up on her friend. She lobbied the Resistance Council to mount a rescue and they promised to consider it, but time was running out. Despairing of help, she put on the Red Cross nurse's uniform she had worn to escort the Jewish orphans from Haarlem and set off for the jail. She told the duty officer she had brought clothes and underwear for a Dutch woman prisoner who had been wrongly arrested and whose boyfriend, a dying German soldier, was desperate to get a message to her.

Truus was shown into a waiting room. A supervisor asked her who she wished to see and she gave Hannie's name. The woman looked through the prison register and said, '*Ist nicht mehr da*' – she is no longer here.

* * *

Joseph Schreieder consulted Willy Lages and together they weighed up the situation. Anton van der Waals had been a useful asset, but he could no longer hope to operate in a country where the Resistance was circulating his description, his mugshot and his last known address. On the other hand, there was no reason to believe the man was known to the intelligence services of the enemy powers.

Ever since Schreieder's Englandspiel operation had cracked the illegal underground's radio communications with London, he suspected they had been routing messages via intermediaries in neutral Sweden. Might it be useful, he asked Lages, to send Van der Waals to Stockholm to see what contacts were active there?

* * *

Three days before Truus Oversteegen's visit to Amstelveenseweg prison, Hannie Schaft had been taken from her cell. It was daytime, not the usual midnight summons for interrogation, and Hannie sensed something was wrong. Ada van Rossem heard her scream as she was dragged down the corridor. A Dutch detective, Maarten Kuiper, and a German officer, Matthaeus Schmitz, took Hannie outside where an SD staff car with two Wehrmacht NCOs in it was waiting.

Maarten Kuiper

They drove to the dunes beyond Bloemendaal and pulled up on a remote dirt road. At his trial after the war, Maarten Kuiper gave his account of what happened.

> We got out of the car. The girl Annie van der Schaft [*Kuiper has misremembered Hannie's name*] was walking next to me and I was talking to her. Schmitz was walking behind. I suddenly heard a shot go off and the girl screamed ... It was not me, but the German who fired into the back of her head ... The shot startled me. I turned and saw [Schmitz] with his 9-millimetre pistol in his hand, pointing it at Annie van der Schaft. The girl cried out, but didn't fall. Schmitz was attempting to fire another shot, but was unable to do so. 'Damn,' Schmitz said. 'My gun is jammed.' [Interrogator's note: *It jammed because there was 7.65-millimetre ammunition loaded in a 9-millimetre weapon.*] The girl was suffering, in a lot of pain. Seeing that Schmitz's shot had been ineffective, I fired a burst from my submachine gun and she died instantaneously ... I delivered this blast of fire standing next to the girl. The suggestion that we sent the girl on ahead of us is incorrect. I have been

interrogated on this matter at least thirty times and I have never made any statement other than the one I have given you now. I have nothing more to add.

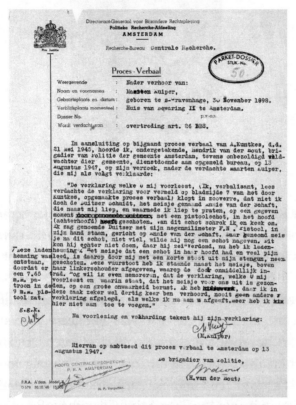

Record of Maarten Kuiper's interrogation, 1947

The four men dug a hole in the sand and threw Hannie into it. In the years that followed, as Hannie, Truus and Freddie acquired legendary status as Resistance heroines, the story of her execution was embellished. It was claimed that Hannie had mocked Schmitz's clumsy attempt to kill her, turning to him and saying, 'Even I can shoot better than that,' and that her murderers were so panicked by what they had done that they failed to bury her properly, leaving a strand of her red hair protruding from her grave. There is no evidence for either story.

* * *

Maarten Kuiper took part in another notorious operation. A
few months before he murdered Hannie Schaft, he was hunting Jews in Amsterdam as part of an SD detachment that had
received a tipoff about a family hiding at 263 Prinsengracht.
The SD men found Otto Frank, his wife and children in a secret
annexe, concealed behind a revolving bookcase. It was accepted
practice to appropriate the valuables of such criminals and
Hauptscharführer Karl Silberbauer needed a bag to carry off
the family's jewellery. He took Otto's briefcase and emptied the
documents in it onto the floor. Miep Gies, one of the people who
had been hiding the Franks, later picked them up. They were
the diary of Otto's daughter.

19

A LAST GAMBLE

Gerrit van der Veen told his daughters how much he loved them. Loekie was eleven and Gerda ten. They were used to their father being away; now he was back and was saying goodbye.

Gerrit van der Veen with Loekie and Gerda

Gerrit told his girls he had important work to do. He didn't hide that it was dangerous; he had to go away now and there was a chance he might not come back for a long time. If that were to happen, Gerrit said, they both needed to be brave; they should do all they could to look after their mother; and if they heard bad things being said about their dad, they should try very hard not to believe them.

* * *

The train that took Anne Frank and her family from Westerbork to Auschwitz was the last. The sixty-six transports before it had ferried 97,000 others to their deaths in the extermination camps; now that the Allies were closing in, Hanns Rauter was eager to declare the deportations completed. He had liquidated the Jewish Council several months earlier, a milestone that he found satisfying. Abraham Asscher and David Cohen had grown arrogant, convinced of their own indispensability; signing the order that consigned them to the mercies of Camp Westerbork ended that chapter.

Asscher would be sent from Westerbork to Bergen-Belsen and Cohen to Theresienstadt, but they and their families would survive. Controversy about their role began as soon as they returned to the Netherlands. The post-war Dutch authorities briefly arrested them on suspicion of collaboration and they were summoned to explain their behaviour to the Jewish Council of Honour. The Council concluded that they had behaved dishonourably 'in assisting the Germans ... in lending support to anti-Jewish measures such as the imposition of Jewish stars ... in the herding of Jews into Westerbork ... and in co-operating in the selection of deportees', recommending that both men should be disbarred from holding public office.

Asscher and Cohen disputed the decision, declaring that they had done their utmost to save people. The ambiguity surrounding their role saw the verdicts overturned in 1950, but not before Asscher had died two months earlier.

It didn't stop the arguments. Hans Knoop, the official historian of the Jewish Council, wrote that Asscher and Cohen had 'issued deportation notices and urged Jews to obey the summonses they received ... Because of them, the deportation of Jews in the Netherlands was done with a greater degree of efficiency than anywhere else in Europe.'

Jacob Presser was more willing to take into account the exigencies of the times. 'Among Jews,' Presser wrote in his definitive history of the Dutch holocaust, 'the spectrum of collaboration ranged from utterly corrupt elements, determined to save their own skins by deliberately and knowingly sacrificing their fellow Jews, to those who, although collaborating, tried to save as many innocent people as possible. [Asscher and Cohen] collaborated and, in so doing, found themselves in a position where they could no longer choose between good and bad, but only between two evils ... But no one has accused the two presidents of the Jewish Council of being collaborators in the strict sense of being corrupt and willing tools of the Nazis.'

Even when it became clear that 'deportation to labour camps' concealed the greatest of all possible horrors, the Jewish Council continued to hand over Dutch Jewry piece by piece, hoping to save at least some parts of it, including themselves. 'They played for time,' Presser wrote. 'Was that wrong? To answer, we must try to imagine ourselves back in those days and remember that very few people thought the war would last as long as it did ... It has been said that if the war had ended in 1942, the Jewish community would have built a monument to Asscher and Cohen as the brave and resourceful leaders by whose hands Dutch Jewry was saved.'

* * *

The important work that Gerrit van der Veen spoke about to his daughters had been necessitated by Arthur Seyss-Inquart and Hanns Rauter's decision to eliminate their prisoners. There were 140 Resistance fighters in Weteringschans prison and 70 of them, including several of Gerrit's friends, were awaiting execution. For a man normally meticulous in his forward planning, Gerrit allowed himself to be hurried into a disastrously underprepared rescue.

Gerrit van der Veen (right)

A sympathetic Dutch guard left a side door unlocked through which the rescuers were able to enter the jail, but things went wrong at once. A guard dog saw them and began to bark, alerting SD troops who ran to investigate. In the ensuing firefight Gerrit was hit twice in the back and had to be carried out by his comrades. They escaped on bicycles, with Gerrit transported on a crossbar to the house of a Resistance doctor, Julius de Clerq-Zubli. A bullet had lodged in Gerrit's spine; he was paralysed from the waist down.

* * *

Anton van der Waals sailed for Sweden on the Dutch freighter *Excelsior*, using papers issued by Joseph Schreieder that identified him as Baron Hendrik Jan van Lijnden, a minor member of the Dutch aristocracy. The ship's captain, F. J. M. 'Jos' Aben, was also an employee of Schreieder's Department IV E. In Stockholm, the two men introduced themselves to the consul of the Dutch government in exile, A. M. de Jong, claiming to be Resistance envoys with proposals for sabotage operations that needed logistical and financial support from London. De Jong took them to meet the representatives of the Dutch anti-Nazi intelligence service, W. A. Gevers-Deynoot and W. L. Lindenburg. Van der Waals told them he wanted to establish a channel of communication with MI6, because he was intending to blow up a number of ammunition depots and the deep-water lock at Maasbracht. Gevers-Deynoot was himself a member of the aristocracy and could find no mention of any van Lijndens in the peerage list, but when challenged, Van der Waals replied that the title was a cover. Gevers-Deynoot and Lindenburg told London they thought he was genuine. 'I am convinced that Baron van Lijnden's proposals are bona fide,' Lindenburg wrote. 'He is measured in conversation and does not make extravagant claims; his seriousness is unmistakable.'

Anton van der Waals spent two weeks in Sweden. He ate well, drank well and had several meetings that he did not mention in his official report. Before he and Aben sailed back to the Netherlands it was agreed they would return to Stockholm the following month, at which time they would receive the assistance they required. Van der Waals told Joseph Schreieder that the mission had been a success, but Schreieder decided that Aben alone would make the next trip. Unfortunately for Aben, London received a tip-off about his true identity; when he returned to Sweden, he was told the British wanted to talk to him in person and he was arrested when he landed at Tilbury.

* * *

Gerrit van der Veen had not lived at his family home for several months; since the raid on the Amsterdam Population Registry, he had been on the move, changing addresses frequently, reliant on the hospitality of fellow Resistance members. One of them was Suzy van Hall, the adopted niece of Walraven van Hall and a member of CS-6's Persoonsbewijzen Centrale forgery division.

Suzy van Hall

Gerrit and Suzy had become lovers. When Dr de Clerq-Zubli told him he would need a safe place in which to operate on his injuries, Gerrit asked to be taken to Suzy's flat. She owned an apartment above the De Spieghel publishing house at 856 Prinsengracht, where she had a job as an editor; she and Gerrit had been living there together. De Clerq-Zubli was able to remove one of the bullets in Gerrit's back, but the other was too close to his spinal cord: a specialist surgeon would be needed if they were to avoid the risk of permanent paralysis.

* * *

The reason Joseph Schreieder declined to send Anton van der Waals back to Sweden was that he had discovered further unsavoury details about his behaviour. Schreieder had investigated Simon den Held's story about Van der Waals murdering a man on his houseboat and found it to be true. The victim, H. W. Mossinkoff, had replied to a newspaper advertisement placed by Van der Waals for a manservant and had been taken on. But Van der Waals had a sinister motive: with his cover blown and his name in the hands of his enemies, he needed a new identity that would be unknown even to his German handlers.

Having established that Mossinkoff had valid ID papers, he shot him and stole them. The fact that Mossinkoff had previously been interned in Camp Vught on suspicion of aiding the Resistance would be particularly useful if Van der Waals needed to switch sides in the event of a Nazi defeat.

* * *

Suzy van Hall cared for her lover, tending his wounds, changing his dressings, massaging his paralysed legs. Dr de Clerq-Zubli spoke to a colleague who specialised in spinal injuries and he agreed to operate. The procedure would need to be done in a properly equipped theatre, for which King Kong enlisted the help of contacts at the nearby Prinsengracht Hospital.

The issue of the Resistance prisoners facing execution in Weteringschans remained and the veteran fighter Johannes Post decided on a second rescue attempt. This time the operation would be better planned. The sympathetic guard, an ex-SS soldier named Jan Boogaard, agreed to admit the rescuers to the Dutch section of the jail and provided a detailed plan showing the way through the central courtyard to the SD wing where their comrades were being held. An hour before their arrival, he said he would poison the guard dogs with cyanide. To ensure that Boogaard was not tempted to betray them, Post told him they would keep his mother under guard until the operation was over. If things went well, he would be given 5,000 guilders, accommodation in a safe house and a pardon from the Resistance for his activities in the SS.

Johannes Post and twelve armed fighters entered Weteringschans prison as planned, made their way to the central courtyard and were met with a hail of bullets. Some were wounded; all were arrested. At the same time, a squad of SD men led by Willy Lages arrived at Boogaard's house at 144 Kinkerstraat and seized the Resistance operatives who were guarding his mother.

* * *

Whoever betrayed Johannes Post, it was not Anton van der Waals. His career as a V-Mann for the Germans was over. With his usefulness gone, he was reduced to lobbying Schreieder for financial help. Schreieder found him temporary lodgings in Zeist, then in Oud Loosdrecht, but Van der Waals became convinced that the Resistance was staking out both locations and demanded somewhere safer. Schreieder put him and his wife into an Abwehr house in Zwolle, later moving them to the Willemspark apartment complex on Zeestraat in The Hague.

Then Van der Waals disappeared. Schreieder found the Willemspark flat empty. He sent detectives to trace its missing occupants, but without success. All Schreieder's V-Men had a number they could call if they felt themselves threatened or in danger of being captured, but Van der Waals did not call it. The possibility that he may have fallen into the hands of the illegal underground was troubling: interrogation of double agents was known to be brutal and bloody; Van der Waals was no hero and he knew too many secrets about Schreieder's operations. Another thought entered Schreieder's head: Van der Waals's trip to Sweden had introduced him to the intelligence agencies of the enemy. Could he be planning to defect?

* * *

Willy Lages wasted no time. The day after Johannes Post's unsuccessful Weteringschans raid, he interrogated the survivors of the operation in the Euterpestraat cells, found none of them willing to co-operate and issued a collective death sentence under the terms of the Schöngarth Order on Terrorism. To the seven new arrestees, he added another eight who had been in jail since the raid on the Amsterdam Population Registry and had them all transported to the dunes at Overveen. Lages oversaw the executions, but the fatal shots were administered by Johan Willem Snoek, a twenty-one-year-old member of the Dutch SS. Haunted by what he had done, Snoek would shoot himself a year later.

Johannes Post

* * *

Gerrit van der Veen waited for the operation that could save his legs. The bullet was pressing on his spine; he was paralysed, incontinent and in pain. He told Suzy she should leave him, but she wanted to stay, so she was in the Prinsengracht apartment, together with Dr de Clerq-Zubli, when the warning came from downstairs that the SS had entered the building. The De Spieghel staff tried to delay them, but the soldiers knew exactly where Gerrit was hiding and forced their way past. They reached Suzy's front door as Gerrit was pulling himself through the skylight onto the roof. In his crippled state, there was no escape.

* * *

Joseph Schreieder became convinced that Anton van der Waals was selling him out. He recalled things from the past that had troubled him then and haunted him now. At the very beginning of their relationship, Van der Waals had proposed a scheme to infiltrate an agent into British intelligence. He had approached the anti-German mayor of Rotterdam, Pieter Oud, with a warning that he was going to be arrested and an offer to help him flee to England. Van der Waals then asked Schreieder if he could accompany Oud to London and operate as a double agent. When that did not work Van der Waals tried again. Shortly before his name appeared in the illegal underground's *Signalementenblad*, he had convinced Schreieder that he should travel to Britain and tell MI6 he was a Resistance man on the run from the Germans. Schreieder had handed over 50,000 guilders to finance the operation and Van der Waals got as far as Paris before his cover was blown and it had to be called off. Van der Waals claimed the money had been stolen, but Schreieder suspected he kept it.

Schreieder tormented himself, wondering if he had missed something about his cunning V-Mann that was now about to bite him. He asked his Abwehr counterpart and Englandspiel co-conspirator, Colonel Hermann Giskes, if he had any qualms about Van der Waals's loyalty and Giskes referred him to his deputy, Gerhard Huntemann. Huntemann said that Abwehr intelligence believed Van der Waals had used his visit to Stockholm to meet the British military attaché.

Hermann Giskes and Gerhardt Huntemann, Abwehr Intelligence

* * *

The SD took Gerrit to the Weteringschans prison he had tried to raid, then moved him to Euterpestraat. Willy Lages was worried that the Resistance would attempt to rescue him and he needed time to complete his interrogation. When Gerrit refused to talk, Lages confronted him with Frans Duwaer, the printer who had helped him and Frieda Belinfante in the early days of the Persoonsbewijzen Centrale, and with Paul Guermonprez, a fellow member of the Resistance Council. None of them flinched; all were sentenced to death.

Gerrit used his farewell letter to declare his love for the three women in his life: for his wife and mother of his two daughters, for Suzy van Hall and for Guusje Rubsaam, who was pregnant with his unborn son. 'My fate counts for little in a world where millions are dying and will continue to die,' Gerrit wrote. 'I knew the risks I was taking so I have no right to complain. As a person, I regret how things are ending; but I have always put duty first. I did what I had to do. I couldn't have done otherwise.'

Gerrit van der Veen asked to be shot standing up and two of his comrades held him erect as they faced the firing squad. Frieda Belinfante fled to Switzerland with the help of her former music teacher, the renowned conductor Hermann Scherchen, then emigrated to Laguna Beach, California, where she lived to the age of ninety. Dr Julius de Clerq-Zubli was deported to the Sachsenhausen concentration camp but returned after the war. And Suzy van Hall survived Ravensbrück and Dachau, dying in 1978 with a photograph of Gerrit in her hand.

* * *

Four days before Gerrit van der Veen was shot in the coastal dunes between Haarlem and the North Sea, there was shooting on other beaches, 400 miles to the west. The news that Allied troops had landed in Normandy did not make the pages of *Volk en Vaderland*, but the majority of Dutch people heard about it. For Anna-Maria, it was a signal of hope renewed.

It was illegal to listen to the BBC. At the start of the war, people had been ordered to hand in all their radio sets, but we had two of them, so we handed one in and kept the other. If you were going to listen, you had to do it secretly; so, in the evenings we went down to the basement where the radio was wired up to a generator that was powered by someone riding a bicycle we had propped up on blocks. That's how we heard about D-Day. We heard the news and we just hugged each other. We were all crying. We listened to a message from Queen Wilhelmina, but the best thing – the thing we loved more than anything – was hearing Vera Lynn. We listened to her singing 'We'll Meet Again' and there were tears running down our faces because we had thought we would not survive – things had been so terrible that we really thought the end was coming for all of us – but then this happened and Vera Lynn was telling us, *No!* We *will* meet again! And I was crying because my brother was away fighting with the British and there had been no word from him, so we didn't know if he was alive or dead. It's not easy to explain it now, all these years later, but Vera Lynn's singing meant so much. It was so moving. She was wonderful.

20

A TRAITOR BEHIND THE TRAITOR?

The penetration of CS-6 had made the group suspect. The unmasking of Anton van der Waals had not put a stop to the betrayals. As a result, the Resistance Council became reluctant to share operational secrets and Kas de Graaf and Bob Celosse struggled to find the support they needed. Of all their Resistance Council contacts, only King Kong seemed to keep faith in them. He suggested they should travel to England and take their case directly to the British Special Operations Executive, which co-ordinated resistance activity in the occupied countries. He would provide a letter of introduction and they could report back to him personally.

De Graaf and Celosse got as far as Paris where they were picked up on suspicion of using false ID documents, but King Kong spoke to a contact and they were released. They travelled onwards via Spain and Gibraltar, from where they flew to London.

* * *

The joy of knowing that the Allies were in France was tempered by growing hardships. Already meagre rations were reduced, heating fuel was scarce and the Germans increasingly vindictive. For Holland's remaining Jews, including Marlies Friedheim, the threat of persecution remained.

> I remember in those later times when I was in hiding at Anna-Maria's, I could sometimes contact my brother Hans via a family from the place where we used to live with our parents. They were the only ones who knew where I was and also where my brother was. We couldn't write because that would have been too dangerous, but our old neighbours would sometimes take messages. We knew what the Germans had done to the Jews; we knew about it and I think many people in Holland also knew. We heard that the transports were no longer leaving from Westerbork, but that didn't stop the Germans rounding up the Jews who were left. They carried on sending people to Westerbork and the camp was full to the seams.

Anna-Maria knew what was being done to Holland's Jews. It was one of the reasons she remained active in the Resistance.

> By the winter of 1944–1945, Westerbork was less well run and people were getting out. Jews who had escaped would come wandering down the road outside the house – it was a sort of country road – going from garden to garden, from house to house. They were starving. We helped them and took them in, but you had to be careful; you couldn't feed them too much food all at once, because their hungry stomachs couldn't cope with it. I can see the poor things now. People helped them, because it was the right thing to do. The conversation was always, 'How can we do this and how can we do that?' It wasn't, 'Why should we do it?'; it just had to be done. No one spoke about the risks.

The people who came from the camps had terrible stories to tell. They wanted to share what had happened to them with someone and then I think they would never tell it again. Some of them had injuries from what the Germans had done to them – beating them and stubbing out cigarettes on their skin and so on. Luckily, we had a medic who could treat them while they were hiding with us; but some of the other stories were so terrible, I can't bear to think of them. There were young girls that the Germans had operated on – medical experiments on them, without anaesthetic.

They told me how they screamed and screamed until they lost consciousness.

* * *

Kas de Graaf and Bob Celosse were put up at Station XIV in Essex and told to wait. The Netherlands Section of Britain's Special Operations Executive (SOE) was plagued by internal conflicts and mutual suspicions that undermined much of its decision making. Its joint section heads, Seymour Bingham and Charles Blunt, were at loggerheads.

The two Dutchmen had proved their bona fides – a lengthy debrief had shown that they were indeed senior members of CS-6 – but Major Blunt was not satisfied. The problem, Blunt said, was the letter.

The thing is, the fellow writes as if we should know him. He says he is a member of the Resistance Council, but shall we really take him at his word? He knows our agents, I grant you – code names, call signs, Uncle Tom Cobley and all – so, fine, he has been working with them; but why have we never had him externally authenticated? Where has he sprung from? And as for his nom de guerre, who on earth goes round calling himself King Kong, for heaven's sake!

Major Bingham allowed himself a show of exasperation. De Graaf and Celosse were undoubtedly genuine, he said, so why worry about the paperwork? If it were left to him, Bingham would fast-track the security clearance and get them up to speed on SOE ops PDQ. When Blunt said he would like to take another look at Chive and Sprout before agreeing, Bingham exploded. 'Chive and Sprout! Good God, man, can't you just forget about Chive and Sprout!'

Major Seymour Bingham, joint chief, SOE Netherlands Section

* * *

A few months after Willem Arondeus and Gerrit van der Veen led the raid on the Amsterdam Population Registry, the Royal Air Force had tried something similar. Six Mosquitos of 613 Squadron were despatched to bomb the Villa Kleykamp on Scheveningseweg in The Hague, where the Germans kept more copies of the population's ID records. Squadron Leader Bob Bateson led the raid and one of the planes was piloted by a twenty-one-year-old Dutch Jew, Robert Cohen, who had rowed across the North Sea in 1941 to volunteer for the RAF.

We flew very low. I located the tower of the nearby Peace Palace (Vredespaleis) and started the nosedive towards the target ... We bombed from an altitude of approximately 18 metres, so lower than the Kleykamp's roof. A sentry outside threw away his rifle and ran. I myself could not see what happened, but my number two told me later that ... one bomb hit the middle of the front door and two others entered through the two large windows.

Now, with the Allied forces drawing closer, the RAF was able to respond to further requests from the Resistance. The Sicherheitsdienst headquarters on Euterpestraat was dive-bombed by twenty-four Hawker Typhoons, leaving the building so badly damaged that the SD had to move its operations to the Hotel Apollo on Apollolaan. There was a growing conviction in the population that the Germans were on the back foot.

Damage to the SD headquarters on Euterpestraat, Amsterdam

* * *

Chive and Sprout were agents – the SOE bosses had a soft spot for codenames with a bit of humour. In real life, they were Johan Ubbink and Pieter Dourlein, parachuted by the RAF into Holland a year earlier and arrested almost as soon as they landed. They had been met on arrival by a Resistance operative, whose name they never learned, but whom they described as 'large, muscular and very genial; walks with a limp'. The Resistance man had given them travel documents, which he said he had obtained from a contact in the German Dienststelle, and taken them on a train from Roosendal to Bergen-op-Zoom. In the course of the journey, a SiPo patrol had carried out a sweep of the train and all three of them were arrested. Ubbink and Dourlein were taken to prison in Camp Haaren in North Brabant; the fate of the Resistance operative was unknown.

Ubbink and Dourlein were no slouches. In the course of their interrogation, Hermann Giskes and Gerhard Huntemann boasted to them that they had successfully infiltrated all of SOE's networks in the Netherlands and consequently had V-Men in many Resistance organisations.

Realising the importance of the information, Dourlein smuggled out a message via a sympathetic Dutch guard to Pieter Jacob Six, the head of the Ordedienst Resistance group. Six passed on Dourlein's warning to Seymour Bingham, who took no action.

The two captured agents were not finished. Their cells were on the second floor of the Haaren detention centre, a former seminary that the Germans had converted for military use. The cells were locked, but a skylight over the door still contained ordinary glass, covered over with plywood. Ubbink and Dourlein squeezed through it, hid in a cupboard then managed to prise open a bathroom window. Under cover of a thunderstorm, they climbed down a rope made from bedsheets, crawled through barbed wire fences, swam across a moat and walked to Tilburg, where they sought refuge in a Catholic church. Three months later, with the help of Jean Weidner's underground escape line, they arrived in Switzerland. The Dutch military attaché in Bern agreed to send a telegram to Seymour Bingham, in which the two agents explained the extent of German infiltration of SOE's Dutch operations and warned that there must be a Nazi mole covering up for them in London. At the end of the message the attaché added his own assessment. 'From interview with agents Ubbink and Dourlein, it transpires there is strong possibility of leakage in London. Over 100 of our agents are in prison.' Bingham filed the telegram and replied that he was unable to help. When Chive and Sprout arrived in London, after two more months on the road, Bingham had them arrested.

Johan Ubbink   Pieter Dourlein

* * *

The improving course of the war was cause for rejoicing, but hope alone could not feed the people. The more the Germans felt menaced, the more they vented their anger. Food and fuel were requisitioned for the occupiers, sent to the army or transported to Germany.

When Dutch railwaymen went on strike to disrupt the Nazi war effort, the Germans took over the rail system and banned civilian deliveries. Anna-Maria had to feed not only her own family but the men and women sheltering in her attic.

The winter of 1944–1945 became known as *De Hongerwinter*, the hunger winter. We had no food, no fuel and no running water. We had to carry it upstairs in buckets. People would roam the countryside begging farmers for food that the farmers didn't have, or scouring the land for wood to burn. This was Holland and one thing we did have was tulips. People would roast them and stew them and turn them into soup. But no one could satisfy their hunger.

One day we looked out of the window and there were German soldiers with guns digging a big trench that went right through our front garden. Well, I loved my garden, so I went out and said, 'What on earth are you doing?' and the soldiers said, 'The Allies are coming. We are digging trenches all around the city; when the enemy comes, we will fight them right here in the trenches.' And of course, they cut all the water pipes, so that's why we had no water. The pipes all froze. It was hopeless.

What was worse, though, was that the Germans brought in forced labour from the concentration camps and made them dig for hours without a break. These were men who were half-starved with no proper clothing. Their situation was much harsher even than ours; they were exhausted and freezing. We went out and gave them warm ersatz coffee and whatever food we could spare. I spoke to one of the Jewish prisoners who did have an overcoat and he told me he was a dentist. In the concentration camp, he had helped a German who had very bad toothache and the German had thanked him by giving him his overcoat. There was human kindness even in those most terrible times.

* * *

Seymour Bingham went to great lengths to keep Ubbink and Dourlein quiet; after their interrogation, he took the unusual step of having them locked up in Brixton jail. When the two men escaped from Haaren, Joseph Schreieder and Hermann Giskes had sent London a wireless message purportedly from one of SOE's own operators, claiming that Chive and Sprout had been turned by the Gestapo and were double agents. Bingham adduced the message in evidence, dismissing Charles Blunt's concerns that its contents could hardly be taken at face value if the warnings of German penetration of the radio network were true.

Without telling Bingham, Blunt sent an enquiry to the Dutch Resistance Council: Could they vouch for the two men, De Graaf and Celosse, who had arrived out of the blue on SOE's doorstep? And could they please tell us who this King Kong is? The reply came via Captain Jan Somer, the head of the Bureau Inlichtingen, the Dutch Intelligence Agency in London. Somer had previously tried to tell his SOE colleagues that things were not right in the Netherlands but had been rebuffed. Now he had something specific: his contacts had heard of King Kong, Somer said, but he was not – repeat not – a member of the Resistance Council and was not empowered to speak on its behalf. As far as his contacts knew, the man's real name was Christiaan Lindemans.

* * *

Sheltering a senior Resistance figure was risky, but Hans Kreisel's presence in the Terbregge house also had benefits. In the harshest days of the Hunger Winter, there were sporadic food deliveries and when the RAF began to drop supplies, Anna-Maria was called on to help in their distribution.

They were hard times for the children; they were going hungry. I remember that winter we kept our young daughter Hanneke and the neighbourhood children amused by building a big snowman. It had coal for eyes and a black hat and a broom in its hand. They loved it; they always said, 'Good morning, Mr Snowman.' But when the snowman melted, they were sad. I said, 'Don't worry; I promise he will come back.' The RAF was starting to deliver more food and they were using the meadows at the back of our house for the drops. The plane would drop four smoke bombs – that was the signal – and then the food parcels. They had cans and sugar and big sacks of flour in them, so we could bake bread. Our job was to rush out to the meadow and collect the parcels and hide them in the house before the Germans came. We hid everything in specific places – sugar here and flour in that cupboard and so on – until the Resistance could come and take it away for distribution. During one of the drops, the air raid sirens went off and my father, who was with us, said we should go down to the cellar. But he carried on gathering up the food parcels and he was on the stairs in the hallway, when a big sack of flour came smashing through the window. It burst open and knocked him off his feet. He was completely covered in flour – he was white all over, from head to foot – and when he came down to the cellar, we all burst out laughing and suddenly I heard the voice of little Hanneke say, 'Oh look! The snowman has come back!' We laughed and laughed. Things like that put life in context.

Not everyone was as fortunate. In the Hunger Winter of 1944–45, 20,000 people died of starvation, including large numbers of children.

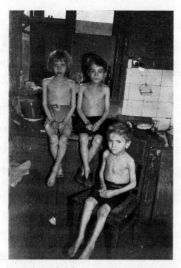

Starving children, winter 1944–45

* * *

Major Blunt knew the name rang a bell. He scoured the transcripts of the Sprout and Chive interrogations for references to traitors and immediately came across Anton van der Waals.

b)   VAN DER WAALS @ DE WILDE @ ANTON, was Haupt V-Mann of
Krimrat. SCHREIEDER of the SD, The Hague.

This man was responsible for the penetration of the Koos
VORRINK group.   In a message from London to BONI, Nr. 34 of
12.11.42, orders were given to contact a certain VENUS; the latter
was a member of the Koos VORRINK group and VAN DER WAALS, after
making this contact, was able to penetrate this organisation.
In order to inspire confidence VAN DER WAALS asked that a B.B.C.
message should be broadcast, and this was done.   This confidence
having been obtained, Koos VORRINK sent the 'VICTORY' messages
through VAN DER WAALS, and these were transmitted on the BONI link.

It is pointed out that this affair – the group being
indigenous – was handled by SCHREIEDER, and III F merely loaned
the BONI link for the purpose.

In the summer and autumn of 1943, black lists, distributed
by one of the Dutch Resistance Groups, described VAN DER WAALS
as being a notorious S.D. agent.

Van der Waals was someone Jan Somer had warned about, but Blunt was looking for another name. The record mentioned it just once: in connection with the betrayal of CS-6.

> S VI ?
>
> either GISKES nor HUNTEMANN know a great deal about this
> organisation. However, it is possible that it was penetrated
> by the Sipo, through LINDEMANS.

Blunt asked Jan Somer to find out as much as he could about Christiaan Lindemans. Somer spoke to a Resistance contact, Karst Smit, who provided a background briefing. It did not make good reading.

> Christiaan Antonius Lindemans. Early thirties, from Rotterdam; qualified car mechanic. Boxer. Known as King Kong due to large physical stature. Slight paralysis in left leg and arm because of motorcycle accident.
>
> Worked with me on the Holland–Paris escape line. Resourceful and reliable. Assisted numerous Allied airmen to flee from occupied territory. Younger brother, Henk, also working in Resistance, captured by SD. Lindemans report-edly in touch with SD and Henk subsequently released.
>
> On next operational run to Paris, agents Victor Swane, Frans van Hugenpoth, plus accompanied Canadian pilot all arrested at Hotel Montholon.

Christiaan Lindemans

* * *

Charles Blunt took the evidence to his colleague. Seymour Bingham was not moved.

'I don't think we need be overly concerned,' Bingham said. 'We all know Somer and his boys have an axe to grind against us. The fact is that De Graaf and Celosse have personally vouched for Lindemans – and Lindemans has vouched for them. We can't be forever second-guessing agents in the field.'

Blunt's anger rose. 'Don't you see?' he said. 'Our ops have been penetrated. The Abwehr are running our transmitters. If De Graaf vouches for Lindemans, it probably means De Graaf is part of the Germans' scheme, too – they all vouch for each other and we end up with a German mole right here in Baker Street!'

Bingham laughed, 'Come on, old chap. Let's not be seeing treachery where treachery doesn't exist. De Graaf and Lindemans and Celosse are just what they claim to be. And in any event, it's too late to change things: Celosse and Cnoops fly tonight.'

* * *

Bob Celosse

Seymour Bingham had sent Bob Celosse for parachute training to the SOE base at Ringway near Manchester, where he did two jumps and came through with flying colours. Bingham had given him the codename Faro and teamed him up with another agent, Tony Cnoops, codename Cricket. By the time Charles Blunt pieced together the intelligence surrounding the penetration of CS-6 and the unreliability of Christiaan Lindemans, Bingham had handed Celosse and Cnoops 50,000 guilders with orders to give the money to Lindemans, who would pass it on to CS-6.

Blunt messaged all agents in the field, 'We have reason to suspect this organisation [CS-6] may have been penetrated by the enemy' and issued 'strict orders' to avoid contact with King Kong.

But it was too late. Twenty-four hours after Celosse and Cnoops parachuted into the Wieringermeer polderland in North Holland, they rendezvoused with Christiaan Lindemans, who expressed his delight at seeing them again. Lindemans drove the men to a safe house on Jekerstraat in south Amsterdam, insisting on providing them with a reliable assistant named Jackie. For the next six weeks, Jackie accompanied them on all their operational sorties, reconnoitring drop zones for the RAF, recruiting members of reception committees, identifying storage locations for arms and explosives, conveying the details to CS-6 and the Resistance Council. It was tiring work. Celosse and Cnoops were both asleep when the SS knocked at the safe house door. When they reached for the revolvers they kept by the side of their beds, they found that Jackie had taken them away for cleaning. Bob Celosse was executed in Camp Vught near 's-Hertogenbosch. Tony Cnoops escaped and survived.

CELOSSE Penetration

> Prisoner heard from GISKES that LINDEMANS was working for him under the designation "C", and states that "C" submitted information on the agent Bob CELOSSE and his collaborators in AMSTERDAM. The Sipo, too, had got into touch with this group through other channels, and although LINDEMANS did not lead directly to the arrest of CELOSSE, Prisoner states quite definitely that LINDEMANS penotrated the CELOSSE

* * *

Hermann Giskes would testify after the war that Christiaan Lindemans, King Kong, was his V-Mann. Shortly after his brother Henk was arrested, Lindemans had made contact via an Abwehr agent codenamed Nelis and asked to see the top man. He walked into Giskes' office and tipped the contents of a briefcase onto his desk. It contained stacks of forged identity cards, the inks and stamps used to make them and wads of foreign currency. Giskes took him on. He agreed to release Henk Lindemans, but kept King Kong's wife in custody, just in case he was thinking of double-crossing him. He would not confirm how many people lost their lives as a result of Lindemans' activities, but he did not demur from the figure of 267 arrests. Of the fifty-six agents parachuted into the Netherlands by the British, forty-three were captured and only eight survived. Eleven RAF planes did not return to base.

* * *

It took time but Charles Blunt was proved right. SOE learned that its operations in the Netherlands had been penetrated from an early stage. Hermann Giskes had captured an SOE radio operator, Hubertus Lauwers, and forced him to continue transmitting to London. By monitoring SOE's replies, Giskes was able to arrest and turn future agents, until he controlled virtually the whole network. Giskes accepted SOE's unmasking of his Englandspiel with good grace and a little British humour, sending the following radio message without encryption:

To Messrs Blunt, Bingham and Successors Ltd. We are aware that you have now started to do business in the Netherlands without our assistance. In light of our long and successful work as your sole agents here, we find this rather discourteous. But never mind. Please be assured that if you decide in the future to come and visit us in larger numbers, you will receive the same reception as your agents did, with the same outcome. So long for now!

Seymour Bingham's protracted failure to act on warnings of German penetration convinced some in the British War Office that Ubbink and Dourlein had been right to accuse him of treachery. He was transferred to a clerical posting in Australia. Kas de Graaf, who had aroused similar suspicions, remained on active service.

* * *

D-Day had engendered hope, but things did not go smoothly. The Allied forces advancing from the west suffered setbacks; the mood of the Dutch people alternated between joy and despair. Operation Market Garden, an ambitious attempt to free western Holland and advance to the Rhine by dropping airborne troops into Eindhoven, Nijmegen and Arnhem, began with initial successes that caused panic in the Reichskommissariat. Arthur Seyss-Inquart ordered the destruction of sensitive documents and the families of German officials were evacuated. A train carrying the wives and children of prominent members of the Dutch Nazi party, the NSB, was bombed en route to Berlin and thirty passengers died. When Resistance newspapers wrongly reported that the city of Breda was in Allied hands, Seyss-Inquart issued a proclamation threatening reprisals against those who welcomed the invaders: 'Order must be maintained. All instructions from the German military must be obeyed. Opposition to German forces will be suppressed with the force of arms. Those who fraternise with the enemy or hinder the work of the German Reich will be shot.'

The news that Allied units were on Dutch soil triggered premature rejoicing. Pim and Anna-Maria were among thousands of people who took to the streets in a moment of national jubilation that became known as *Dolle Dinsdag* – Crazy Tuesday.

But the troops of Market Garden ran into fierce German opposition. Heavy casualties and a chastening withdrawal led to recriminations; it was rumoured that the Allied battleplan had been betrayed to the German High Command. The planned liberation of the Netherlands was set back by several months.

An Allied inquiry sought to understand how the Germans had known to move the 9th and 10th Panzer divisions to Nijmegen and Arnhem, just in time to thwart the advancing British, American and Canadian forces. When Abwehr agent Nelis, the man who had introduced Christiaan Lindemans to Hermann Giskes, was captured some months later, he pointed the finger at his former comrade. Lindemans, Nelis claimed, had used his Resistance sources to learn of the Allies' plans and passed them on to the Germans.

* * *

Arthur Seyss-Inquart apologised to his wife. It was hard for him
to see her go, but she would be much safer in Salzburg; and then
there were the children to think of: 'Let them spend a couple
of months having fun with their grandparents and we'll all
meet again in the summer; things may get bumpy here, but the
Führer has the situation under control and the emergency won't
last.' As he waved his family off from Amsterdam Centraal, he
knew he would never see them again.

* * *

The closer the Allies got, the more confident the Resistance
became. Attacks on the occupying forces grew bolder, the set-
tling of accounts with traitors more bloody. The Dutch SS man
Hermann Heinrich Pennings was shot in the head as he cycled
past the post office on Coolsingel boulevard in Rotterdam, but the
bullet lodged in his jaw and he survived. In a letter to his wife from
the Rotterdam Naval Hospital, Pennings demanded vengeance.

> I got shot right in the head. I lost consciousness and came to
> with a lot of people standing round me. When I set out that
> morning, I had no idea such a thing was going to happen,
> but I was luckier than some of the others. Romer and Koster
> bought it and they've executed twenty terrorists as reprisals.
> There's an Ordepolitie guy in the same ward as me who took
> a bullet in the shoulder – I think they'll shoot another twenty
> for him. As for me, I hope they put dozens of them up against
> a wall and let them have it.

We do not learn if Pennings was disappointed that the authorities shot only ten civilians on his account. The men were

executed in front of the Utrecht Insurance building, opposite the post office, and their bodies left to lie, with a written warning to others.

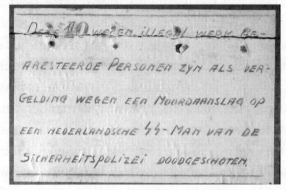

'These ten people took part in illegal work and were shot dead in response to an assassination attempt on a Dutch SS man.'

The collaborator and NSB activist Pieter Marsman was gunned down on the pavement of Veenendaalkade in The Hague. Two days earlier, Marsman had betrayed the leader of the Resistance's Organisation for Help to People in Hiding (LO), Leo Voogd, who would later be shot. Marsman's own sons, who themselves worked for the LO, confronted their father and were suspected of involvement in his killing.

Pieter Marsman

Johan van Lom was the man who informed the Germans about the meeting of Walraven van Hall's National Support Fund at which the Resistance's leading financiers were arrested and later executed. He had gone into hiding but was tracked down following a wiretap by Wim Sanders of the Resistance's Political Crimes Bureau, the body that pursued traitors. In a building on Keizersgracht, Van Lom was interrogated for several hours by Sanders and four others. He confessed and claimed the SD had blackmailed him by threatening to tell his wife about his affair with her sister. Sanders gave him a vial of poison and Van Lom drank it, but he was still alive an hour later so they shot him and dumped his body in the Keizersgracht canal.

The multiple slayings convinced many collaborators that the time had come to save themselves. Some of them sought refuge on evacuation trains to Germany; others, including Anton van der Waals and Christiaan Lindemans, explored the possibility of offering their services to the enemy.

* * *

For Anna-Maria, the final months of the war were the most difficult. So many Resistance fighters had been betrayed, so many
executed or sent to the camps. Hans Kreisel, to whom she had
become close, continued to participate in active operations. With
every instance of German repression, every hostage murdered,
she saw Hans's anger grow. When she spoke to him about the
future and the prospects for a new life in a world at peace, he
smiled but said little. His focus was on the present; Anna-Maria
feared his plans were leading him into danger.

Attacks on the occupying forces increased and reprisals
became indiscriminate. When two Wehrmacht officers were
killed at the Oldenallerbrug bridge near Putten, General
Friedrich Christiansen sent SS units to surround the town and
arrest its inhabitants. The women were locked in the church
and men and boys in the school. A hundred houses, nearly the
whole town, were burned down.

The women were released, but 602 men between the ages of
eighteen and fifty were deported to the Neuengamme concentration camp, from where only forty-eight returned. As with
the razing of Lidice in Czechoslovakia and Oradour-sur-Glane
in France, the horror of the Putten raid inflamed the thirst for
vengeance.

21

DOING JUSTICE

Anton van der Waals and Christiaan Lindemans had, between them, destroyed CS-6 as an effective fighting force. The majority of its operatives had been killed or forced to flee; but those who remained were looking for revenge and their betrayers knew it.

As soon as Allied troops crossed the border into Holland, Van der Waals reported to Unit 15 Field Security of the Canadian Intelligence Corps and presented himself as a Resistance operative who had spent the war infiltrating German espionage. The Canadians handed him over to British Special Counterintelligence, who wasted little time in establishing his true identity. Ever resourceful, Van der Waals admitted everything, including his lengthy employment by the SD, and offered to put his extensive knowledge at the Allies' service as they hunted down German war criminals in the newly liberated territories. After some deliberation his offer was accepted. Van der Waals was attached to the British intelligence division combating *Unternehmen Werwolf* – Operation Werewolf – that was suspected of running an undercover network of SS saboteurs.

There is some mystery about what happened next. Van der Waals evidently proved his worth to the British, because at the end of hostilities, they would take him with them to Berlin, where he managed to combine his service to the Crown with a surreptitious visit to the Soviet embassy. Soviet military intelligence appears to have hired him and taken him to Moscow where he spent two months before his British handlers realised he was no longer responding to their messages.

Christiaan Lindemans' self-preservation strategy was even more eventful. When the Germans fled from the Netherlands, Hermann Giskes instructed him to stay behind, make contact with Allied intelligence and offer himself as an agent, with the aim of discovering their plans. Giskes gave him the codes he would need to pass through the front lines and identity papers affording him the highest level of security clearance. Having made his way to Brussels, where British troops were engaged in street-to-street fighting, Lindemans volunteered to join them. He fought bravely in the battle to capture the Brussels Gare du Nord, killing two German soldiers and wounding two others. His new comrades reported that he fought 'as if he had nothing to lose'. He didn't.

His acts of bravery brought Lindemans to the attention of a British intelligence officer, Peter Baker of IS9 D Group (Western Europe), who was looking for reliable Dutch speakers to be sent into Holland to prepare the ground for the Allied advance. Lindemans was keen. Baker carried out the proper security checks and received a positive recommendation from SOE in London, signed by a Captain Kas de Graaf. De Graaf could have mentioned that he and Lindemans had successfully vouched for each other in the past but did not. In addition to his Abwehr papers, Lindemans now possessed Allied security clearance and an IS9 pass identifying him as 'Christiaan de Vries, in the service of His Majesty Prince Bernhardt of the Netherlands'.

Over the course of several weeks, Christiaan Lindemans showed great courage in crossing and re-crossing the front lines. On each side he would meet with senior intelligence officials, delivering detailed reports on what he had learned from his contacts with the enemy and receiving instructions for his next assignment. His British and his German handlers all expressed complete faith in his loyalty.

* * *

Allied troops advance into southern Holland

Hitler ordered his troops to defend Fortress Holland. British and Canadian forces had advanced into the south of the country, but most of the big cities remained in German hands. When Hanns Rauter gave instructions for all Resistance prisoners to be brought together in the central prison in Scheveningen, word spread that he was planning to use their release as a bargaining chip with the Allies. Discussions took place in the Reichskommissariat. Hopes rose. Then, citing Adolf Hitler's *Niedermachungsbefehl* – the order to shoot terrorists and saboteurs – Rauter moved the prisoners to Camp Vught, where he instructed Erich Deppner to select 450 for immediate execution. A month later, the forty-seven remaining agents sent by SOE to work with the Resistance and captured as a result of Giskes and Schreieder's Englandspiel were transported to Mauthausen concentration camp. They were also shot.

Hans Kreisel said the Resistance Council was left with no alternative; he told Anna-Maria its vengeance would be spectacular.

* * *

The last weeks of war brought both joy and despair. Anna-Maria's young brother Rein had left home immediately after the German invasion to sail to England and join the free Dutch forces, but his boat had sunk and Rein was feared drowned.

We had been close and I mourned his loss. As children, we were thick as thieves. We defied our parents' warning never to skate under the Boterbrug bridge because we were certain to fall through the ice, and Rein rescued me when I did exactly that.

When I was at Leiden and Rein was studying engineering, he used to say, 'I can't be bothered taking a girl to the dance: you come with me' and we would be the best dancers in the room. The end of the war would mean confirmation that my brother was dead. I was in the garden in Terbregge; it was spring and even now I can see the roses. A jeep pulled up and a man came out of it in British army uniform with a sten gun on his shoulder. I didn't recognise him, but he shouted 'Riet!' – that was my pet-name in the family – 'Come and have a go at this!' I fired my brother's sten gun before I even hugged him. My shoulder ached for days … I was crying. I loved him so much. Firing my brother's gun … for me, it meant the war was over.

* * *

It wasn't. In the early hours of 7 March 1945 Hanns Rauter was being driven from his headquarters at Didam, east of Arnhem, to take part in the last-ditch defence of Apeldoorn. His BMW staff car was flagged down outside the village of Woeste Hoeve by a group of men in SS uniforms. It was 1.30 a.m. and the night was dark.

Rauter's car ambushed, Woeste Hoeve

When the driver pulled up, one of the men jumped onto the bonnet and shot him twice through the windscreen. Rauter, who was sitting in the front passenger seat, and his adjutant Erwin Exner in the back drew their revolvers, but Resistance fighters on either side of the car opened fire with machine guns.

They quickly checked all the occupants and disappeared into the woods.

Damage to Rauter's car

A Wehrmacht patrol came across the bullet-riddled car at 3.30 a.m. and heard groans from inside. Hanns Rauter had been hit in the leg and the jaw. Two bullets had passed through his lungs and he had lost two pints of blood, but he was not dead. The Wehrmacht took him to the Apeldoorn military hospital for an emergency operation that saved his life and cost hundreds of others.

Rauter in hospital

From his hospital bed, Rauter demanded to see mugshots of all known local Resistance members. He identified the man who had jumped on the bonnet of his car as Geert Gosens, a leader of the Apeldoorn Resistance, then phoned Eberhardt Schöngarth and ordered the execution of 300 hostages. Todeskandidaten from Apeldoorn, Amersfoort, Amsterdam, Assen, Almelo, Utrecht and Zwolle were put on buses and driven to the scene of Rauter's ambush. A firing squad of fifty Waffen-SS and Ordnungspolizei was waiting. The prisoners were told why they were being killed, and were taken out of the buses in groups of twenty and shot. The time between each round of executions was around five minutes. The Ordnungspolizei then laid out the bodies on either side of the road and brought local inhabitants from their homes to see them. A thirty-year-old German private named Ernst Gräwe, who refused to take part in the killing, was shot through the head by his commanding officer.

Ernst Gräwe

* * *

Four weeks later tanks of the Canadian South Saskatchewan regiment entered Camp Westerbork. The Germans had fled, leaving 876 Jewish inmates to greet their liberators.

Liberation of Camp Westerbork

The Canadians transformed the camp into a holding facility for suspected collaborators. It was the signal for Holland's surviving Jews to emerge from their hiding places. For Marlies Friedheim, the end of Westerbork was the end of a nightmare.

When the war ended, I carried on living with Anna-Maria. That may seem strange, but she and I were like sisters. Her daughter was just a baby when I first came and I loved her very much. Did I tell you, I'm her godmother? The reason Anna-Maria helped me was because she believed it was the right thing. On the whole, I would say the Dutch were good people. There were some who weren't, of course, but that is true of all people.

The years after the war were hard. The Germans were gone, but the problems weren't. My brother Hans went to reclaim our father's business, but the authorities wouldn't let him. When the Germans invaded, they seized all Jewish businesses, but they tried to force my father and his partner to keep the factory open and run it for the Nazis. My father said, No! He said right away he would never work for the Nazis. But his partner agreed and stayed on working for the Germans. So, when my brother tried to reclaim the business, the Dutch police turned him away because they said our dad had collaborated. It was heart-breaking to hear such a lie. It was only because we had the company records proving that my father refused to collaborate that Hans was able to reclaim the business. After that, he and I rented a small flat in Amsterdam and we lived there together until he got married and I got married. Hans had four children, a son and three daughters, and I had my son and my daughter. We stayed close with Anna-Maria and with the Jansen family and the Griffioen family, the farmers who saved us from Westerbork, and Hans kept in touch with his two old schoolteachers who sheltered him during the war. When Hans died in 2006, it was such a blow.

Hans and Marlies in 2006

* * *

When Crazy Tuesday – *Dolle Dinsdag* – panicked the Germans, Hanns Rauter had decreed that Camp Vught must be closed before it could fall into Allied hands; all prisoners were to be moved out or eliminated. Mies and Jan Canada Boissevain had been put on separate trains, one taking female prisoners to Ravensbrück, the other taking the men to Buchenwald. Mies had organised the women on her train, assigning the strong to care for the weak, corralling every voice for communal singing. In Ravensbrück, she formed self-help groups, offering physical and spiritual support, counselling, education and exercise sessions.

Mies Boissevain, prison photo

Four months later she learned that her husband had starved to death. She refused to be broken, continued to help her fellow inmates, vowed she would survive and give testimony.

She did. In April 1945 Ravensbrück was liberated by the Red Army and Mies was flown to Sweden by the Red Cross. She weighed less than four stone. When she returned to Amsterdam she rang her sister, Hester, and announced 'I'm back' with a cheerfulness that brooked no argument.

Mies Boissevain resumed her feminist campaigning, drawing up an all-women list to contest the city's municipal elections. She called it Practical Politics because, she said, that was what men lacked. She did not hide her war trauma: she spoke openly about the cruelty and the loss, naming those who abetted the Germans, demanding justice for her family. But her talent was for optimism. She devoted herself to creating the template for a National Skirt, sewn from patches of fabric representing hope for the future, travelling through Europe and North America to promote the symbol of renewal, processing her traumas by sewing them into the clothes she wore.

Mies Boissevain and her 'National Skirt'

* * *

Hermann Giskes and Gerhard Huntemann, whose double dealing caused the deaths of scores of Allied agents, successfully claimed that they were soldiers fighting for their country. Neither was ever charged; both went on to have careers with US intelligence.

Joseph Schreieder was interrogated by British and American officers, who found him 'frank and co-operative'. He argued that he had done everything possible to prevent the ill-treatment of Allied prisoners and had actively engaged with representatives of the Resistance to minimise bloodshed. He cited a series of meetings he had held towards the end of hostilities with the right-wing, monarchist Ordedienst, to discuss joint post-war efforts to combat communist subversion.

Joseph Schreieder in Allied custody

In the anti-Soviet climate of the time, it gained him credit. The CIA took Schreieder on as an agent, codename Cobalt, and in 1957 he joined West German intelligence where he had a successful career before retiring in the mid-1960s.

Willy Lages

Willy Lages and Ferdinand aus der Fünten were put on trial, found guilty of war crimes and sentenced to death. But their execution was delayed by legal arguments and in 1952 their punishment was commuted to life in prison. Lages was released in 1966 and Fünten in 1989.

Ferdinand aus der Fünten

Erich Deppner, the mass murderer of prisoners of war, was captured by the Red Army and taken to a Soviet labour camp, but he was released in 1950 and returned to Germany. Despite knowing about his past, the West German secret service, the Bundesnachrichtendienst, hired him and refused requests for his extradition. Deppner died in 2005, aged ninety-five.

The leniency shown to the killers at the top did not extend to lesser folk. Ans van Dijk, the lesbian milliner who was coerced into betraying her fellow Jews, received little compassion at her trial. She saw her appeal for a royal pardon refused and was shot.

Ans van Dijk

* * *

Marlies Friedheim retained her capacity for hope. The pain of war shook her but did not defeat her. In 1948 she met her future husband, a British physicist named Bert, in Edinburgh where she had gone to improve her English. After they married, they moved to Ireland and then to Australia.

> When I first came to Australia, nobody had any idea what we had been through during the war. At first, I thought they were superficial people, but it isn't that: how could they ever understand it when they hadn't been through it? I always thought after the war that people would have learned from what happened and it would never happen again. But I was wrong. You can see it happening again in the world. For a long time, I couldn't face going back to Germany, where we came from. But my mother had had a close friend there who wasn't Jewish and she begged me to come. She was in her nineties and she said she wanted to make up for the harm Germany had done. So, I went; but when people came and shook my hand, I couldn't help wondering what exactly that hand had done ... They all said they hadn't done anything, but somebody must have.

* * *

Hanns Rauter

Hanns Rauter had murdered tens of thousands of Jews in the name of an idea and hundreds of Dutchmen because they dared to shoot at him. At his trial he stood by his actions: he did not consider himself guilty. He put on a show of military conviction. But the newsreels show his hands fidgeting nervously, his fingers gripping and un-gripping his thumbs.

Rauter's final letter to his lawyer was full of master-race entitlement:

I wish to thank you for the help you offered me in this difficult court case. I regret that you were unsuccessful, but ... in such a politically motivated process, it was not your fault. I do not feel guilty. I could not have acted any differently. Now, I voluntarily offer my person as a peace offering to the Dutch people, whom I hold so dear. These are my last wishes:

I ask to be allowed to die without being tied up. I declare on my honour that I shall not attempt to flee or offer the soldiers a moving target.

If my body is released by the Dutch authorities, which should surely be possible now, four years after the war, I ask you to ensure that it is buried in a German military mausoleum alongside my SS comrades.

Rauter. Scheveningen. 23 March 1949

Two days later, Hanns Albin Rauter was taken from Scheveningen prison to the Waalsdorpervlakte dunes where he was allowed to walk to his execution unbound and without handcuffs. On hearing the firing party load their weapons, he ripped the blindfold from his eyes and shouted 'Feuer!'

Arrest of Anton Mussert, 1945

Anton Mussert was captured by the Resistance in May 1945. When he was sentenced to death six months later, he remained convinced that Queen Wilhelmina would pardon him. She didn't.

Arthur Seyss-Inquart was a defendant in Nuremberg where the transcript of his interrogations reveals a man acutely aware of his own guilt, reduced to deceit, evasion and lies. His efforts failed. He was convicted and hanged.

* * *

Even for the sharpest of criminal minds, good luck rarely lasts for ever. Anton van der Waals and Christiaan Lindemans tried hard to save themselves but neither succeeded.

Having belatedly realised that Van der Waals had given them the slip, his British handlers contacted their Russian counterparts and asked if they could have their agent back. Moscow did not reply. But a chance sighting in the Soviet sector of occupied Berlin raised the possibility that Van der Waals had returned. A British surveillance operation confirmed it was him and undercover detectives cornered him at the Brandenburg Gate. MI6 ruled that his flirtation with the Russians amounted to desertion. He was sent to a detention camp near Hanover, where he might have remained and eventually been released were it not for two Rotterdam policemen he had betrayed during the war. Leendert Ridderikoff and Jan van den Ende had been members of the Ordedienst Resistance group, before Van der Waals turned them over to the Germans. They had spent nearly four years in Sachsenhausen and returned in 1945 determined to track down their tormentor. As a result of their efforts, Anton van der Waals was extradited in July 1946 to stand trial in Holland.

In proceedings that lasted more than a year a court in The Hague heard details of his betrayals from his victims and, damningly, from his former boss, Joseph Schreieder.

Anton van der Waals in court

Van der Waals maintained that for the whole of the time he was employed by the SD, he had been a British double agent, reporting regularly to an English intelligence officer, known to him as Jonny Verhagen. But the court did not believe him. The judges described him as 'an extremely clever and mendacious traitor, cold and unfeeling, with a complete lack of emotional empathy ... a man whose callous nature left him indifferent to the suffering he knew he was inflicting and interested only in what might be to his own benefit.' There seemed to be no political or ideological motivation for his actions, the court said, but a 'special ability to gain the trust and confidence of strangers' allowed him to take advantage of the German occupation to manipulate people for his own ends with impunity.

Despite pleas for clemency from his lawyers and from his wife Corrie, Anton van der Waals was sentenced to death. On the night before his execution on 26 January 1950, he confessed to all the charges against him and admitted that his claim to have been working for 'Jonny Verhagen' of British intelligence was a lie.

Christiaan Lindemans, too, had a 'special ability' to fool people. Captain Baker of British intelligence admired him so much that he took him on as his personal assistant and they went on missions together to infiltrate agents through the lines. At the end of one sortie, Baker left his protégé in a safe house owned by Jan Kooy, a Dutch policeman, who found Lindemans boastful and inconsistent in his account of his activities during the first part of the war. Kooy searched Lindemans' possessions and discovered his German security pass. Lindemans claimed it was a fake, but Kooy had him locked up in a police cell. When Peter Baker heard what had happened, he hit the roof. Lindemans was promptly released and returned to British HQ where Kas de Graaf was again called upon to reassure London that his friend was 'certainly no traitor'.

It was only after the Abwehr agent Nelis, who had helped recruit Lindemans, was captured by the Allies that the story began to unravel. Nelis confirmed that Lindemans had worked as a V-Mann for Hermann Giskes ever since the arrest of his younger brother, Henk, and that his apparent service to the British was a cover for his continued collaboration with the Abwehr. When his British handlers confronted him with Nelis's revelations, Lindemans sighed and shrugged and said, 'Yes. That's right.' He was taken to St Gilles prison in Brussels and from there to Camp 020, a maximum-security detention centre, where he was interrogated by Lieutenant Colonel R. W. G. Stephens of British intelligence. 'Tin Eye' Stephens got Lindemans to confess to everything, writing in his report that he had never come across such treachery. 'If I have not yet plumbed the depths of human degradation,' Stephens wrote, 'I am at least near it in [Lindeman's] confession . . .'

Colonel Stephens recommended the death penalty but acknowledged that it would be up to a Dutch court to make the decision. For the next two years, Lindemans was held in Scheveningen prison where Resistance operatives had been tortured and killed as a result of his betrayal. A Dutch counter-intelligence officer, Oreste Pinto, who visited him in jail, reported that the former King Kong was now nervous and physically frail. 'Is there no mercy?' Lindemans asked on Pinto's final visit. A week later he killed himself by taking an overdose of phenobarbital, supplied to him by a nurse he had befriended in the prison hospital.

* * *

My conversations with Anna-Maria continued in the living room of a small bungalow near Worthing. Her wartime experiences had sent her life in unexpected directions.

> War puts pressures on you and Pim and I drifted apart. After our daughter, we had a son who died when he was sixteen. He looked at me and said, 'Mum, my watch has stopped' and moments later his life stopped.
>
> Pim went to Argentina. They were looking for musicians to play in a band and Pim was perfect for them, because he could play every instrument. He ended up staying there. Our daughter used to write to him, but he never really wrote back. I think he died when he was around seventy.
>
> The person I stayed closest to was Hans Kreisel, the Resistance fighter who came to live with us and pulled off so many daring operations.

Hans Kreisel (left), Tulpenrallye winner, 1957

He was always a heartthrob and a bit of a playboy. He went back to being a rally driver and won all the big prizes, including the Tulpenrallye, the Dutch equivalent of the Monte Carlo Rally.

My brother Rein, who had fought with the British, was looking for a new start after the war and he emigrated to South Africa.

When I finished writing, I thanked Anna-Maria and expressed my admiration for the vividness of her memory. She laughed.

I have always had a photographic memory. I can still recite screeds of Ovid that I learned in school. When we were children, my brother Rein challenged me to memorise the number plates of the vehicles that we drove past in our parents' car: he wrote them down to check on me and at the end of the journey, I could recite them all.

There's a last story I want to tell you. When I was married again and had moved here to England, I met Vera Lynn. It was before one of her concerts and I was taken backstage. I told her how we used to listen to her on the radio powered by the stationary bicycle, and how important she was for all of us in those dark days. She was so lovely and so gracious. She asked if she could tell the audience that I was there that evening and remind them of the time when the world was oppressed and no one knew if we would ever see peace. She wanted to tell people that those things must never happen again.

Anna-Maria van der Vaart, aged 90

Marlies Friedheim died in Australia in 2020 shortly after her hundredth birthday. Anna-Maria died in March 2024 at the age of 104. Her name, and that of her husband, Pim, has been honoured by Yad Vashem, the World Holocaust Remembrance Center, as one of the Righteous Among the Nations.